# Keepers of the Sacred Chants

# Keepers of the Sacred Chants

The Poetics of Ritual Power in an
Amazonian Society

Jonathan D. Hill

The University of Arizona Press / Tucson and London

The University of Arizona Press
Copyright © 1993
Arizona Board of Regents
All Rights Reserved

♾ This book is printed on acid-free, archival-quality paper.
Manufactured in the United States of America

98  97  96  95  94  93    6  5  4  3  2  1
Library of Congress Cataloging-in-Publication Data
Hill, Jonathan David, 1954–
    Keepers of the sacred chants : the poetics of ritual power in an Amazonian society /
Jonathan D. Hill.
        p.      cm.
    Includes bibliographical references (p.      ) and index.
    ISBN 0-8165-1135-7 (acid-free paper)
        1. Curripaco Indians—Rites and ceremonies.   2. Curripaco Indians—Religion and
mythology.   3. Curripaco Indians—Oratory.   4. Discourse analysis—Venezuela—
Gavilán.   5. Gavilán (Venezuela)—Social life and customs.   I. Title.
F2270.2.C87H55   1993                                                         93-5028
299′.883—dc20                                                                       CIP
British Library Cataloguing-in-Publication Data
A catalogue record for this book is available from the British Library.

*To the memory of Alan P. Merriam,*
*whose untimely death in March 1980*
*prevented him from seeing this work*
*reach completion and*
*whose dedication to the anthropology of music*
*continues to inspire the living.*

# Contents

# Figures

# Acknowledgments

Many people and institutions have helped me at various stages of preparing this book. Fulbright-Hays, Doctoral Dissertation Research Abroad Program, and the Social Science Research Council (SSRC/ACLS), Latin America and the Caribbean Program, provided funding for twelve months of field research in Venezuela in 1980–81. In addition, SSRC/ACLS gave money to support me during the first six months of the dissertation write-up phase in early 1982. Fulbright-Hays, Faculty Research Abroad Program, supported my return visits to the Venezuelan Amazon in the summers of 1984 and 1985. Research facilities, time, and office space for writing the first chapters of this book were generously provided through a Postdoctoral Research Fellowship at the Department of Anthropology at the Smithsonian Institution in 1988. I am very grateful to Fulbright-Hays, SSRC/ACLS, and the Smithsonian Institution for their financial support of my work over the past eight years. However, the findings and opinions contained in this book are my own and do not necessarily reflect their views.

I am very thankful to the Venezuela Education Ministry, Division of Indian Affairs, for granting me permission to reside in Wakuénai (or Curripaco) villages along the Guainía and Casiquiare rivers in 1980–81 and in various neighborhoods and communities of Arawak-speaking peoples in the western parts of the Federal Amazon Territory during 1984 and 1985. Dra. Nelly Arvelo-Jimenez of the Department of Anthropology,

Venezuelan Scientific Research Institute (IVIC), taught me a great deal about indigenous affairs in Venezuela and helped me to bring this wider perspective to bear on my specific research interests in Arawakan societies of the Upper Río Negro region. As a Professional in Training in Dra. Arvelo's Laboratory of Ethnology, my work benefited from periodic discussions with Dra. Arvelo and several other anthropologists at IVIC, including Erika Wagner, Alberta Zucchi, and Dieter Hienen, among others.

In addition to the Department of Anthropology at IVIC, the Center of Ecology provided invaluable technical assistance by helping me to transport personal necessities and scientific equipment between Caracas and the field. Dr. Rafael Herrera and Dr. Ernesto Medina, co-directors of the Man and the Biosphere Project Number 1 in Tropical Ecology at IVIC and in San Carlos de Río Negro, helped me in numerous ways. I can only hope that my research has had, and will continue to exert, a positive effect on the increasingly fruitful dialogue and collaboration between ecologists and anthropologists in IVIC and at other centers for Amazonian studies. I am particularly thankful to Andrea Nemitt, Dr. Howard Clark and his wife, Kathleen Clark, Carl Jordan, Chris Uhl, Robert Buschbacher, and Robert Sanford for sharing their knowledge of the nutrient-poor, blackwater ecosystems of the Upper Río Negro region and for their open-mindedness toward anthropological research that by its very nature is not always clearly related to the objectives of the ecological sciences. Few ethnologists are fortunate enough to have such sophisticated and up-to-date sources of knowledge about the specific environments of the peoples where they carry out fieldwork.

Dra. Isabel Aretz and Dr. Luis Felipe Ramon y Rivera, co-founders and directors of the Instituto Interamericano de Ethnomusicología y Folklore (INIDEF), were kind hosts in 1980-81 and introduced me to Jose Jorge de Carvalho, Ronny Velasquez, Yolanda Salas de Lecuna, Igor Colinas, and other Latin American scholars of musical culture. It was an honor to be affiliated with INIDEF during 1980–81 and to contribute copies of my original field recordings to the archive, a collection of indigenous and folk music of Latin America that was unparalleled in any other South American country.

Among the many people who supported and advised me as a graduate student at Indiana University before, during, and after my fieldwork in 1980–81, I am most grateful to Emilio Moran, Ivan Karp, Anya Royce, Anthony Seeger, John MacDowell, and Michael Herzfeld. Emilio Moran deserves special thanks for setting up initial contacts for me with Venezuelan scientists at IVIC and thus providing my first opportunity to experience life in the Amazon Basin and in Venezuela as a whole. Emilio took time to read copies of my field notes and sent me comments in the mail, a favor that has paid off in the long run by helping smooth the difficult, yet creative, transition from the field to the writing desk. He also gave me sound practical advice on how to adapt in difficult field conditions.

It is with great sadness that I no longer benefit from the intellectual and personal guidance of Dr. Alan P. Merriam, the late ethnomusicologist and professor of anthropology at Indiana University who served as my principal adviser throughout the three years of graduate studies leading up to my fieldwork with the Wakuénai of Venezuela. Dr. Merriam's death in 1980 came as a shock to me and also to my Venezuelan colleagues in anthropology, ethnomusicology, and folklore. His teaching and advice contributed greatly to the development of my research interests and would no doubt have been equally valuable in bringing the project to completion.

I would also like to thank Terence Turner, Ralph Nicholas, Leonard Meyer, A. K. Ramanujan, and many other outstanding teachers who initiated me into the intellectual worlds of anthropology and music as an undergraduate student at the University of Chicago. Many thanks also to Bela Nagy and Peter Graham Swing at the Boston University Tanglewood Institute for sharing their musical talents during seminars in 1973 and 1974.

During the past ten years, many of the specific topics and issues contained in this book were developed in lectures and short publications. Many people responded generously with comments and criticisms. Robin Wright, my co-author in two of these publications, has greatly improved my understanding of indigenous history in the Upper Río Negro region. Gerard Behague at the University of Texas wrote extensive comments on an earlier version of my analysis of *málikai* chants in childbirth rituals, and his insightful questions were very helpful in my subsequent fieldwork and publications. The number of other people whose intellectual criticism has helped to shape this book is too great for me to treat each one individually, so I list them here in alphabetical order: Ellen Basso, Michael Brown, Janet Chernela, William Crocker, Stephen Hugh-Jones, Jean Jackson, Mark Johnson, Ken Kensinger, Waud Kracke, Betty Meggers, William Merrill, Salikoko Mufwene, Donald Pollock, Alcida Ramos, Irene Silverblatt, Richard Smith, Terence Turner, Norman Whitten, and Johannes Wilbert.

I am especially grateful to my parents, Lee and Dorothy Hill, for helping me and my son, Alexander, pull through the difficult times between jobs and grants. Without their support, I could not have afforded many of the shorter publications and papers that led to this book.

Finally, I am deeply appreciative to the people living along the lower Guainía River in Venezuela for their warm-hearted readiness to teach me about their culture and to let me share in their way of life. The Wakuénai have endured a multitude of external forces that threaten their sociocultural identity and physical existence, and yet their way of life prevails as a sensible and human means of coming to terms with basic problems of existence in the equatorial, riverine environment that they inhabit. This book is dedicated to the humanness and sensibility of the Wakuénai people and to the future of these qualities in their lives and, hopefully, in our own lives as well.

# Glossary of Indigenous Terms

*áati*  Hot pepper used in everyday cooking and in sacred food (*kárid-zámai*) prepared during rites of passage; in *málikai* chants for initiation, *áati* is an important category of spirit-names.

Amáru The primordial human female of myth and the mother of Kuwái; in *málikai* chanting and singing, Amáru is an extraordinarily powerful category of spirit-names for "hot things," including steel tools, firearms, and contagious diseases brought to the region by white people.

*déetu*  A large, shiny black species of coconut palm weevil; the adult form of white *mútsi* palm grubs; also the name of flutes played by guests to "suck" fermented drinks out of their hosts during the late-night period of *pudáli* exchange ceremonies.

*dzáato*  A hallucinogenic snuff made from the bark of trees (*Virola calophylla*) and used only by shamans as a means of entering into communication with spirits of the dead during curing rituals.

*dzákare*  Village or place; also used extensively as a way of mapping out sung and chanted journeys in performances of *málikai*.

*dzámakuápi*  "Two-snakes," or a species of vine used for making sacred musical instruments and ritual whips for initiation.

*dzáwiñápa íhwerrúti*  "Great Jaguar-Bone," or large conical trumpets played in male initiation rituals to represent the jaguar-ancestors.

*dzáwináitairi*   Master shamans who are said to have powers of clairvoyance and of controlling witchcraft and other supernatural forces.

*dzéema*   Tobacco; invoked in the language of *málikai* in order to combat disease-causing spirits as well as to protect ritual subjects from powerful spirit-names.

Dzúli   A younger brother of Iñápirríkuli and the first owner of the sacred songs and chants, called *málikai*.

*éenu*   Sky; in *málikai* chanting and singing, *éenu* is used as a category of powerful spirit-names that includes some wild palm species and all types of lightning.

*éenunái*   A category of spirit-names that includes most forest animal species; *éenunái* spirits are said to reside in the dark netherworld (*íyarudáti*) of the dead, where they are kept as domesticated animals whose movements are controlled by shamans.

Eenutánhi   The celestial home of Amáru after the events related in the cycle of myths about Kuwái; Eenutánhi is described as the region where the sky begins, where the sun rises, and where rivers run in a continuous circle.

Héemapána   "Tapir-house," or the house of recently deceased members of the highest ranking sib of the Waríperídakéna phratry.

Hérri   The first male initiate in myth.

*hekwápiríko*   The world of living human beings; also inhabited by fish and other aquatic animal species making up the category of *umáwari* (anaconda) spirit-names.

*hínimái*   Evil omens, or events that portend unavoidable death.

Hípana   A village along the Aiarí River in Brazil, the place regarded as the center, or "navel," of the world where the mythic ancestors emerged from the ground and where Kuwái is brought down to the ground in myth and in initiation rituals.

*hliépule-kwá éenu*   "Umbilical cord place in the sky," or the celestial umbilical cord that connects the sky-world of mythic ancestors with the world of living human beings on the ground at Hípana; the celestial umbilical cord is musically evoked in the opening and closing songs for initiation rituals.

Iñápirríkuli   "Made-from-bones," the name of the trickster-creator of myth and father of Kuwái.

*ínyapakáati dzéema*   To blow tobacco smoke; the indigenous term for the activity of performing *málikai*.

*íyarudáti*   The dark netherworld of recently deceased persons and the place where shamans travel in songs to retrieve the lost souls of their patients.

Káali   A younger brother of Iñápirríkuli and mythic originator of cultivated plant species and all things associated with horticulture, including *pudáli* exchange ceremonies.

*kadápu*   Sacred ritual whips made of a vine, called *dzámakuápi*, used only for striking male and female initiates at the end of their periods of ritual fasting.

Kálimátu   The wasp-person sent up to the sky-world by Iñápirríkuli to lure Kuwái into coming down to the ground at Hípana.

*kapéti*   Ritual whips used for marking time in collective dance-songs called *kápetiápani* performed in *kwépani* ceremonies and in male and female initiation rituals.

*káridzámai*   Sacred food of the mythic ancestors consisting of hot-peppered, boiled meat over which *málikai* songs and chants have been performed.

*kémakáni hliméetaka hekwápi*   The powerful sound that opened up the world, or Kuwái's humming and singing-into-being the various species and objects of nature during the first creation.

*képinái*   A category of spirit-names that includes most bird species; like *éenunái* spirits, *képinái* are said to reside in *íyarudáti*.

*kérramu*   A newborn infant prior to the time when its parents undergo a rite of passage to end the period of fasting and seclusion.

Kuwái   The monstrous, primordial human being whose musical voice and instruments powerfully opened up the world.

Kuwaikánirri   A younger brother of Iñápirríkuli who was the first victim of witchcraft and whose cure consisted of traveling up to the home of the bee-spirits, or Kuwái-people.

Kuwáinai   Bee-spirits, or "Kuwái-people," who mediate between the world of living human beings and mythic ancestors in the sky-world.

*kwépani*   Kuwái-dance, or ceremonial exchanges of wild fruits over which the sacred flutes and trumpets of Kuwái are played.

*liakúna*   Spirit-name, or "place"; in *málikai* chanting and singing, each of these names consists of two parts, a generic name (e.g., *umáwari*, *éenunái, or képinái*) and a specific name.

*lidánam*   Shadow spirits, or spirits of recently deceased persons living in *íyarudáti* but capable of returning to the world of the living.

*likáriwa*   The celestial paradise of Iñápirríkuli, where the mythic ancestor spirits live, a place of eternal light and total purity.

*likáriwa*   The human body-shaped soul, or the individual identity, which must remain connected to a collective, animal-shaped dream soul during a person's lifetime.

*línupána*   The supernatural danger, or power to cause harm, that inheres to varying degrees in all things created by Kuwái's musical naming power.

*líwanápu éenu*   "The corner of the sky," or the place where Kuwái went to live after the events related in myths about Kuwái and Amáru; also the spirit-name for *kadápu* whips used in male and female initiation rituals.

Máapakwá Makákui   "Great Honey Place," or the most powerful place of the bee-spirits (Kuwáiñai), the center of ritual healing powers invoked in *málikai* counterwitchcraft songs.

Máhnekánari   "Nobody Knows"; an alternative name for Kuwái referring to the fact that no one knew the identity of his father.

*máhnetímnali*   Poison-owner, or sorcerer, who causes illnesses that must be reversed by shamans.

*málikai*   A complex genre of mythically powerful speech, including spoken, chanted, and sung performances in various sacred ritual contexts.

*málikai limínali*   Chant-owner, or ritual specialists who know how to perform and interpret *málikai* prayers, chants, and songs.

*malírri*   Shaman, or ritual curer.

*málirríkairi*   Shamans' songs.

*máliwéko*   House where spirits of the dead keep *éenunái* and *képinái* spirits in *íyarudáti*.

*molítu*   A species of small frog (unidentified) and namesake of short flutes played in sacred ceremonies and rituals; symbol of Iñápirríkuli's recapturing of Kuwái's sacred flutes and trumpets from Amáru and the women in myth and also a child of Káali used to schedule horticultural activities.

*mútsi*   White palm grubs that mature into *déetu* insects; in myth, the food used to lure Kuwái down to his fiery death at Hípana.

Mútsipáni   *Mútsi*-dance, or the mythic home of Amáru on the Aiarí River.

*pudáli*   Ceremonial exchanges of meat and manioc products between affines.

*tsépani*   Final dance-music of *kwépani* ceremonies, evoking the mythic episode in which Kuwái ate and vomited three boys who had prematurely ended their ritual fast and uniting the five fingers of Kuwái's mythic hand.

*umáwari*   Anaconda; in *málikai* chanting and singing, *umáwari* is the category of spirit-names that includes fish and aquatic animal spirits, which are said to reside along with people in *hekwápiríko*.

*wadzúhiakau nakúna*   "We go in search of the names," or the more dynamic process of moving through a variety of different categorical and place names in *málikai* chanting and singing.

*wakáitaka yénpiti*   "We speak to our child," or female initiation rituals.

*wákapétaka yénpitipé*   "We show our children," or male initiation rituals.

*wakéetaka nakúna papíniritsa*   "We heap up the names in a single place," or the more static process of invoking a large number of specific names within a single place or category before moving to a new category of spirit-names.

*waliáduwa*   Sacred flutes played in sets of three during *kwépani* ceremonies to represent the outer three fingers of the mythic hand of Kuwái; term means "new-like" and refers to the implicit theme of social renewal in *kwépani* ceremonies.

*wálimerú*   Recently initiated girl.

*wálitáki*   "Newly fasted," or recently initiated males.

Wámidzáka Ipérrikána   "The one who is like our older brother"; an alternative name for Kuwái; as the first human being to be born from a human mother (Amáru), Kuwái is like an older brother to all human beings born after him.

*yárinárinai*   An indigenous term for white people.

Keepers of the Sacred Chants

# 1

## An Introduction to Wakuénai
## Ritual Poetics

On a hot, sunny afternoon in August, 1981, the headman of Gavilán sang a mythic tale of bee-spirits, flowers, and honey, stopping from time to time to exhale the cooling, sweetening powers of these primal healing substances into a tightly covered pot of manioc beer. In a small clearing behind the house, the headman's brother inhaled hallucinogenic snuff to make the spirits of the dead visible in the sky and sang for the return of a dying child's lost soul to the world of the living. The shaman vividly acted out his musical retrieval of souls from the world of the dead by sucking at the sky through the feathers of his sacred maraca, carrying deep breaths of tobacco smoke across the clearing, and blowing smoke onto the heads of the patient and her family. A small crowd of people gathered to watch the ritual, and the shaman blew tobacco smoke onto the head of each person present.

Across the eastern channel of the river surrounding the island-village, dark clouds appeared above the green canopy of the rain forest and began to move toward us. By then the shaman had sung and snuffed himself into a deep trance, and he worked to capture the cooling winds of the approaching storm with his tobacco, stones, and maraca. The winds ceased, and the air became sultry and still. The shaman sang at the storm cloud, which blocked out all sunlight and dropped heavy rains over the manioc gardens across the river. He finished a song and stood up to talk to the cloud, mumbling questions through the feathers of his maraca until a loud crash of thunder obliterated the sound of his voice. For several minutes he spoke like this to the storm cloud that hung over the manioc gardens but that did not cross over to the village, and the gathering of participants sat spellbound by the shaman's magical conversation with thunder.

When the rains finally began to fall, those gathered took shelter in the small cooking area behind the adobe-walled house. I perched next to Siderio, the headman's son, on the step of the doorway between the house and kitchen, a position where we could simultaneously listen to the headman's singing of the mythic journey of the first witchcraft victim and the shaman's musical journeys to the houses of recently deceased persons. Heavy tropical rains pounded against the thatched roof, producing a background din of natural sound that was punctuated by frequent explosive peals of thunder from nearby lightning bolts. In less than ten minutes, the rain began to let up, and the thunder became a distant rumbling over the forests to the west, the place where the sun falls and where shamans search through the houses of the dead. In the coolness produced by the late afternoon storm, no one moved except the shaman, who stood up between songs to search the eastern sky for shadow-spirits. Inside, the headman continued the steady rhythmic pulse of sung mythic speech, musically naming-into-being all the classes of bee-spirits and flowering fruit trees to sweeten the patient's heart and to turn around the lethal process of an uncontained mythic ancestral power spreading sickness and death among the living.

I tape recorded the sounds of the two curers at work but did not feel like taking notes or doing anything else that could create an intellectual distance between me and the rest of the gathering. As we listened to the headman's musical journey through the center of the world and the shaman's agitated travels to and from the edge of the world, we felt surrounded by a kind of energy, or power, that emerged from the voices of two men who had been practicing their art of ritual healing for decades and who were popularly esteemed as the most competent and powerful healers in the entire Upper Río Negro region of Venezuela. We were in a musically produced space-time of reversed mythic creation, a process of creating a feeling of unity between the musicality of speech, the mythic meanings of speech, the physical movements or postures of individual bodies, the forces of nature, and the grief shared by a community of people.

The curing ritual marked a major shift in the way I approached my project of documenting and interpreting indigenous performances of musicalized ritual speech. The shaman's musical dialogue with the spirits of the dead touched off an interior dialogue within me. I had intellectually prepared for this moment through years of training in universities and months of fieldwork on indigenous language, narratives, rituals, and social organization. I had carefully taken notes on beliefs about various kinds of ritual power and mythic beings, including the belief that young men training to become shamans had to learn how to call upon and converse with wind, rain, thunder, and lightning. However, none of this prior intellectual activity prepared me for the feeling of power that ran through the shaman's musical linking together of natural forces and a community of people united by a common sentiment of grief over the impending death of a child. Before retiring to my hammock that night, I wrote in my diary about this feeling and the tension between it and the intellectual project of documenting and interpreting the shaman's ritual activities.

When I awoke the next morning, the feeling of tension had not disappeared but had been transformed into a kind of physical energy that drew me deeper into the grief-laden underworld of the shaman's singing-into-being of the various spirits of sickness and death. The headman and other people were distracted that morning with the activity of bartering for gasoline from a Ministry of Environment launch that was making a rare trip from Maroa to San Carlos de Río Negro. As the shaman set up a small screen of palm fronds and laid out an array of tobacco, hallucinogenic snuff, stones, and other sacred objects, I set up my remote stereo microphones, camera, notebooks, and a small chair off to his side. Any lingering doubts about the appropriateness of taking photographs and writing down my thoughts and observations were replaced by an almost diametrically opposed feeling that I not only could but had to write down every detail of the shaman's activities and the day's unfolding ritual drama. It was as if my inscription of events, rather than acting as a barrier of distanced intellectual observation, had become a necessary and desirable part of the ritual process. Although I did not become consciously aware of the indigenous explanations for this change until several weeks later, I was emotionally "plugged in" to the circuits of ritual energy and wrote about these feelings in my diary.

"By noon, when the mother and child came outside, I felt as tuned as a concert piano. The heat was horrible, but I scarcely even felt it. My hand wrote page after page of notes, but it didn't hurt at all, it just flowed along without effort. My little chair was hard and uncomfortable, but I felt comfortable nevertheless. I had eaten only two arepas with coffee at nine, but I felt no hunger at all. And so it went" (Hill, field diary, August 6, 1981: 278–79).

From that time on, I no longer had to request information about ritual and ceremonial events but was told about them, sometimes in advance, and asked to be present with my tape recorder, notebooks, and camera. In the process of experiencing and documenting the curing ritual, I had moved from a distanced, intellectual level of understanding to a more intuitive, emotionally charged way of connecting with the social universe of the Arawakan Wakuénai. At the same time, the headman and other people in the village had begun to actively participate in my research project.

What accounted for this dual process of crossing cultural boundaries? From the perspective of a historically oriented North American anthropologist, the indigenous response could perhaps be attributed to their desire to have a permanent record of their most valued cultural performances in the face of centuries of external pressures by missionaries, traders, and others who have denigrated, extirpated, and shown little or no willingness to understand, much less appreciate, the value of indigenous ritual performances. Although this line of reasoning was consistent with the indigenous concern for ritually powerful ways of speaking as a means for asserting cultural continuity between mythic ancestors and living human descendants, to explain the sudden emergence of indigenous interest in my project in such intellectually historical terms was not entirely satisfactory. I had previously discussed the rationale and probable results of my research with people in the village, but it was unlikely that they were so strongly motivated by my descriptions of government ministries, musical archives, research institutions, academic publishers, and university classrooms.

The real reasons emerged several weeks later in a series of conversations with the village headman and keeper of *málikai,* Hernan Yusrinu. The shaman's musical journeys through the underworld are a process of searching for and retrieving the patient's body-soul, which has been lost or stolen due to the actions of poison-owners or spirits that cause sickness. Shamans use the feathers of their sacred rattles and tobacco smoke to capture their patients' wandering body-souls, and they seek to restore these souls to their proper place by blowing tobacco smoke over the top of their patients' heads. Upon learning this, I asked Hernan why his brother had also blown tobacco smoke over the heads of the patient's family members as well as everyone else present at the ritual gathering. Hernan responded by making an analogy: each person's body-soul is like the compression inside a motor, so the shaman seeks to gather up the collective forces of everyone present by blowing tobacco smoke over their heads. In other words, blowing tobacco smoke over people's heads links their body-souls together to form a collective force that helps the shaman attract the patient's body-soul back from the underworld of spirits of the dead to the world of the living.

Hernan elaborated upon his analogy by commenting that his brother's curing powers worked very much like my tape recorder and writing. Just as the tape recorder and notebooks pulled in the sounds and sensations of the curing ritual, so also were the shaman's singing and smoke blowing a way of pulling in the patient's body-soul. With that statement I began to understand the curing ritual, the release of physical energy I had felt, and my changing relations with Wakuénai people of the village in a new light. From indigenous perspectives, the curing ritual embodied an overlapping, or alignment, between my study of ritually powerful ways of speaking and the actual practice of those rituals. However, this insight did not fully prepare me for Hernan's next statement: "My brother was afraid that his songs would break your tape recorder. But when you began to record his songs and write in your notebooks, he felt that your work was good for you and that it helped him to gather up compression." This commentary confirmed my earlier understanding of the curing ritual as a convergence of shamanistic practice and the study of those practices, but it also puzzled me. Why all the analogies with machines and writing, and why the fear that the shaman's musical and other ritual activities would destroy the tape recorder?

The answers to these puzzling questions became clearer after I had been studying the principles of spirit-naming in *málikai* chants performed during childbirth rituals. Hernan had made it clear that whites, mestizos, and other people who were not born into the Wakuénai social world as members of one of the various hierarchically ranked patrilineal families were not included in, or affected by, the dynamics of indigenous ritual performance. Indeed, the invocation of the Tobacco Spirits of the White People, and Hernan's somewhat ironic interpretation of this spirit-name, hinged upon this exclusion of whites and other outsiders. White people, Hernan explained, did not have collective, animal-shaped dream souls like those of the Wakuénai, so when white people became parents they were able to return to work immediately after the birth without going through a period of fasting, seclusion, and other ritual restrictions.

For this reason, the spirit-name of the Whites' Tobacco was invoked in childbirth rituals that mark the end of the period of seclusion and fasting for Wakuénai and other indigenous parents.

Although I fully grasped the ironic twist of logic in Hernan's explanation, I could not reconcile the idea that White people were excluded from the ritual powers surrounding childbirth and yet at the same time remained susceptible to the lethal effects of indigenous witchcraft. "White people do have collective dream souls," Hernan continued, "but their dream souls take the form of books and papers. The missionary's soul is a Bible, the merchant's soul is a financial record, and the anthropologist's soul is his notebook." That explained the convergence: the very paper and ink with which I was writing down Hernan's answers to my questions were material embodiments of a dream soul, and since the words I was recording concerned indigenous spirit-names, musical sounds, body-souls, and other ritually powerful forces, my project had become a collaborative construction of an anthropological identity, or dream soul, a synthesis of Hernan's knowledgeable interpretations and performances with my ongoing inquiries into those same realms of indigenous thought and action.

After a brief moment of silence, Hernan continued his answer to my question. "A witch can attack a White man's dream soul at night while he sleeps, killing the victim by ripping the book in half, just as a witch cuts up the animal-shaped souls of Wakuénai victims." That observation made me a bit nervous about the safety of my fieldnotes, but it also explained why the shaman had been afraid that his musical searches among the spirits of the dead could have broken my tape recorder. If the tape recorder had broken, it would have meant that indigenous witches had destroyed the emergent anthropological dream soul. The fact that my tape recorder did not break and that my writing was felt as "good," both for my purposes and the shaman's curing practices, meant that the anthropological identity was resistant to witches, spirits of the dead, and other disease-causing spirits, and that it was therefore capable of helping to "gather compression" and "pull in" body-souls.

The dialogue between Hernan and me continued over the remainder of my stay in Gavilán in 1981 and during return visits in the summers of 1984 and 1985. The importance of the initial dialogue triggered by the curing ritual of August 1981 was twofold: on the one hand, our conversations located and defined the anthropological process of inquiry within indigenous frameworks of understanding ritual power; on the other hand, our discussions opened up a cross-cultural metadiscourse about the principal genres of ritually powerful speech, the ideas and episodes transmitted in narratives about mythic and historical pasts, and the complex interrelations between ritually powerful speech and narrative discourse. By grounding the process of anthropological research in Wakuénai ways of understanding ritual power, our conversations about writing and dream-souls transformed the meaning of the fieldwork from a process of accumulating knowledge based on alien assumptions and questions into a process of creating knowledge together within the framework of indigenous assumptions. Because of this change, Hernan and his brother were able to understand my project of inscribing ritually powerful speech as an activity that was inside their sphere of control. For my part, the transition embodied in our discussions of writing and dream-souls was a matter of allowing Hernan and his brother to take on a more active role in defining and structuring the questions and directions of the research. To be sure, I continued to ask questions that only an anthropologically trained outsider could have raised and that were probably regarded as irrelevant curiosities by the Wakuénai people of Gavilán. However, when the subject was directly related to performances of ritually powerful speech and its interpretation, I had become keenly aware that Hernan and his brother were master-poets whose understanding of historical, social, linguistic, and other dimensions of ritual power were at least as sophisticated as the theories I had learned in undergraduate and graduate studies in anthropology and related disciplines. In effect, they became my teachers rather than mere informants.

The translations and interpretations of ritually powerful speech that form the primary subjects of this book aim at demonstrating how senior, highly ranked Wakuénai ritual specialists understood their practices in the early 1980s. This book is more of an exercise in the imaginative potentials of ethnographic inquiry than an attempt to compare Wakuénai ritual power to other indigenous religions or to social theories of power. The methodological approach to ritual power taken in this book follows from the way Wakuénai ritual specialists understand their practices. In the most general sense, chant-owners and shamans evaluate their own and other specialists' ritual powers not only in terms of their command of the overall repertoire of performance genres and subgenres, but also by how well they can relate specific formal features of the language of ritual performances to specific concepts and episodes that are related in mythic narratives. Even nonspecialists know the literal meanings of many of the words used as spirit-names in *málikai,* but they do not know the precise nuances of mythic meaning that such names embody, nor do they understand the poetic processes of using taxonomies of spirit-names to create complex arrangements of visual, tactile, auditory, and synesthesic imagery that embody the life-giving powers of the mythic ancestors. To become a powerful keeper of *málikai,* it is necessary to know that some spirit-names are more powerful than others because they "have stories," to have a detailed understanding of those stories, and to be able to explain how the stories influence the form and context of spirit-names invoked in performances of *málikai.*

These two indigenous ideas, that ritual power inheres in the breadth of knowledge across genres and subgenres of performance and in the ability to interrelate the form and context of ritual language to narratives, are fundamental to the organization and contents of this book. The goal is to focus broadly on the major subgenres of *málikai,* as well as the less complex genre of shamans' songs (*málirríkairi*), to provide an understanding of how the overall repertoire informs and energizes the performance of each specific subgenre. Performances of *málikai* counterwitchcraft songs, for example, are based on the metaphor of "turning around" destructive processes by restoring properly mediated relations between mythic ancestors and their living human descendants. Understanding these metaphorical means of "turning around" witchcraft requires a knowledge of spirit-naming processes that are employed in the ongoing creation of human relations with mythic ancestors during childbirth and initiation rituals. At the same time, specific performances of *málikai* counterwitchcraft songs derive much of their expressive force against a background knowledge of mythic narratives about bee-spirits, flowers, and honey, as well as other narratives about the coming-into-being of socialized individual humanness and collective processes of social reproduction. In short, this book aims to replicate as closely as possible the manner in which Wakuénai ritual specialists understand their ritual powers by ranging broadly across (sub)genres of performance and by weaving back and forth between the language of ritual and the mythic stories that are evoked in rituals.

## The Arawakan Wakuénai of Venezuela

The Wakuénai people living in Gavilán during the early 1980s were related by complex ties of kinship and marriage to an extensive network of people living along the lower Guainía and Negro rivers in Venezuela, the upper Guainía and Cuyarí rivers in Colombia, and the Içana and Aíarí rivers in Brazil (see Figure 1.1). Social relations among these widespread

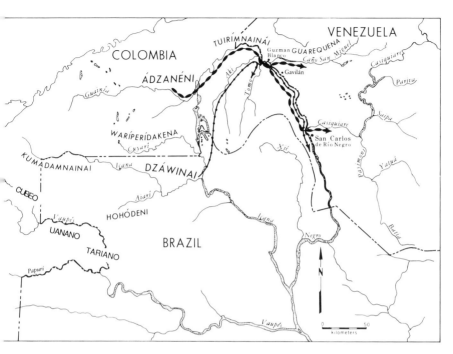

1.1    *Map of the Northwest Amazon region (adapted from Hill and Moran 1983: 120)*

local peoples were undergoing rapid change in the 1980s, due to the division of Wakuénai ancestral lands among three nation-states, the schism of Wakuénai peoples into nominally Protestant and Catholic converts, and various other forces. Despite all the changes taking place and a centuries-long history of interethnic relations characterized by enslavement, forced relocation, depopulation, and indebtedness, the Wakuénai continued to organize themselves into hierarchically ranked phratries, or groupings of five or so patrilineal sibs whose members regarded themselves as descendants of a set of ancestral mythic brothers.

Along the lower Guainía, the phratry had ceased to be a territorially based set of patrisibs occupying a continuous stretch of riverine territory, yet it still served to demarcate the boundary between classificatory kin and marriageable outsiders and to differentiate between higher and lower social statuses. These two dimensions of phratric organization, or the regulation of marriage and the serial ranking of patrisibs according to the order of mythic ancestral emergence, were explicitly linked together by the prescription that members of highly ranked sibs in one phratry intermarry only with members of highly ranked sibs in other phratries. The headman of Gavilán and his brother, for example, were members of a highly ranked sib from the Dzáwinai (Jaguar-People) phratry, and their wives and other in-laws were members of the most highly ranked sib from the Waríperídakéna (Pleiades'-Grandchildren) phratry.

The prevalence of ranked social organization and hierarchies of ritual specialists among the Wakuénai and their Eastern Tukanoan neighbors to the south and west sets the Northwest Amazon region apart from all other contemporary indigenous societies of lowland South America. Hierarchically ranked forms of social organization like those found in the Northwest Amazon today were undoubtedly more widespread and common in Amazonia and adjacent areas prior to the arrival of European peoples, diseases, and technologies. Previous studies of rank and hierarchy in the Northwest Amazon have focused mainly on Eastern Tukanoan groups, who are perhaps most renowned for their practices of language group exogamy and institutionalized multilingualism (Jackson 1983). Ethnographic studies of the Wakuénai and other Northern Arawakan peoples still lag far behind the extensive literature focused upon Eastern Tukanoan peoples (Goldman 1963; Reichel-Dolmatoff 1971, 1975; C. Hugh-Jones 1979; S. Hugh-Jones 1979; Arhem 1981; Jackson 1983). This book fills a major gap in the ethnology of the Northwest Amazon region by providing a detailed account of the dynamics of ritual power among the Arawakan Wakuénai of Venezuela.

Some general background on the Upper Río Negro region and its peoples is contained in the accounts of early explorers who traveled through the region (Humboldt 1852; Spruce 1970) and in reports written by early ethnographers (Koch-Gruenberg 1909; Nimuendaju 1950 [1927]; Tavera Acosta 1927). A more detailed account of Wakuénai social life and religion appeared in *Vida Indiana* (1912) by Martin Matos Arvelo, who served as Prefect of Maroa in the 1890s and early 1900s. Although he was not formally trained in anthropology, Matos Arvelo wrote a sensitive, informative ethnography based on years of direct interaction with the Wakuénai of the Guainía River, including initiation into the cult of Kuwái. More specialized studies include articles on social change and kinship terminologies (Galvão 1959, 1964; Oliveira and Galvão 1973; Oliveira 1975; Hill and Moran 1983; Hill 1984a; Wilbert 1966), social organization (Hill 1984b, 1985b; Journet 1981), mythology (Saake 1968), history (Wright and Hill 1986; Hill and Wright 1988), religion (Hill 1985a), and ceremonial exchange (Hill 1987a, 1987b). In addition, ecologists have published a number of studies focusing on the region's nutrient-poor rain forests and acidic blackwater rivers (Jordan 1979; Jordan and Uhl 1978; Herrera, Jordan, Medina, and Klinge 1978; Clark and Uhl 1988; Sanford, Saldarriaga, Clark, Uhl, and Herrera 1985; Saldarriaga and West 1987).

Throughout the Northwest Amazon region, ritual hierarchy is intrinsically connected to the ecology of blackwater rivers and to competitive, egalitarian relations of exchange among phratries and language groups. European colonizers nicknamed the Río Negro "The River of Hunger," a label that resonates profoundly with Wakuénai sacred myths and rituals that establish the individual's ability to control hunger through ritual fasting as the most basic means of becoming fully human. The Upper Río Negro region is characterized by nutrient-poor soils, highly acidic rivers, and tightly closed cycling of forest nutrients (Herrera, Jordan, Medina, and Klinge 1978). Fish and other animal biomass is extremely low, even by Amazonian standards, and more than 250 mm of rain falls even during the so-called dry season months of January to March. The region lies almost directly along the equator where there is considerably less variation in rainfall between wet and dry seasons than in areas to the north, such as the llanos of Colombia and Venezuela.

Despite high amounts of rainfall during all months of the year, the Río Negro and its tributaries rise and fall more than 7 m on a regular and predictable schedule, and this hydrological cycle has profound consequences for both human and nonhuman populations inhabiting the region. When the rivers fall during dry-season months, fish and aquatic animal species are concentrated in shallow, narrow channels, which become relatively productive sources of meat for human consumption. Hunting also becomes more productive as floodwaters recede, allowing men to use dogs for tracking peccary, tapir, deer, and other forest animals. These conditions abruptly change with the onset of heavier rains in April and the rising of rivers to form vast areas of flooded forest. Fish and other aquatic animal species migrate into this semi-terrestrial environment, where they spawn and fatten up. At the height of the April-to-August wet season, more than 65 percent of the forests are flooded, and the productivity of both hunting and fishing drops to precariously low levels. After the long wet season, river levels fluctuate during the months of September to December, providing somewhat improved hunting and fishing conditions. Cultivation of bitter manioc in swidden gardens provides a steady source of calories throughout the year. However, the extremely nutrient-poor soils of the region do not allow indigenous horticulturalists the option of producing protein-rich grain crops in sufficient quantities to buffer against the scarcity of fish and game meat during long wet seasons.

The seasonal alternation between relative abundance of hunting and fishing resources during dry seasons and nearly total absence of such resources during wet seasons is both materially and meaningfully integrated into social organization and ritual performances of the Wakuénai and other indigenous peoples of the Northwest Amazon region. Beginning with Mauss's famous "Essai sur les Variations Saisonnaires de Sociétiés Eskimos" (Essay on Seasonal Variations of the Eskimo) (1968), anthropologists have taken a keen interest in studying and understanding how peoples with simple technologies adapt to dramatic shifts in the availability of local food supplies. Laughlin (1974) has demonstrated how the range of reciprocal food sharing cycles inward to only the closest consanguineal relatives during periods of drought among the So of East Africa. With the end of drought-triggered deprivation, the ranges of balanced and generalized reciprocity gradually open up into wider networks of exchange among affinally related groups and with strangers who are outside local networks. The contraction and expansion of socioeconomic relations are closely tied to natural cycles of drought and rainfall, which in turn directly influence the efficiency and productivity of subsistence activities. This "accordion effect" leads to flexible, dual forms of social organization, especially in societies where seasonal changes entail shifts, not only in the number of basic resources, but also in their type and quantity. The concept of diaphasis, or the "tendency for an adaptive infrastructure to integrate constraints on social action and coordinate them with recursive environmental change" (Laughlin and Brady 1978:21), has great utility for understanding Wakuénai social relations as a dynamic process of opening and closing, or expansion and contraction, that is integrally connected to the natural rhythms of falling and rising river levels in the Upper Río Negro region (Hill 1984b, 1989). Moreover, this duality is not limited to a simple one-to-one parallelism between ecological and social processes but is embodied within the cycle of narratives about the two-fold creation of the world during the time of primordial, mythic human beings, integrated into the ritually powerful musical naming processes of *málikai,* and collectively enacted in exchange ceremonies.

The Wakuénai practice two distinct types of exchange ceremony, each concerned with different features of social organization that are grounded in contrasting ecological conditions of abundance versus scarcity. *Pudáli,* or ceremonial offerings of food and other gifts between affinally related groups, expands the range of reciprocal giving and taking in conditions of relative abundance. The ideal time to begin a cycle of *pudáli* exchanges is at the very beginning of the long wet season, a brief period of superabundance when Leporinus fish migrate and spawn in newly flooded forests and are captured in great quantities as they return to the river channels. Ceremonial dances in *pudáli* celebrate this cultural ideal through the playing of large trumpets, whose low bass sounds are said to replicate the sound of rivers and streams rumbling with migrating, spawning Leporinus fish (Hill 1983, 1987b). In practice a local group may initiate a *pudáli* exchange with actual or potential affines during any season of the year when they experience a sizable surplus of fish or game meat. After an opening, male-owned ceremony in which guests offer presentations of smoked meat and trumpets to their hosts, the latter agree to sponsor a female-owned *pudáli* in which processed manioc pulp is given to the initiators of the cycle. *Pudáli* ceremonial cycles are concerned with the dispersal, or expansion, of local patrisibs through forming widespread networks of trade and intermarriage. *Pudáli* ceremonies also coordinate these dynamic social processes with natural processes of fish migrations and spawning, a brief period of superabundance that marks the beginning of the long wet season and that acts as a release mechanism for ceremonial exchange.

A distinctly different type of ceremonial exchange called *kwépani* (dance of Kuwái) takes place only when there is an abundance of wild palm fruits. Although guest groups are invited to participate in these sacred events, the exchange of wild fruits does not serve as a means for expanding affinal relations but for constructing a ritual hierarchy of adult males through performances on sacred flutes and trumpets that are strictly taboo for women and children. Whereas *pudáli* opens up an arena for competitive, egalitarian relations between men and women from different kin groups, *kwépani* narrows the range of social relations to mediate symbolically the passing down of sacred ritual power from a senior generation of specialists and male elders to a younger group of apprentices and adult men (Hill 1993a). *Pudáli* ceremonies are occasions for joyous feasting in times of abundance, whereas *kwépani* ceremonies require people to fast on a diet of wild fruit juices in solemn commemoration of mythic ancestors. Although some of the wild fruit species exchanged in *kwépani* ripen during dry season months, the great majority of these fruit species ripen during May and June at the height of the long wet season. During the early 1980s, the most common time for holding *kwépani* ceremonies in the Venezuelan Río Negro region was mid to late

June, precisely when the productivity of hunting and fishing had bot-
tomed out and would stay close to zero for several more weeks (Hill
1984b).

Dual ceremonial complexes similar to those of the Wakuénai have been
reported among various Eastern Tukano-speaking peoples of the Vaupés
Basin in Brazil and Colombia (Jackson 1983; S. Hugh-Jones 1979;
Reichel-Dolmatoff 1971). The contrast between food exchange ceremonies concerned with transcending local social boundaries and wild
fruit ceremonies emphasizing continuity of male-controlled ritual power
within local groups is highly salient throughout the Northwest Amazon
region. Nevertheless, important symbolic, social, and ecological connections integrate these two types of ceremonial exchanges. As Jackson has
pointed out, "The food exchange rituals are concerned with reciprocity.
The fruit and initiation rituals are concerned with growth, fertility, and
continuation. In a deeper sense these two types are linked, the one ensuring the continued production of people and food and the other ensuring
the proper exchange of these between groups of people" (1983: 202).
Indeed, closer examination of the symbolism of musical performances,
dances, and other dimensions of *pudáli* and *kwépani* has revealed that
the two types of ceremony are grounded in a common underlying symbolic process of metamorphosis, or self-generativity and transformation
(Hill 1993a).

The constant interplay between ritual hierarchy and social equality,
always situated in the fluctuating seasonal cycles of rising and falling river
levels, is what makes the Wakuénai so fascinating and challenging for
anthropological study. The complexities of mythic meanings, musical
sounds, and other dimensions of Wakuénai ritual and ceremonial performance are in many respects more readily comparable to ritual speech
genres in larger, more hierarchical societies such as the Kuna of Panama
(Sherzer 1983) or the Kogi of highland Colombia (Reichel-Dolmatoff
1987) than to ritual performances among Gê, Tupí, and Carib-speaking
peoples of lowland South America. At the same time, these complex hierarchical processes of meaning construction are very firmly rooted in
basic practical objectives of everyday survival in a nutrient-poor, blackwater rain-forest environment that affords a tremendously rich diversity
of useful and edible natural species but only an impoverished number of
individuals within each species.

Performances of ritually powerful speech are usually not directly tied
to ecological scheduling, for the timing of such performances is necessarily determined by human social events such as childbirth, the onset of

puberty, and occurences of illness and death. Wakuénai shamans and keepers of *málikai* are not full-time specialists who control nonspecialists' behavior through coercion but individuals who participate directly in the daily activities of production: manioc gardening, fishing, hunting, gathering wild plants, house and canoe building, and so on. As leaders of their local communities, the keepers of *málikai* are expected to demonstrate a heightened concern for aesthetic and moral dimensions of village social life, but they are in no way exempt from practical activities of producing foods and other basic resources. For example, if a headman wishes to improve the appearance of the village before the arrival of visitors from another community, he (and perhaps his adult sons) will begin clearing weeds, picking up garbage, and otherwise beautifying the village. Wakuénai ritual specialists are elders who lead by example and persuasive organization of collective sentiments. Because they are not exempt from everyday productive activities, they cannot lose touch with the basic ecological conditions facing the local community. The complex webs of meaning and musicality that specialists employ in ritual performances are inseparable from basic concerns for survival, growth, and health.

Just as the power of ritual specialists is relativized by its grounding in everyday, practical activities of economic production, so also is the specialized vocabulary of *málikai* constrained by its grounding in the experiential worlds of nature and society. The objects of ritual discourse are, at least at one level, no different from the most commonly experienced objects of everyday life: natural species and materials used in extracting foods and other necessities from the environment and basic human physiological processes experienced in the course of the life cycle. Although *málikai* does not significantly alter the objects of everyday experience and discourse, the language of *málikai* creatively reformulates the same range of natural and social phenomena into a more hyperanimate, powerful world of mythic beings and the presocial, cosmological processes whereby the experiential world originally came into being. *Málikai* is thus a masterful poetic synthesis of the practical, ecological knowledge of natural species upon which human society depends for its survival and the mythic significance of these species as verbal metaphors for the socialization of individual human beings.

The construction of ritual hierarchy in performances of *málikai* and other genres of sacred speech is a historically dynamic process of using the diversity of natural species in the Upper Río Negro region as a poetic tableau of colors, sounds, textures, and other imagery to mediate between categories of social being. This process of defining individual humanness and collective social relations as a poetic transformation of natural diversity is both pragmatically situated in the cyclical alternation of dry and wet seasons and historically engaged in the long-term development of interethnic relations between the Wakuénai and expanding political economies of colonial and national states. Performances of ritually powerful speech coordinate transitions between hierarchical and egalitarian modes of social organization in changing ecological conditions and also in contexts of irreversible historical change.

The historical significance of ritual hierarchy as an indigenous resource for symbolically appropriating historical change is perhaps best illustrated by nineteenth-century millenarian movements in which charismatic leaders mobilized local ancestor cults of the Wakuénai, Baré, and Baniwa into cults of resistance to the political economy of indebtedness. The Wakuénai remember these movements in narratives about the Rubber Boom era (ca. 1860–1920) (Hill 1990; Hill and Wright 1988). Taken together with written historical accounts about the nineteenth-century movements, these narratives provide insight into how the Wakuénai understand the past as a process of opening up a shared historical space-time with Western peoples. At the same time, these narrative counter-discourses socialize the raw events of political coercion, economic exploitation, and even genocide by placing them within the framework of indigenous concepts of reempowerment through shamanistic reversals of sickness, decay, and death. These same processes of transforming disempowerment through ritually organized collective action were very much in evidence during the early 1980s along the Río Negro of Venezuela. In July of 1981, for example, a Wakuénai shaman coordinated a series of sacred ceremonial performances that specifically aimed to protest the unfair economic practices of merchants working along the river (Hill 1993b). In short, ritual hierarchy among the Wakuénai is an art of "practical signification" (Brown 1985) that both grounds human social relations in the natural ecology of the Upper Río Negro region and that dynamically transforms them in the ongoing history of interethnic relations in the region.

## The Musicality of Speech and the Semantics of Musical Sound

As a form of verbal art, *málikai* can be understood as a process of linking the experiential world of objects, species, and persons together with a conceptual universe of powerful mythic beings. However, this ritual in-

tegration of everyday social life and primordial mythic power is not re-
ducible to a purely verbal, semantically encoded conveyance of attributes.
*Málikai* is also a musical art that includes spoken, chanted, and sung
speech as well as all the subtle gradations and mixtures of these varying
degrees of musicality. The most central idea of this ethnography of ritually powerful speech is that there are systematic correspondences between
the verbal construction of meanings embodied in the language of *málikai*
and the musical creation of meanings instantiated in the tones, tempos,
rhythms, volumes, and timbres of speech. Although cast in terms of a
general theory of language, Paul Friedrich's recent definition of poetry
provides an elegantly concise model for understanding the culturally specific semantic and musical processes embodied in *málikai*:

> Poetry . . . is the symbolic process by which the individual mediates
> between the music of a natural language and the (nuances of) mythic
> meaning. To create felt consubstantiality between language music and
> myth is the master trope of poetry—"master" because it is superordi-
> nate to and in control over such lesser figures as image, metaphor,
> and paradox. (Friedrich 1986:39)

In performances of *málikai,* Wakuénai ritual specialists use the lyrical,
rhythmic qualities of speech to explore poetically the outer limits of
meanings originating in narratives about the coming-into-being of humanness and human social relations during mythic space-times.

Describing and interpreting these complex interweavings of mythic
meaning and musical sound require sensitivity to the inherent difficulties
of translation. Recent works on the interrelations between narrative and
music in lowland South America have demonstrated that the boundaries
between spoken speech and sung speech are by no means clear-cut (Seeger 1986; Graham 1986). In many cases, the musicality of speech is con-
ceptually and pragmatically integrated within genres of spoken speech,
such as narratives and ceremonial dialogues (Basso 1985; Sherzer 1983;
Sherzer and Urban 1986; Urban 1986). By focusing upon actual mani-
festations of language use and the indigenous theories of meaning which
inform these activities, these studies have contributed to a deeper understanding of the musical dimensions of spoken and sung speech in lowland
South America. Broad, *a priori* distinctions, such as Lévi-Strauss's opposition (1969:27) between musical language and articulate speech,
have given way to a fine-grained concern for the rhythm, tonality, meter,
timbre, and in short, musicality of all speech varieties (Sherzer and Urban
1986). Methodologically, this approach has required researchers to rec-

ognize that transcription and translation of indigenous speech genres are themselves complex, analytical procedures rather than a simple, literal rendering of texts.

This study of ritually powerful speech among the Wakuénai builds upon the growing number of discourse-centered ethnographies by providing detailed, line-by-line transcriptions and translations of specific performances of *málikai*. The method employed here closely resembles the works of Seeger (1986) and Graham (1986) by exploring contrasts and similarities across (sub)genres of ritual performance and through paying close attention to musical as well as verbal dimensions of ritual speech. This study does not attempt to make broad comparisons across widely separate areas of lowland South America but instead works inward from the more general concerns of interpretive social anthropology into the intricacies of meaning and power embodied in specific performances of *málikai*. The theoretical perspective that informs this study is intracultural, historical, and interpretive; mythic narratives and ritual discourse are understood as ongoing processes of creating linguistically and culturally differentiated forms and meanings in specific historical and ecological contexts (Sullivan 1988; Turner 1988; Eco 1990; Hill 1988; Whitten 1978).

The decision to take an interpretive, historical approach to mythic narratives does not mean that the narratives themselves cannot be treated as instances of discourse. For a number of pragmatic reasons, I chose to take the discourse of ritually performed speech as the primary focus of study. My fieldwork with the Wakuénai during the early 1980s was constrained by constant struggles to obtain official permits from the Venezuelan government and to get local and regional officials to authorize the permits that I had received from the national government. Under the circumstances, I had to establish priorities, and I chose to focus on exact documentation of the language, sounds, and indigenous interpretations of *málikai* and other genres of ritual and ceremonial performance rather than mythic discourse. To some extent, my research priorities reflected indigenous concerns for having performances of *málikai* recorded and studied as a means of helping to preserve for future generations a performance tradition that was clearly central to the social regeneration and historical persistence of their culture. These considerations in no way imply that mythic narratives do not in themselves play an important role in cultural continuity, nor that these narrative performances are lacking in musical and other stylistic and poetic qualities worthy of special attention. Such detailed transcriptions and translations of mythic discourse would make an extremely valuable study, and perhaps someday I will be able to return to the field with that specific goal in mind.

My decision to focus on *málikai* also had to do with the fact that only chant-owners with great experience and talent were able to produce the kind of metadiscursive commentary on the meanings of *málikai* in relation to mythic discourse. In the Venezuelan Río Negro, Hernan Yusrinu was one of only a handful of individuals of this stature, and he was already elderly in 1984. Sadly, I learned in November of 1991 from my Venezuelan colleagues, Omar Gonzalez and Silvia Vidal, that Hernan had died in October 1991. It was best that I chose to focus on *málikai* in the early and mid-1980s while Hernan was still actively practicing in Venezuela. I can always return to study mythic narratives and obtain fully nuanced interpretations of these performances, but I could not hope for comparable depth of indigenous interpretation of *málikai* chanting and singing.

My approach to mythic narratives in chapter 3 draws heavily on post-structuralist modes of myth analysis (Munn 1969; Turner 1985) and pragmatic theories of meaning construction (Eco 1990). The analysis of mythic narratives as practical, ecologically and historically situated processes of meaning construction aims at identifying underlying principles that are broadly significant in a wide variety of ritual and social contexts. Once identified, these principles of meaning construction provide a guideline for entering into the fine-grained details and interminglings of musical sound and mythic meaning in specific performances of ritually powerful speech. Most importantly, the myth analysis in chapter 3 allows micro-linguistic analyses of ritual discourse to be understood in relation to broader relations of cultural meaning rather than broken apart into a number of isolated shreds and patches.

Even the most ardent proponents of discourse-centered approaches to culture are beginning to acknowledge the danger of an overly narrow preoccupation with discourse itself. For example, in a recent book advocating a discourse-centered approach to culture, Greg Urban uses the popular aphorism about failing "to see the forest for the trees" to characterize this weakness. "So much effort goes into dissecting the textual tree, . . . not just for its gross morphology but for the microarchitecture of its venation, for the configuration of its stamens into anthers and filaments, that the forest of social life in which it thrives cannot be glimpsed" (Urban 1991:8). Like the ethnoscience movement of the 1960s, with its insistence on excluding anything but the narrowest of semantic relations from cultural analysis, discourse theory of the 1980s and 1990s provides no clear ways of moving up the scale from narrower to broader semantic and cultural relations of meaning unless it can be successfully synthesized with interpretive theories of meaning construction. Elevating discourse from a method of study into a theoretical approach to cultural analysis is a mistake for anthropology if it leads to the abandonment of semiotic, post-structuralist, and other pragmatic theories of cultural meaning. In this study, a discourse-centered approach to ritually powerful speech is employed as a method for exploring broadly significant processes of meaning construction as these are embodied in precise, micro-level details of mythic meaning and musical sound.

The complex interactions between verbal and musical dimensions in Wakuénai ritual performances are in a general sense intelligible within the framework of Paul Friedrich's theory of poetry as the creation of a "felt consubstantiality between language music and myth" (1986:39). As a point of departure, Friedrich's definition of poetry anticipates new theoretical developments as researchers begin to examine the linguistically and culturally specific ways in which people understand and apply the interactions between sound and meaning. In the case of Wakuénai ritual specialists, the integration of language music and mythic meaning is overdetermined in mythic narratives about the primordial human being, whose singing and humming voice named-into-being all the species and objects of nature and "opened up" the closed, primordial world of the trickster-creator. The Wakuénai refer to this mythic event as "the powerful sound that opened up the world" (*kémakáni hliméetaka hekwápi*). Adapting Nancy Munn's analysis (1969) of the concept of naming power in Murngin myth and ritual, I refer to the Wakuénai concept of a world-opening verbal sound as "musical naming power." The concept of musical naming power means that language music and mythic meaning are in constant tension as parts of a unified process of meaning construction. Therefore, I have found it necessary to amend Friedrich's original definition of poetry by developing two new terms that seek to capture the irreducible, dynamic interactions of language music and mythic meaning.

"Musicalization" is the more powerful, dynamic process of transforming the basic semantic categories of mythic being into a musically dynamic, expanding universe of places and spirit-names. "Mythification" is the complementary, less powerful process of stabilizing the language music by using the verbal categories of mythic being to construct a relatively steady flow of vocal sound. In musicalization, the musicality of speech activates the poetic potentials of semantic, taxonomic thought, resulting in expanding, chaotic, highly complex patterns of meaningful sound. In mythification, the semantic activity of naming unfolds primarily within rather than between categories of mythic being, constraining the explosive, chaotic creativity of language music to produce orderly, bounded patterns of meaningful sound. I will use these terms, "musicalization" and "mythification," as a shorthand at various points in this book with the understanding that they refer to the mutual interaction of the musicality of speech and the classificatory power of language.

According to Wakuénai mythic narratives about the primordial human being, the twin processes of musicalization and mythification originated during the transition from a primordial mythic space-time of undifferentiated animal-humans to a differentiated, cultural universe inhabited by fully human beings who empowered themselves by socializing the raw creativity of musical naming power and who began to make their history by playing musical instruments that embodied the power of mythic ancestors. The cycle of narratives about the Amáru and her child, Kuwái, outlines a two-fold process of mythic creation in which the world created and opened up by musical naming power shrinks back to its original size when the trickster-creator pushes Kuwái into a great bonfire. After this symbolic death of the child and contraction of the cosmos, Kuwái returns in the form of trees, vines, and other plant materials used for making sacred flutes and trumpets. Amáru and her female companions steal these sacred instruments, and the world opens up for a second time as the trickster-creator gives chase to Amáru, who plays the musical sounds of the mythic ancestors in different places along the Río Negro. In both parts of the myth cycle, musical sound and verbal meaning form tightly integrated partners, but the valences of musical and semantic dimensions are reversed in the second part of the cycle.

In the first mythic creation, the explosive creativity of musical naming power becomes socialized into semantically intelligible speech. This socialization, or mythification, of musicality takes two stages to reach completion: (1) a dialogical speech in which Kuwái reveals the secrets of his life-giving powers to a messenger sent from earth; and (2) a monological performance of *málikai* songs and chants for initiation that is perfectly memorized by Dzúli, the prototypic keeper of *málikai*. To become fully socialized, the creative force of musical naming power must be not only transformed into verbally intelligible speech but engraved into human consciousness as poetically thickened speech that is semantically richer than the language of everyday social life. Mythification stabilizes musical naming power and makes it into a source of continuity. *Málikai* originates in myth as a form of poetic speech that directly embodies the mythic power to create socialized individual humanness. Keepers of *málikai* are thus in the first instance specialists in the production of cultural continuity through mediating between mythic ancestors in the sky-world and their living human descendants on the ground, between generations of living human beings, and between different stages in the human life cycle.

The first mythic creation is the story of how an originally ambiguous, potentially destructive unity of musical naming power and the species and objects of nature becomes differentiated into semantically distinct categories of mythic being. The original unity of signifying musical sound and signified objects first opens up into vertically distinct worlds, or the semantic space between words and things in everyday human speech. However, this newly created semantic distance does not remain for long in the limbo status of arbitrariness but is soon transformed into the motivated, chanted, and sung language of *málikai,* thus placing the potentially unlimited semiosis of verbal signs under the control of ritual specialists whose primary objective is to produce cultural continuity.

The second mythic creation reverses the valences of language music and mythic meaning by relating the transformation of Kuwái's first creation of the world into an expanding, musical universe of diverse peoples and places. In other words, mythification transforms into musicalization; the relatively stable, continuous process of transmitting *málikai* to Dzúli gives way to a more dynamic, transformational battle of the sexes for control over the sacred flutes and trumpets of Kuwái. The ability to produce musical sounds on sacred instruments endows men and women with the power to mediate the social distances between adult masculinity and femininity and between groups of people who speak different languages or dialects. Linguistically and culturally separate categories of social being are understood and symbolically controlled as a historically dynamic, musical expansion of the world.

These two complementary processes of meaning construction—the mythification of language music and the musicalization of verbal meaning—form the middle ground between narratives about the genesis of ritual power and actual performances of *málikai.* Underlying both processes is the indigenous concept of liakúna, or "spirit-name." The term liakúna translates most directly as "name" or "place," but more accurate renderings would be "sacred identity" or "soul." Each of these spirit-names consists of two distinct parts, a generic term that refers to a category of mythic being and a specific term that refers to distinctive physical or spiritual attributes of a particular species or type of object. For example, the spirit-name for *cabezon* turtles combines the generic classifier umáwari ("anaconda," or "prototypic water-animal spirit") with the everyday term for parakeet (*kúlikúli*) and the adjectival suffix -*áduwa* to form *umáwari kúlikúliáduwa* (parakeet-like water-animal spirit). This spirit-name is a poetic metaphor that draws upon the similarity between the bright yellowish green coloring of parakeets and that of the underside of *cabezon* turtles. As a verbal art of spirit-naming, *málikai* is an ongoing process of coupling, decoupling, and recoupling categories of mythic being and specific attributes, such as colors, textures, sounds, shapes, sizes, and temperatures. This concept of sacred meaning as an integration of generic and specific identities originates during the first mythic creation, when Kuwái reveals that his body unites trees, water, vines, stones, and all the other material elements of the world into one being. Each spirit-name used in *málikai* embodies this mythic concept of sacred power as a synthesis of all things in one being, and the entire set of spirit-names making up performances of *málikai* form complex verbal images of the primordial human being of myth.

In talking about *málikai*, Wakuénai ritual specialists distinguish between two distinct principles of spirit-naming. The first is an essentially taxonomic process of invoking a number of specific spirit-names within a single category of mythic being and only gradually moving on to other categories. This process is called "we heap up the names in a single place" (*wakéetaka nakúna papínirítsa*), and it establishes the basic framework of semantic categories that describe the first mythic creation: fish, aquatic animals, forest animals, birds, wild and domesticated plants, and other life forms. "We heap up the names in a single place," or the mythification of language music, poetically mediates between vertically distinct "places" in the cosmos, human society, and the individual life cycle. "We heap up the names" constrains both the potentially unlimited semiosis of verbal signs and the creative force of language music by placing the diversity of natural objects and species into a relatively stable set of generic categories of mythic being.

The second spirit-naming principle is a dynamic transformation, or inversion, of the building of continuity and stability. *Wadzúhiakaw nakúna*, or "we go in search of (or chase after) the names," is a hyperanimated activity of movement through a wide variety of generic categories of mythic being. For example, the specialist may commence by invoking two or three specific names that fall within a single category, then move through several distinct categories, attaching only a single specific name to each category and creating a highly dynamic image of sacred power as an activity of "searching." "We go in search of the names," or the musicalization of verbal categories of mythic meaning, poetically constructs the displacements of Kuwái away from and back to the center of mythic power during the second mythic creation and the struggle between men and women for control over sacred flutes and trumpets. "We go in search of the names" explodes the relatively stable, verbal categories of mythic being into a historically dynamic, expanding musical universe of changing relations between men and women and among a diversity of linguistically and geographically separate peoples.

The contrast between the two principles of spirit-naming is schematically illustrated in Figure 1.2. The diagram slightly oversimplifies actual ritual practices in two ways. In employing the first principle, "we heap up the names," Wakuénai ritual specialists always include a few names within categories of mythic being that do not belong on the basis of the primary semantic meanings of those categories but that are placed there because of particular mythic or spiritual attributes. This shifting, or marking, of especially powerful species and objects is common to other languages that have noun classes or nominal classifiers (Dixon 1983), and its presence here indicates that the more stable process of mythification is always connected to the more dynamic process of the musical expansion of mythic categories. Conversely, in employing the second principle, "we go in search of the names," Wakuénai ritual specialists always make at least minimal use of the first principle of "we heap up the names" by enlarging one or more categories to include at least two-to-three specific names. Again, the more powerful, dynamic principle of musicalization is defined in relation to the less powerful, stabilizing principle of mythification.

The specific ritual performances of *málikai* described and interpreted in this book demonstrate in numerous ways how the twin principles of mythification and musicalization form a relative hierarchy of more-to-less powerful ways of speaking rather than a clear-cut dichotomy between powerful and powerless principles of meaning construction. In sets of performances constituting complete ritual events, the principles of musicalization and mythification are used in tandem, but one of the two principles is dominant over the other in any given performance of *málikai*. In childbirth rituals, for example, an initial set of chanted-and-sung performances aims at searching for the ancestral tobacco spirits of the newborn infant. This dynamic, musicalized search gives way in a second set of chanted performances to a relatively stable, gradual process of heaping up the spirit-names of all edible fish, aquatic animal, forest animal, and bird species so that the infant's parents can end their pe-

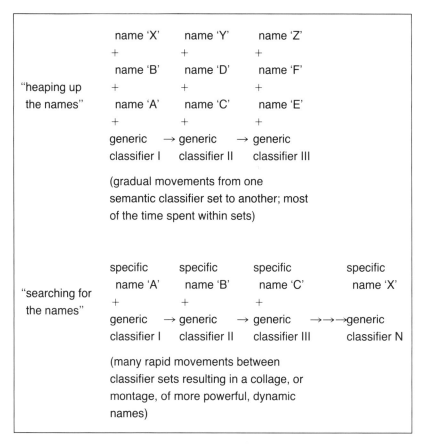

1.2   *Comparison of "heaping up" and "searching for" the names*

riod of ritual fasting. In other words, musicalization transforms into mythification over the course of childbirth rituals, just as musical naming power transforms into ritually controlled language during the first mythic creation.

The relative dominance of one or the other principle of spirit-naming is expressed simultaneously in verbal and musical dimensions of performance. When the more dynamic principle of searching for spirit-names acts as the dominant principle of naming, as it does in the first set of chants during childbirth rituals, the performer's voice becomes musically dynamic through such techniques as microtonal rising of pitch, rapid or accelerating tempo, and augmentation of volume. When the more stabilizing principle of heaping up the spirit-names is dominant over the more dynamic principle, the performer's voice becomes a steady, rhythmic pulse of sound with only minimal change in pitch, tempo, and volume. This fusion of naming processes and musical sounds forms the central core of the poetics of ritual power in Wakuénai social life, the "felt consubstantiality" between the musicality of speech and the semantics of musical sound, an overdetermined nexus of musical meanings and meaningful sounds.

## *The Research Setting*

Finding a suitable research site for studying Wakuénai ritual power was not an easy task. In my first visit to the Upper Río Negro region, I traveled to several small villages of Curripaco and Yeral-speakers along the lower Casiquiare River as part of a group project on human ecology in the Upper Río Negro region.[1] These visits in April and May, 1980, produced useful data on indigenous horticultural practices and gave me a chance to start learning the Curripaco dialect of Wáku. However, they also raised great doubts about the feasibility of my plans to carry out research on indigenous narrative, musical performance, and ritual, since the peoples living along the Casiquiare had all joined an Evangelical Protestant sect of the New Tribes Mission.[2] In mid-May, I had my first encounter with Curripaco-speakers from a "Catholic" village of the lower Guainía River. The village headman and about a dozen other people had traveled downstream in a large dug-out canoe, laden with manioc breads, tins of manioc flour, and bottles of pepper sauce to sell in San Carlos de Río Negro. The National Guard had stopped them in the port and threatened to confiscate all their products, allegedly because they did not have Venezuelan *cedulas* (ID cards). The local representatives of the Office of Indigenous Affairs intervened, and the villagers were able to sell their products to the townspeople of San Carlos and buy small quantities of fishhooks, ammunition, soap, and other goods from the local merchants. I met briefly with the village headman and several of the other men from Punta Bella,[3] and they were receptive to my request to visit their village in the near future. I waited in San Carlos for several days for news from other members of the human ecology project, but none came. Since there was no gasoline available for travel by river, I packed up a few of my fieldwork materials and headed by plane up to Maroa, hoping to work my way back down the Guainía and Negro rivers to San Carlos through short journeys between neighboring villages or hitching a ride with one of the motorboats that occasionally made the trip from Maroa to San Carlos.

After a promising start, my trip came to an abrupt end in Sebucan, a large village of Guarequena-speakers, where I came down with a serious case of dysentery in June. Although I was disappointed to have to return to San Carlos by plane from Maroa, my stay in Sebucan had allowed me to broaden my survey of indigenous horticultural practices in the region and to conclude that my plans to study indigenous narrative and ritual could be carried out in Wakuénai villages along the lower Guainía between the Caño San Miguel and the mouth of the Casiquiare (see Figure 1.3).

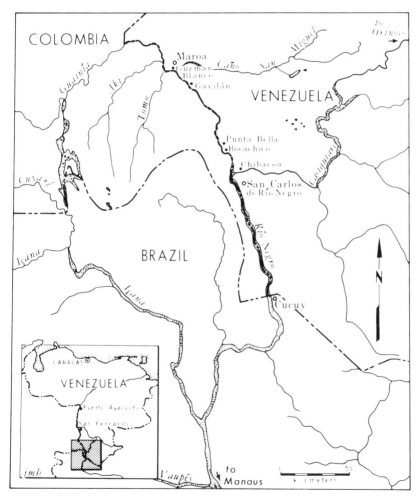

1.3  *Map of the Venezuelan Río Negro Basin (adapted from Hill and Moran 1983: 115)*

I returned to the region in late September 1980 to spend three months living in Punta Bella on the lower Guainía River. The village turned out to be an excellent place to work on language because all but two individuals spoke the Curripaco dialect of Wáku. It was in Punta Bella that I gained my first understanding of the complex cycles of narratives about the distant mythic space-time of Iñápirríkuli, the trickster-creator; the transformational space-time of the primordial human beings, Amáru and Kuwái; the more recent, human space-time of the spirits of the dead; and the legendary, historical times of the rubber boom and the villainous dictator, Tomás Funes. However, social relations in the village were somewhat tumultuous, due primarily to tensions between the Curripaco headman and his two Yeral-speaking sons-in-law.[4] These problems erupted into open hostilities when the Catholic sisters from San Carlos proposed the establishment of a village "store" where they would exchange items of clothing and food in return for indigenous handicrafts. The headman strongly opposed the sisters' plan, correctly perceiving that it would undermine the fragile leadership he exercised as an organizer of the trade in surplus manioc products with the townspeople of San Carlos. The two Yeral sons-in-law welcomed the sisters' proposal, thereby infuriating the headman. The situation put me in the awkward position of trying to keep a balance between my obligation to reciprocate the hospitality of my hosts and the need to maintain cordial, or at least neutral, relations with the Catholic missionaries, who represented a powerful force in the territory that I could not afford to alienate or offend.

After a brief trip to Caracas in late December, I returned to Punta Bella in the dry season months of January through March 1981 to continue my studies. The sisters had decided not to force their project on the villagers, so I was able to get a lot of work done on language, narrative, social organization, and other topics. However, it was becoming clear that I would need to move to other villages farther upstream to complete my studies because there were no practicing shamans or other ritual specialists living in Punta Bella. I had learned a great deal about ritual power and the complex set of mythic beings and events that inform Wakuénai ritual practices, but I still had no direct knowledge of how these rituals were actually performed.

I spent the months of April, May, and early June in a long and disappointing struggle to regain permission to enter the field. Although the national office of indigenous affairs (DAI) had granted my request for a permit to continue working in villages along the lower Guainía until the end of 1981, the governor of the Federal Amazon Territory decided to block the entry of all foreign researchers into the region. When I finally managed to return to Punta Bella in late June, the sisters' proposed village "store" was in full evidence, located in the home of one of the headman's Yeral sons-in-law, who managed the exchanges of handicrafts for clothing and food. The project had exacerbated factionalism in the village, and in early July I decided to hitch a ride upstream with the Department of Hydrology.

In contrast to Punta Bella, the village of Gavilán was older and more established. Social relations in Gavilán centered around a core group consisting of a patrilineal, patrilocal extended family from a highly ranked sib of the Dzáwinai ("Jaguar-People") phratry.[5] Members of the village occasionally traveled to Maroa to purchase fishhooks and other necessities, but they were not actively engaged in trading surplus manioc products with the townspeople. The village headman and his brother were known throughout the area as powerful ritual healers and diviners. Although nominally Catholic, the village was the strongest center of indigenous religion along the Venezuelan side of the lower Guainía. For some time, the villagers had participated in the Catholic sisters' project of trading handicrafts for clothing and food, but they had successfully resisted the sisters' frequent calls to increase the amount of trading.

Gavilán proved to be a nearly ideal location for my research on ritual power. Through my earlier fieldwork in Punta Bella, I had gained a working knowledge of the Curripaco dialect and a general understanding of the mythic powers evoked in sacred rituals. As a result, I was quickly able to establish a dialogue with Hernan Yusrinu, a chant owner (*málikai limíinali*) and village headman. Although I was slowed at first by having to learn the Curricarro dialect of Wáku in order to understand people in Gavilán (but not to be understood by them), Hernan and several other men and women in the village soon began to take a keen interest in my studies of *málikai* and other genres of ritual power. The people of Gavilán were skillful teachers, and they would often correct me if I made a mistake.

Because so much of the mythic knowledge embodied in the language of *málikai* is esoteric and specialized, Hernan was the only individual in the village who could teach me about these performances. He had an outstanding memory and a gift for interpreting both the nuances of mythic meaning and the subtleties of everyday social events. In his youth, Hernan had studied *málikai* with one of his father's brothers at Tonowí, a village on the Içana River in Brazil. As an adult, he had learned the art of divination from a father-in-law living along the Aiarí River. In 1981

Hernan was already an old man whose grandchildren were approaching marriageable age, and on several occasions he expressed concern for passing his knowledge on to a member of the younger generation. "Who is going to chant over the food of these children when I'm gone?" Ideally, an old man would have had several adult sons and brother's sons from whom a successor would step forward. Hernan had only one surviving son, Siderio, the others having died as youths. In 1981 Siderio did not show much interest in memorizing the complex taxonomies of spirit-names in *málikai* or in exploring the symbolic interrelations between spirit-naming in *málikai* and narratives about mythic space-times.

As is often the case in the open-ended process of ethnographic inquiry, each round of answers generates a still larger set of new questions. When I left Gavilán in November 1981, I knew that there were many questions that I had not yet even asked. Fortunately, I was able to return to the lower Guainía for brief visits in the summers of 1984 and 1985 as part of a general survey on interethnic marriage patterns and other social changes among the Wakuénai and other Arawak-speaking peoples of the Venezuelan Amazon Territory.

The processes of entering the field were just as difficult as they had been in 1980–81. The local authorities and townspeople of the Río Negro still looked upon my work with suspicion, wondering how anything worthwhile could come from associating with the Curricarro-speakers of Gavilán. However, returning to the village after a period of nearly three years' absence was a truly satisfying experience. Siderio had started learning how to perform *málikai* from his father but was having trouble memorizing the various sets of spirit-names. Hernan asked me if I could loan my tape recorder to Siderio to help him memorize the taxonomies of spirit-names and other features of the language of *málikai*. The next day I went to work with Siderio, showing him how to change batteries, plug in external microphones and earphones, clean the recording heads, adjust the volume level, and so forth. Siderio learned quickly how to use and care for the equipment, since he was already familiar with cassette tape recorders and had seen me using and maintaining them on numerous other occasions. In return for loaning him the use of my tape recorder for a year, I asked Siderio to record performances of *málikai* and other events.

When I returned to Gavilán in July 1985, Siderio had made considerable progress in learning *málikai* by listening to tape recordings. Hernan had become seriously ill after an injury to his foot during the dry season and was afraid that he might never recover his health. He and Siderio had made a number of recordings of *málikai* specifically for the purpose of learning the language of chants and songs. In these recordings, the songs and chants were not performed in the usual style but spoken clearly and slowly so that Siderio could first learn to recite verses without musical intonation. After learning the language of the chants and songs, he could listen to recordings of them as they are actually performed in ritual contexts. In addition to their primary purpose of helping Siderio to learn *málikai* from his father, these practice tapes also provided me with valuable insights into the indigenous processes of teaching and learning *málikai,* and they allowed me to make detailed transcriptions of some of the more complex chants and songs. The tape recorder had added a new element to the processes of orally transmitting *málikai* from one generation to the next, yet it did not change the basic, underlying pattern of memorizing spirit-names and verses, inquiring about the esoteric meanings of names, and adding musical dimensions of tonality, rhythm, tempo, and timbre.

By the end of the dry season, Hernan had partially recovered from his illness and was strong enough to perform the long series of *málikai* songs and chants for the puberty initiation ritual of Rosa, one of his granddaughters. In Siderio's recordings of these performances, his father's voice is noticeably weaker than it had been in the recordings I had made in 1981.[6] Only a few weeks later, Hernan had fully recuperated, and Siderio recorded over ten hours of *málikai* songs and chants, instrumental music, women's drinking songs, ritual advising of initiates, and other social activities during a male initiation ritual. By the time of my visit to Gavilán in July and August 1985, Hernan was in good health and, as usual, made extensive commentaries as we listened to Siderio's tape recordings of the two initiation rituals. I had brought along a new tape recorder to make copies of Siderio's recordings and to make new recordings of the narratives about Venancio Camico, the leader of an important millenarian movement in the late 1850s (Wright and Hill 1986; Hill and Wright 1988). I gave this new equipment to Siderio as a permanent gift along with a fresh supply of batteries and blank cassette tapes, hoping that he would continue to use them to study with Hernan.

From the perspective of our highly technological social world of computers, libraries, universities, and other institutional means for guaranteeing the endurance of cultural knowledge over passing generations, the oral transmission of mythic knowledge and ritual competence from father to son seems like a slender, delicate thread of continuity. In the 1980s, the Wakuénai found themselves increasingly enmeshed in an array of powerful outside institutions and agents, some of which are explicitly devoted to extirpating indigenous forms of religion. Sophie Muller and other members of the New Tribes Mission, for example, continued to wage a campaign of propaganda among the Wakuénai, openly denigrating the activities of chant-owners and shamans. Along the Içana River in Brazil, a gold rush and increasing militarization threatened to destroy the fragile, nutrient-poor ecology of blackwater rivers and, along with it, the indigenous subsistence economy of fishing and horticulture. Illegal drug traffic and political insurgency had crept into Wakuénai villages along the Cuyarí and upper Guainía rivers in Colombia. And in Venezuela, government social planners looked to the Amazon Territory for solutions to the severe economic crisis brought on by a collapse of the oil economy.

Amid the din of ethnocidal and neocolonial voices of the 1980s, the sounds of the Wakuénai chant-owner teaching his artistry to an only son could easily seem like the dying gasp of a lone poet, lamenting the end of his people's way of life. To accept this conclusion as inevitable is, I believe, premature or even erroneous. The Wakuénai have experienced and survived a long and tortured history of interethnic relations with the whites, including forced labor campaigns and severe depopulation in the eighteenth century, the deprivations of debt peonage during the rubber boom, and the culture of terror practiced by Tomas Funes and his soldiers in the early twentieth century. To Hernan, Siderio, and the people of Gavilán, the musical naming power of Kuwái was, and still is, not a fragile thread connecting the present to an unchanging mythic past but "the powerful sound that opened the world."

# 2

# The Regional and Historical Contexts of Wakuénai Ritual Poetics

The poetics of ritual power in Wakuénai society is situated in the larger, regional context of ranked, patrilineal societies in the Northwest Amazon region and in the long-term historical context of colonial domination and the tripartite division of Wakuénai lands among three separate nation-states during the nineteenth and twentieth centuries. The point of departure for this regional historical perspective is a version of the origin myth that explains how the Wakuénai came to be displaced from the center of mythic power by the whites at the same time as they managed to retain control over the historical definition and transformation of their unique social identity as "The People of Our Language."

This same narrative shows how the Wakuénai interpret their historical relations of trade and intermarriage with Eastern Tukanoan peoples of the Vaupés basin to the south and west as a consequence of the arrival of the whites. The myth of origins is an ironic allegory of colonial history. In the narrative, the Wakuénai have used the poetic processes of mythification and musicalization to understand the loss of life, land, and autonomy brought on by the arrival of Western peoples during the colonial period as the beginning of a process of renewing and redefining their social identity. The myth also provides historical insight into regional ethnopolitical relations between the Wakuénai and their Eastern Tukanoan neighbors by directly connecting these relations to the arrival of Western peoples in the region.

The myth of origins embodies a political process of mediating between the construction of hierarchical relations within local communities and the formation of a regional network of relations with other peoples. Mythification, or the establishment of cultural continuity through verbal signification, acts as a vehicle for connecting present social conditions to a remembered past in which the Wakuénai formed part of a vast region of riverine, Northern Arawakan societies that extended from the Central Amazon floodplains near Manaus up to the lower Orinoco basin. Musicalization, or the dynamic transformation of social identities through musical performance, has allowed the Wakuénai to interpret the profound changes in their own and other peoples' identities through centuries of colonial and nation-state expansion in the Upper Río Negro region. In the narrative of origins, the Wakuénai use the twin principles of meaning construction to understand their place in this broader regional history.

## *The Myth of Emergence as Ironic Allegory of Colonial History*

Ongoing social processes of changing historical relations among the Wakuénai, their Tukanoan and Arawakan neighbors, and nonindigenous peoples of Venezuela, Colombia, and Brazil are not external to the conception and performance of ritually powerful ways of speaking. The opening up of historical relations with Western immigrants to the Upper Río Negro is interpreted within the narrative framework of Amáru's travels away-across horizontal space from the center, or place of ancestral emergence, to remote downstream locations at the margin of indigenous territory. The introduction of steel tools, epidemics, losses and migrations of peoples, and other profound historical changes are not absorbed, or "frozen," into preexisting categories of mythic being but enter directly into the dynamics of indigenous ritual power at the highest levels of meaning.

The intrinsic connection between historical transformation and ritual empowerment is compellingly demonstrated in Hernan Yusrinu's rendering of a narrative about the autochthonous emergence of mythic ancestors. The story of mythic emergence is not truly a narrative account of mythic creation like the Kuwái myth cycle, with all its complex, embedded transformations (see chapter 3). Instead, the story of mythic emergence is a poetic transformation, based upon Kuwái's powerful ways of speaking (*málikai*), of spoken narrative discourse into a litany of more and less powerful names and naming processes. This litany is secretly taught to initiates during their period of fasting. Unlike the musicalized transpositions of mythic taxonomies into poetic genres of speech in *málikai*, the litany of ancestral emergence is a prosaic listing of mythic names within the framework of a highly simplified version of the hierarchy of more-to-less powerful ways of speaking.[1]

The litany of ancestral emergence shows that historical changes associated with the arrival of white people in the Upper Río Negro region are both fully integrated into the vertical dimension of power relations between mythic ancestors and human descendants, and excluded from the more powerful, dynamic dimension of horizontal relations of exchange.

> *Néni, médzeníka hwa nawíki, Hípana.*
> Then, we human beings were born, at Hipana.

> *Úpika, médzeníka yárinárinai, phiúmi yárinárinai.*
> First, the white people were born, all the white people.

> *Hnetédali médzeníka hwá nawíki, phiúmi hekwápiriko nawíki.*
> Later, we human beings were born, all the human beings in this world.

> *Hnetédali lídiahliúna nanaíkika pawéniríko.*
> Later he searched for their sib names in a hole.

> *Nepítiwana Hérri hálepiwanai ienípe,*
> They [the whites] receive the name "Children of Herri and the Whites,"

> > *liphiáleta dzéema.*
> > he blows tobacco smoke.

> *Hnetédali wáma nána nanaíkika, nepítiwana Hérri hálepiwanai ienípe;*
> Later we will go look for their sib names, now they receive the name "Children of Herri and the Whites;"

> > *waphiálewa dzéema.*
> > we blow tobacco smoke.

In the litany, the white men (yárinárinai) are clearly distinguished from indigenous peoples (hwá nawíki, or "we human beings") through being the first-born, or raised from the hole in the ground and given a Tobacco spirit-name by the trickster-creator. Being first-born makes the white people more powerful than indigenous people, since the first-born, or older brother, peoples are always the most highly ranked. Having given them all a single Tobacco spirit-name, Iñápirríkuli sets them aside and promises to give them powerful sib names (nanaíkika) later, after searching for the ancestral spirit-names of Wakuénai sibs.

> *Wapinétaka wadzúhiakaw nanaíkika hwá nawíki, phiúmi*
> *hekwápiríko.*
> We go to chase after the ancestral sib names, for all people in this world.

> *Úpika, nepítiwana márherriwátsa,*
> First, they [the *Waríperídakéna*] receive the male Tobacco spirit-name,

> *néni nepítiwana márhéna.*
> then they receive the female Tobacco spirit-name.

> *Néni nepítiwana Kutérruéni,*
> Then they receive the name "children of the *kutérru*-bees,"

> *néni nepítiwana Túmiéni,*
> then they receive the name "children of the túmi-ants,"

> *néni nepítiwana Makúliéni.*
> then they receive the name "children of the Makú [workers]."

> *Liphiáleta dzéema.*
> He blows tobacco smoke.

In this section of the litany, the more powerful way of speaking, or "chasing after the names," is used to organize lists of powerful sib names within the Waríperídakéna phratry. The four sibs are ranked in serial order according to their emergence, and all four sibs receive a single pair of Tobacco spirit-names, or grandparents. In everyday contexts, members of all four sibs are referred to as Waríperídakéna, and the members of all four sibs regard one another as patrilateral, parallel cousins who form "one kin" (*nukítsiñápe*). The litany continues in this manner through all the other Wakuénai phratries inhabiting riverine territories along the Içana and Guainía rivers and their tributaries.

After naming all these peoples, the litany continues as a "search" for the powerful sib names that includes the Tariano, Cubeo, and Uanano. These groups are distinguished from the Wakuénai with the phrase "after the white people" (*hnetédali yárinárinai*). All three groups are ambiguously included in and excluded from the category of *hwá nawíki*, or fully human beings. The Cubeo, due to their historical and geographic proximity to Wakuénai phratries of the upper Içana and Guainía rivers, receive four different names. Déetana (a species of snake), Otiarírria, (a species of tree), and Kuphémnainai ("Fish-Masters") are Cubeo subgroups living along the Vaupés River. The Cubeo phratries living along the Cuduyarí River, where Goldman (1963) did his field research, are named Akárinai, or "ant-people," because they are so numerous. The Uanano are lumped into a single name, Puínai (translation unknown). By "heaping up" entire peoples, or language groups, into a single spirit-name, the litany excludes the Uanano and Tariano from the social category of fully human beings who are differentiated according to a ranked order of more-to-less powerful sib names. The Cubeo, however, are much closer to being regarded as fully human beings, since they are differentiated into four subgroupings. Taken together, the Tariano, Uanano, and Cubeo form a quasi-phratry of peoples who became part of the Wakuénai social order at some point after the arrival of white people in the eighteenth century.

Having completed the "search" for ancestral spirit-names and tobacco spirits, Iñápirríkuli returns to the white people, the first people created. As in other narratives about Iñápirríkuli, the litany depicts the trickster-creator as a master of reversal and transformation.

*Néni, ñétim yúhakáwa; wakéetaka nanaíkika.*
Then, there are too many people; we heap up their sib names.

*Nepítiwana liwakéetanhim dzáwi-ñápirríkuli,*
They receive the name "the heap of the jaguar made from bone,"

*nepítiwana yáranárinai.*
they receive the name white people.

*Nepítiwana nadzákare Venezuela-kwá, Colombia-kwá, Brazil-kwá.*
Their places receive the names Venezuela, Colombia, and Brazil.

The white men have been tricked, for they are both included as the first-born, most powerful, peoples, but are too numerous to be given powerful sib names that must be actively "searched for" rather than merely "heaped up into a pile." Naming the places where the white men live is a poetic opening up of the shared historical space-time of interethnic relations between fully human beings and the whites. Nevertheless, the white men lack powerful ancestral names, so they are unable to fully participate in the construction of meaningful social history.

The litany of ancestral emergence is a verbal process of reempowering indigenous peoples who have lost political and economic control over their ancestral lands by ambiguously including and excluding the initially greater power of the white people, who were the first-born. This same process of ironically inverting colonial history is evident in the indigenous belief that white people have dream-souls that take the form of books or papers. According to this view, the white people have failed to become fully human, socialized beings because their books and writing have un-naturally divided them up into occupational specialties. Thus, teachers' souls appear in their sleep as textbooks, missionaries' souls as Bibles, merchants' souls as financial logs, and so on. These denaturalized dream-souls are beyond Otherness, or naturalized social being, and can thus not take part in the social creation of meaning except as semi-human beings who are alienated from nature and society. White people's dream-souls, or "books," are vulnerable to the horrifying effects of witchcraft, but the whites can only become participants in the creative, transformative pow-ers of Kuwái's powerful ways of speaking at the less powerful level of "heaping up the names."

Other indigenous peoples are arranged in the intermediary space be-tween "searching for" and "heaping up" the names according to the depth of historical and social interactions they have had with fully human beings, or the Wakuénai. The Cubeo, Tariano, and Uanano are included in the search for powerful sib names, and they receive names of natural species like those of the Wakuénai ancestors. The Baniwa, Guarequena, Piapoco, and other peoples with whom the Wakuénai have developed extensive social relations only in the recent historical past are given the same Tobacco spirit-names as the white people. However, the social dis-tance between Wakuénai and other Arawak-speaking peoples has been rapidly diminishing in recent decades through intermarriage, ritual co-participation, and a variety of everyday contacts.

The litany of sib ancestral emergence is an inversion of colonial and neocolonial structures of political-economic domination that historically developed between whites and indigenous peoples from the early eigh-teenth century. In essence, the litany affirms that the human social world into which individuals are born and raised has undergone irreversible changes due to the arrival of "older," more powerful beings. At the same time, however, the litany negates the relationship of political domination that the whites established over indigenous peoples by asserting that the whites are beyond Otherness, or naturalized social being, and thus are unable to take part in indigenous processes of social reproduction. The exclusion of white people from indigenous social reproduction is partially offset in the litany by the ambiguous inclusion of Eastern Tukanoan and Arawakan peoples of the Vaupés and Cuduyarí rivers into the social universe of exchange relations. The litany of sib ancestral emergence provides a discourse on historical transformations that began with the arrival of white people, along with their superior technologies, infectious diseases, and alien forms of political authority, and continued through the period of indigenous recovery in the early nineteenth century.

The story of ancestral emergence is an ironic, mythic trope of colonial history, an indigenous counterdiscourse to Western myths of New World history as a process of the Civilized taming the Savage. Like all other narrative accounts that are primarily about the past, whether oral or written, the myth of ancestral emergence forms part of an ongoing process of historical interpretation that is situated in contemporary social contexts and that actively shapes social relations in the present. The narrative character of Iñápirríkuli prefigures all Wakuénai narratives about mythic and historical pasts and provides an indigenous model of subjectivity as a process of creating a reflexive, interpretive distancing between the acting subject and the immediate situation. The trickster always finds a way to cope with difficult situations, not by directly confronting dangerous, powerful beings but through concealing knowledge and intentions to imagine a future way to break out of present entanglements. The narrative character of the trickster-creator is thus an ideally suited symbolic vehicle for creating an ironic distancing from past and present systems of sociocultural domination into which Western peoples have forced the Wakuénai and their indigenous neighbors throughout the Upper Río Negro region.

The Wakuénai are quite aware of Trickster's social meaning and openly compare Trickster's ability to turn the tables on his rivals with the coping mechanisms that men and women use in everyday social life to confront danger or difficulty. One elder explained Trickster's meaning to me by analogy with the present. If an indigenous man, he explained, is taken captive by soldiers because of some accusation against him, the man will show no fear or anger to the soldiers. Instead, he will be thinking all the time of a future moment when he will be able to escape from or perhaps even destroy his captors, if necessary by resorting to witchcraft. Again, the comparison with Trickster's ability to escape danger through concealing emotions and knowledge while constructing imagery of a future reversal of the present situation is based on an indigenous model of sub-jectivity as the ability to create interpretive distance from the immediate present.

The trickster-creator's ability to both create the whites as "older broth-ers" and also exclude them from the more powerful process of "searching for the ancestral names" provides the Wakuénai with a symbolic model for coping with difficult situations in the present. From the perspective of disempowered peoples, or that of marginalized subcultural groups within a national society, the first necessity is to construct shared understandings of the past that acknowledge their situations of relative powerlessness but do not deny the possibility of a restoration of their autonomy in an imag-ined future. The trickster-creator embodies this double-sided interpretive process by enabling the Wakuénai to understand their relative lack of power in contemporary interethnic relations in terms of their own ways of poetically constructing history as an ongoing search for the names of mythic ancestors.

## Colonial Transformations

Like other indigenous peoples living in the Venezuelan Amazon Territory during the 1980s, the approximately 1,600 Wakuénai found themselves increasingly enmeshed in a national political system that placed high value on the elimination of cultural differences and the rapid assimilation of indigenous minorities. As a nominally democratic state, Venezuela in the 1980s might be expected to implement a more enlightened policy toward its indigenous Amazonian peoples than the policies of conquest and genocide practiced during colonial state formation. The addition of a veneer of democracy, however, through asserting the full citizenship status of Amazonian indigenous peoples served only as an ideological instrument for further strengthening the policy of incorporation. By as-serting that Amazonian indigenous groups enjoyed the legal rights of all Venezuelan citizens, the government preempted any basis for the grant-ing of collective land titles, Biosphere Reserves, or other special forms of protection. The rhetoric of democracy formed part of a more general process of constructing an ideological double bind that simultaneously placed indigenous Amazonian peoples in two contradictory social stat-uses: (1) full citizens who must be treated as the equals of all others and (2) lawless savages who must be incorporated into the life of the nation. In effect, the rhetoric of democratic equality was used to produce greater social inequality through denial of indigenous Amazonian peoples' rights to participate in the nation's legal system.

The language of government officials describes the expansion of state control in Amazonas as a rational process of bringing law and order to a lawless, barren region in which illegal political and commercial agents were free to manipulate indigenous groups to act against the interests of the nation-state. This way of speaking implicitly removes indigenous minorities from the centuries-long history of state formation and ethnic group formation in the region. The indigenous groups living in Venezuela's Amazon Territory in the 1980s were not pristine, indigenous groups but tribal societies that came into being through missionization, warfare, and other processes of state formation during the colonial period.

Aside from the veneer of democratic equality and economic rationality, contemporary interethnic relations in the Venezuelan Amazon Territory are a direct outgrowth of colonial systems of conquest and domination. The ideological double-bind in which the Wakuénai and other Amazonian peoples are currently entangled is simply a new manifestation of an older colonialist paradox, or "a contradiction between the impossibility and the necessity of creating the other as the other—the different, the alien—and incorporating the other within a single system of social and cultural domination" (Sider 1987:7). As Taussig (1987) has demonstrated, the colonial mode of producing reality is a largely unconscious process in which the dominant society projects the imagery of lawlessness and savagery onto colonized peoples, thereby metaphorically inverting the actual historical processes of domination by brute force. Colonialist discourse severs the targets of sociocultural domination from the real historical and social contexts of their actions by using inverted metaphors to construct images of the other as dangerous and lawless, and thus requiring the imposition of law and order.

From the very first contacts between European conquerors and colonized Amazonian peoples, the Europeans sought justification for their systems of domination by depicting Amazonian peoples as lawless savages who needed assistance from powerful outsiders to "protect" them from their own lawlessness. Many of the first European contacts with indigenous peoples of the Venezuelan interior, for example, were made by the German explorer Nicolas Federmann as part of his ill-fated search for the legendary El Dorado. On September 27, 1530, Federmann's expedition arrived in the territory of the Aymanes and found that the local inhabitants had destroyed several of their villages and surrounding fields to deny them to the European conquerors. Federmann sent three captive Indians with gifts for the local chiefs and this message:

> To tell them the cause of our arrival and that if they wished to come and receive us as friends, they would be pardoned for all that had occurred, would be our allies, and would be protected against their enemies. But if they refused my offerings, they would be persecuted, their fields would be devastated and their country ruined, they would be reduced to slavery together with their children and, finally, they would be treated in every possible way as the enemy incarnate. On the second day, at about eight, a chief arrived with about seventy Indians, unarmed, as was their custom when seeking peace. . . . I had him baptized along with all his companions (Federmann 1916 [1557]: 37, translation mine).

In this passage we hear the language of conquest in the conqueror's own words. Significantly, the first action taken by the conquerors after coercing the Aymanes' "friendship" with threats of genocide was to encompass symbolically the local inhabitants into the mythic space-time of Judeo-Christian cosmology. Like newborn infants, the Aymanes were perceived as presocial, non- or semi-human beings who required a ritual passage to become human beings in the eyes of the conquerors. In such historical moments of first contact and the mythic incorporation of indigenous South American peoples, we can see the historical production of "peoples without history." Perhaps a funeral rite would have been more appropriate for the occasion; what armed conquest and the imposition of alien systems of production and meaning did not accomplish, the spread of contagious diseases from the Old World brought to completion. The Aymanes, Caquetios, and most other indigenous peoples of the Venezuelan interior had ceased to exist by the end of the colonial period. The survivors of this "Great Dying" (Wolf 1982) had become conquered peoples who lived and worked on *resguardo* lands belonging to Jesuit, Franciscan, and Capuchin missions.

That the Wakuénai phratries of the Upper Río Negro region survived the colonial period is due in part to their geopolitical location at the remote boundary between expanding European empires and also to their ability to draw upon the poetics of ritual power as a resource for redefining their social identity in radically changed historical conditions. Linguistic reconstruction shows that the Wakuénai phratries of the Içana-Guainía drainage area formed the center of a much greater number of peoples who all spoke languages of the Northern, or Maipuran, branch

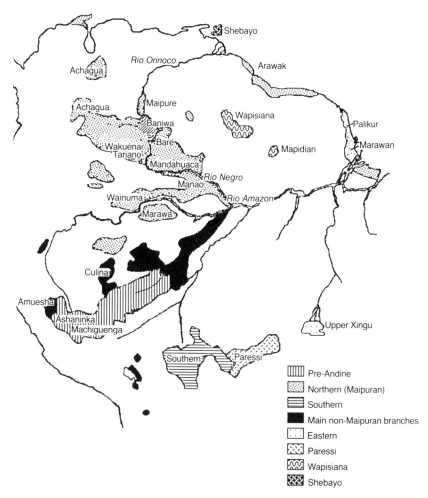

Pre-Andine
Northern (Maipuran)
Southern
Main non-Maipuran branches
Eastern
Paressi
Wapisiana
Shebayo

2.1   *The distribution of Arawakan language groups (adapted from Key 1979: 74)*

of the Arawakan family (see Figure 2.1). In male initiation rituals, Wakuénai chant-owners construct an image of this immense region of interconnecting, riverine territories through naming the various places where Kuwái and Amáru traveled during the second opening up of the world after Kuwái's fiery death and transformation into the sacred ancestor flutes and trumpets. Place naming in these songs and chants begins and ends at Hípana, the place of mythic emergence and the center, or "navel," of the world where Kuwái and Amáru are ritually linked to the world of living human beings via a cosmic umbilical cord. Between the opening

1. from Hípana to Mútsipáni, Amáru's home on Caño Waraná
2. down Caño Waraná, up to the headwaters of the Aiarí
3. over to the middle Vaupés and up to the headwaters
4. down the Vaupés to São Gabriel (*Kúrukwí-kwa*)
5. down the Río Negro to Manaus (*Bárra-kwa*)
6. down the Amazon to the open sea (*Tsówai-kwa*)
7. up the Amazon and Río Negro to the middle Içana
8. up to the headwaters of the Içana
9. down the upper Guainía and Cuyarí rivers
10. down the middle and lower Guainía to Caño Pimichín
11. down the Temi, Atacavi, and Atabapo rivers
12. down the Orinoco to the open sea (*Tsówai-kwa*)
13. up from the mouth of the Aiarí River to Hípana

2.2  *List of horizontal movements in* málikai *chants for male initiation*

and closing songs, a long series of chants outlines a horizontal journey across the world through the naming of places along the Aiarí, Içana, Vaupés, Negro, Atabapo, Orinoco, Guaviare, Inírida, Guainía, Cuyarí, and Içana rivers (see Figures 2.2 and 2.3). In these chants, the Wakuénai ritually construct a mythic map of their world as the center of a much larger region, which corresponds almost exactly to the distribution of Maipuran Arawakan language groups at the time of first contact with the whites.

The ritual naming of places in *malikái* chants embodies a historical consciousness of a past when the ethnopolitical situation of the Wakuénai differed profoundly from that of the present and integrates this historical awareness into the framework of the coming-into-being of the world in mythic space-times. Historical records lend support to the indigenous view of a past in which the regional political situation of the Wakuénai was very different from that of the more recent past. Portuguese slave trading and revenge warfare led to the extinction of the Manao and other Northern Arawakan language groups of the lower and middle Río Negro in the early eighteenth century. To the north, Spanish missions, called *reducciones* (reductions), imposed a regime of religious conversion and political-economic domination upon the Maipure, Achagua, and other Northern Arawakan peoples of the middle Orinoco basin. Portuguese explorations from the south reached as far north as the confluence of the Guaviare and Orinoco rivers. Throughout the first half of the eighteenth

2.3 *Map of spatial movements in* málikai *chants for male initiates' food*

century, the Portuguese raided Arawakan peoples of the Upper Río Negro region for slave labor. Approximately 20,000 indigenous people were taken into slavery and removed from the region in the fifteen-year period between 1740 and 1755, resulting in the extermination of entire language groups (Wright 1981). Alarmed by the Portuguese incursions into their colonial territory, the Spanish sent a heavily armed expedition in the 1750s under the leadership of Francisco Solano to found mission forts at San Fernando de Atabapo, Esmeralda, San Carlos de Río Negro, Solano, San Miguel, and other strategic locations along major rivers.

By the 1760s, the Wakuénai and other surviving Northern Arawakan peoples found themselves caught between two colonial powers contending for control over the Upper Río Negro region and its inhabitants. The Wakuénai phratries of the Içana-Guainía drainage area managed to remain numerous during the early colonial period and probably absorbed refugees from other Arawakan groups (Wright 1981:134-35). The official abolition of traffic in indigenous slaves in 1767 coincided with the expulsion of Jesuit missions from the Portuguese colonies, but slavery was perpetuated under the new name of *descimentos* (descents), or forced labor campaigns. In the *descimentos,* armed military expeditions brought Arawakan and Tukanoan peoples from the Vaupés, Içana, and Negro rivers to work in plantations and extract forest products in areas far downstream (hence the name "descents"). A series of epidemics devastated indigenous populations of the Upper Río Negro in the 1780s, leaving vast areas virtually uninhabited. At the end of the century, the collapse of the Portuguese colonial government in Manaus and the failure of Spanish missionaries and military to establish a stable colonial structure allowed indigenous groups to return to their ancestral territories and recover from severe depopulation.

During the early nineteenth century, the Wakuénai regained a sense of social autonomy through renewing the ritual ties between local patrisibs and specific ancestral lands and through forming new alliances among phratries. Along the Içana River and its tributaries in Brazil, the Waríperídakéna phratry negotiated a trade with the Hohódeni for permission to cut gardens within the latter group's territory. In return, the Hohódeni received permission to send fishing expeditions in Waríperídakéna territory (Wright 1981: 18). The early nineteenth century was thus a period of recovery and reconstitution for the Wakuénai after they had suffered heavy population losses due to disease, slavery, and forced relocation during the late eighteenth century.

Spanish and Portuguese colonialism of the eighteenth century transformed the Wakuénai from a relatively autonomous society who defined themselves primarily in relation to other riverine, Arawak-speaking peoples to the north and south into a colonized society of escaped slaves, or refugees, whose main concern was to survive the onslaught of Western diseases, missionization, and military campaigns. The Wakuénai who escaped enslavement during the 1740s or the *descimento* program of the 1770s did so by fleeing upstream into remote headwater regions of the Içana-Guainía drainage area. In some cases, the Wakuénai remember the migratory histories of specific groups during the colonial period and the story of their return to ancestral territories after the collapse of colonial governments in the region (Wright 1981). In other instances, such as the narrative of mythic emergence that Hernan Yusrinu told to me in 1981, the Wakuénai commemorate the immense changes of the colonial period through the metaphorical displacement of indigenous ancestors from the mythic center of power by the whites, or "older brothers," and the subsequent reempowerment of mythic ancestors through the trickster-creator's acts of deception.

At some point during these colonial transformations, the Wakuénai began to redefine their regional history from one based on relations with other Arawak-speaking peoples living in downstream locations to one in which relations with Eastern Tukanoan peoples became increasingly important. The story of mythic ancestral emergence expresses this shift in regional ethnopolitical relations as an extension, or amendment "after the whites," of the trickster-creator's original search for the ancestral names of Wakuénai phratries and patrisibs. Although it is impossible to set an exact date for this change, increasing relations of trade, warfare, and intermarriage between the Wakuénai and their Eastern Tukanoan neighbors would most likely have begun during the last two decades of the eighteenth century, after the demise of downstream Arawakan peoples and the establishment of permanent colonial settlements at choice downstream locations, such as São Gabriel and San Carlos. Wakuénai phratries, or remnants of phratries, fleeing to the headwaters of the Içana and Guainía entered into territories already inhabited by Eastern Tukanoan peoples, resulting sometimes in a process of "Tukanoization." The Tariano, for example, were a small group of Arawak-speaking refugees who became part of the Eastern Tukanoan regional network of exchange based on the principle of language group exogamy. The greater elaboration of Cubeo ancestral names in the Wakuénai myth of emergence reflects an even deeper historical process than trade and intermarriage, since "one of the Cubeo phratries was, in fact, once Arawakan" (Goldman 1963 : 26). In other words, the Cubeo historically came into being through the Eastern Tukanoans' absorption of Arawakan groups who were fleeing diseases and slavery along the lower Içana and Guainía rivers. Although the evidence is less clear for Uanano ethnogenesis (Chernela 1983), the Uanano are also situated in the intermediate space between Northern Arawakan and Eastern Tukanoan territories, and their political organization is transitional between the territorially based phratries of the Wakuénai and the geographically dispersed phratries of the Central Vaupés basin (Jackson 1983).

The colonial period brought a variety of new, outside forces to bear upon the Wakuénai and other indigenous peoples of the Upper Río Negro region. Exactly how and when these colonial transformations developed is still being investigated through ethnohistorical research. In their efforts to understand the colonial period, the Wakuénai have not frozen historical changes into a static mythic order but have actively integrated the arrival of Western peoples into the poetic processes of "searching for" and "heaping up" the spirit-names of their mythic ancestors.

## The Rubber Boom as Historical Reemergence

The period of recovery for the Wakuénai and other indigenous groups of the Upper Río Negro region lasted well into the nineteenth century but came to an end in the 1840s when the newly independent state of Brazil began to implement a policy called the Directorate, a policy that gave local administrators authority to force indigenous groups to perform "public service labor." Resistance to the new policy was met with military force, and in the 1850s the program resulted in widespread abuses of indigenous labor. Along the Negro-Guainía River in Venezuela, San Carlos de Río Negro and Maroa emerged as centers of trade, boat building, and rope making. Despite the growth of such industries, severe shortages of food were a frequent problem in these towns, and indigenous laborers revolted against the system of debt peonage on several occasions (Spruce 1960).

The millenarian movement led by Venancio Camico arose against this background of hunger and deprivation along the Río Negro in Venezuela and the abusive Directorate policy of public service along the Içana River in Brazil. In 1858, Venancio began to prophesize that the world would end in a fiery conflagration on St. John's Day. Venancio was captured and returned to San Carlos but later escaped from prison and fled to the Aki River (a tributary of the Guainía River). Although the millenarian movement of 1858 had ended in abrupt military defeat, Venancio Camico continued to preach resistance to the white's economy until his death in 1903. By 1900, the shaman-prophet's vision had become incorporated into the ritual advice given during male initiation: "The White men are thieves who buy our wares cheap and sell their merchandise to us at high prices. That is why they are rich and we are poor. Know that the Whites are your enemies. Hide your hatred because it's strong and treat the Whites with distrust because they are traitors" (Matos Arvelo 1912: 86, translation mine). Venancio's movement was a historical rite of passage for the Wakuénai, Baniwa, and other Arawak-speaking peoples of the Upper Río Negro region. The colonial political economy of indebtedness and military force could no longer be regarded as a purely alien power, external to the indigenous social order but had to be exorcized from within.

The division of Wakuénai ancestral lands into Portuguese and Spanish, and later Brazilian and Venezuelan, administrative sectors was a strategic advantage from the beginning of contact with the whites until well into the twentieth century. In the 1850s, for example, Venancio Camico traveled from San Carlos de Río Negro and Maroa in Venezuela to start his movement among the Wakuénai of the Içana in Brazil. When Brazilian authorities broke up the movement, Venancio's followers fled to safety up the Cuyarí and Caño Aki. After a brief imprisonment in San Carlos, Venancio escaped and went to live on the Caño Aki among his followers until his death in 1903. In the early twentieth century, the Wakuénai and Baniwa of Venezuela escaped devastation by the military forces of Tomas Funes by fleeing to the Içana River in Brazil. Many children and grandchildren of these refugees have returned to Venezuela over the past fifty years to found new villages along the lower Guainía.

A rich variety of narratives and family histories records the more recent historical changes that began with Venancio Camico's messianic movement on St. John's Day of 1858, on the dawn of the Rubber Boom, and ended with the death of Tomás Funes, in 1923. The Wakuénai and other peoples of southernmost Venezuela use the historical figures of Venancio Camico and Tomas Funes to construct a historical discourse about the culture of terror that developed during the Rubber Boom. Venancio and Tomas Funes have become symbolic vehicles for establishing a chronotype that opens up in the space between indigenous revitalization and the auto-destruction of the whites' structure of political domination through military force. Underlying this chronotype of doubly reversed power is a background of genocidal annihilation, a culture of terror that transformed the Wakuénai and other indigenous peoples of the Upper Río Negro region from colonized populations into those who survived a holocaust.

The following narrative account of Venancio Camico and Tomas Funes is widely told throughout the Upper Río Negro region by many different peoples and in several different languages. The version presented here is a condensed summary translated from Hernan's performance in the Curricarro dialect of Wáku and is similar to the version recorded by Wright among the Hohódeni of Brazil in 1977.[2]

A man who knew about Venancio, who knew that he was a saint, who knew that Venancio could tell which people were sorcerers (*dañeros*) who had poison to kill others, told Funes about Venancio. Funes sent a commission of soldiers to fetch Venancio from his home on the Aki River. They took Venancio up to Funes's house in San Fernando where Funes asked Venancio if it were true what the others said about him, that he was really a saint. "No, this is false, what the others say. A saint is different because he doesn't eat manioc bread and meat. But I'm a normal human being and eat manioc bread and meat," Venancio replied. Then Funes asked him if it were true that he had many followers who brought gifts to him in payment for cures. Again Venancio denied what the others had told Funes. But Funes wanted to make sure that Venancio was telling the truth, so he ordered him to enter a coffin. Soldiers stood guard on all sides to make sure that Venancio did not run away. After Venancio had lain down inside the open coffin, Funes ordered it to be nailed shut, tied with a cord, and weighted with a rock. Then he sent his soldiers to throw the coffin into the Río Orinoco where it is very deep. After one hour, the soldiers raised up the coffin and took it back to Funes. When they opened the coffin, it was totally empty inside. The soldiers explained that Venancio must have escaped because the cord was not strong enough and the nails had not been placed very closely together.

So they went to fetch Venancio and encountered him at his home on the Aki River. Again they ordered him to enter a coffin that was waiting inside Funes's home in San Fernando. This time they tied the coffin shut with a rope instead of a mere cord and spaced the nails only three fingers' width apart. They weighted down the coffin with a stone and threw it into the same deep part of the river. Again it was empty when they brought it back to Funes' house, and again the soldiers explained that there were not enough nails used to shut the coffin and that the rope was too thin.

The third time, they put nails very closely together, only one finger's width apart, and tied the coffin shut with a very thick rope made of rawhide. After waiting the usual one hour, they raised up the coffin and untied the stone. This time they felt that the coffin weighed more than the other times and were certain that they had finished off Venancio. They told Funes so when they reached his house with the coffin, but they were all surprised when the coffin was opened and there was a huge anaconda (*umáwari*) inside. At that moment, Funes decided that Venancio was really a saint and that he could never kill him no matter how hard he tried.

Five months passed, and Funes sent his soldiers to fetch Venancio from his home on the Aki River again, just for a friendly talk. Funes told Venancio when he arrived that he now believed that Venancio was truly a saint since he'd survived three times underwater. Then Venancio pronounced a punishment on Funes, saying that he'd be killed one day in a revolt by his followers. Funes felt guilty about what he'd done and offered Venancio money, but Venancio wouldn't accept. Funes was very vexed about his refusal of his offer and continued to feel guilty until his death.

The formal style of this narrative requires some consideration in itself prior to any interpretation of substantive elements and their intertextual relations with the Kuwái myth cycle and other genres of indigenous narrative. The historical situation of interethnic contact is not merely a series of events taking place between two distinct social formations but a process, or structure of events, that forges social contradictions within and between peoples into a totally new historical patterning of power relations. Indigenous narrative representations of this historical structure of power are qualitatively different from narratives that seek to embody reflexively the coming-into-being of socialized human individuals and the institutions of social reproduction. "Instead of an integral, self-embedding, self-reproducing system of transformations, one is left with a cleavage between mutually exclusive and external processes of replication. . . . In form, the narrative consists of an irreversible externalization, as contrasted with the reversible self-embedding or internalization, of a process of productive transformation" (Turner 1988: 276). The narrative account of Venancio Camico and Tomas Funes very clearly belongs to the "contact" literature of "irreversible externalizations." The narrative consists of a single episode repeated almost identically three times. Three times Venancio is taken by military force from the indigenous center of power at Makareo to San Fernando de Atabapo, and three times Venancio escapes shamanistically back through the underwater, underworld space of death from San Fernando to Makareo. Finally, the third time, the soldiers open Venancio's coffin to find a giant anaconda, thereby effecting a double reversal of Venancio's movements downward from the surface to the bottom of the river and backwards from San Fernando to Makareo. The soldiers' release of the anaconda from Venancio's coffin is an externalization, or letting out into the open, of a doubly reversed culture of terror, a simultaneous return upward from the bottom of the river and forward into the center of the whites' political power.

The importance of spatial movements in the narrative about Venancio Camico and Tomás Funes is an inversion of the indigenous cycle of myths about Kuwái and Amáru and the idea of an opening up of historical space-time between peoples through playing the sacred musical instruments in different locations. In the journeys of Kuwái and Amáru, the goal was to bring the sacred musical instruments, or the process of musically transforming language and society, back to the center of mythic power at Hípana. In the narrative journeys of Venancio Camico, the objective is to remove forcefully an alien form of power from the mythic center of the indigenous society (which has shifted now to Makareo on the Aki River) to the whites' capital at San Fernando de Atabapo.

Corresponding to the differences in narrative style is an equally important difference in the forms of power embodied in narrative structure. The relationship between the whites' center of power at San Fernando de Atabapo and the indigenous center of power at Venancio's home, Makareo, is a dehumanizing, coercive power of brute military force rather than the socializing power of mythification and musicalization. The multiple interments of Venancio into the coffin and deep down into the chthonian underworld invert the socializing descent of Kuwái from celestial home to fiery transformation on the ground into a macabre scenario of death by drowning. The unwilling, coerced movements of Venancio from surface to the bottom of the river also invert the myth of Kuwái's birth, an escape from death inside the maternal womb to life outside, into a confinement to death inside the tomb from life outside. The horizontal dimension of power relations, or the inclusivity versus exclusivity of political relations among peoples, is also contaminated by the unnatural, alien power of the whites to militarily coerce the movements of indigenous peoples. The repeated dislocations of Venancio away-across the world and his returns to the center of indigenous power through the chthonian underworld of death do not produce and mediate between categories of Otherness, or naturalized social being, but construct a denaturalized social relation between a dominating alien power and the unwilling victims of the culture of terror. The horizontal dimension of power relations has transformed beyond the naturalized space-time of death to reach a denaturalized rottenness that is progressively tying up, weighting down, and suffocating the indigenous social order from the inside out. The manageable dilemma of being the "Other's Other" has now become the sickness of a people's alienated consciousness of being "Other People's" dominated slaves. This affliction has worked into both the vertical dimension of socialization and the horizontal dimension of social reproduction. Venancio Camico, the indigenous shaman and hero, must negate the negation of his people's power by releasing a doubly reversed, chthonian source of indigenous power into the center of the whites' military power.

Venancio Camico's "initiation" into the military class structure of the whites is a narrative prototype for the indigenous experience of progressive desocialization, alienation, and death in the historical structure of interethnic relations during the Rubber Boom. Like the narrative function of Kuwái as a prototype for the opening up of socialized individual humanness into a pattern of collective institutions for social reproduction, the narrative function of Venancio Camico is to demonstrate how the individual's negation of desocializing, alien power opens up into a collective historical process of defining a new social identity through the negation of a people's collective, alienated consciousness of powerlessness. When understood as a prototype of the historical emergence of a new social consciousness, the outward and downward movements of Venancio Camico can be interpreted as historical metaphors for the forced relocations of indigenous groups to labor in the whites' rubber camps and the extermination of indigenous peoples who refused to go work in the camps. In the narrative about Venancio Camico and Tomás Funes, the Wakuénai represent the culture of terror as a Hobson's choice between two forms of collective death, the firing squad and the bottom of the river.

The emergence of an enormous anaconda from the coffin is a synthetic image of Venancio's successful transformation of his individual, shamanistic negations of denaturalized power into a collective negation of the genocidal, dehumanizing power structure of Funes and his soldiers during the Rubber Boom. The anaconda is a metaphor for the coming-into-being and reemergence of the Wakuénai and other indigenous peoples of the Upper Río Negro region as peoples who survived a holocaust. The narrative about Venancio is a double reversal, or negation, of contaminations that have seeped into both vertical and horizontal dimensions of power. The anaconda doubly reverses Venancio's repeated movements downward from the surface to the bottom of the river and back across the world to the center of indigenous power into an explosive release of power upward from bottom to surface of the river and from outside to inside the whites' center of military power.

The upward movement from underwater to river's surface is paralleled by a reversal of the repeated movements from life outside to death inside the tomb. Life, or the anaconda, is now inside the tomb and is allowed to escape as death in the outside world. The natural behaviors through which anacondas kill and eat their prey provide apt metaphors for the reversibility of the vertical dimension of power relations. Like the increasingly thick ropes that Funes's soldiers used to tie Venancio's coffin, the anaconda forms a constricting braid of death around its victims. And like the coffin that carried Venancio down to the underworld, the anaconda swallows its victims whole. The anaconda also eats its victims more than once by vomiting up the partially digested remains before returning to eat its own vomit (Drummond 1981), a disgusting behavior that resembles both the repeated interments and escapes of Venancio and the final vomiting forth of doubly reversed power into the denaturalized space of Funes and his soldiers. Moreover, the anaconda's rise and release is not a self-generated transformation but is carried out by Funes's henchmen themselves, the agents of their own death and alienation.

The anaconda's release also reverses the horizontal dimension of power relations. Whereas the narrative began with the forced removal of Venancio from his center of power at Makareo, the penultimate episode portrays the reverse action of an indigenous, re-naturalized social power that forces the soldiers to flee from Funes's capital at San Fernando de Atabapo. In effect, the initial process of forcefully excluding Venancio from the indigenous society and including him as a dominated subject of the whites' society is reversed into the historial reempowerment of Venancio and the indigenous society within the military power structure of the whites.

In the final episode of the narrative, the contact situation between Funes's soldiers and Venancio has been socialized, or converted from brute military force into a dialogical process of asking and agreeing. Venancio's refusal to accept Funes's offer of money and gifts is a transformation of the historical situation of contact that developed during the Rubber Boom. The refusal to accept monetary compensation reverses the indigenous situation of coerced economic dependency into a renewal of partial autonomy. The military power structure's destruction is a self-generating process set in motion by Venancio's mythically powerful speech act. Instead of an internalization of self-generated creative powers, the narrative about Venancio Camico and Tomas Funes concludes with the externalization of self-generating powers of dehumanization and collective annihilation.

The narrative about Venancio Camico and Tomas Funes is a mythic trope of historical consciousness through which the Wakuénai and other indigenous peoples of the Upper Río Negro continue to carve out an enduring social identity in the aftermath of Rubber Boom terror. As an indigenous interpretation of history, the narrative is less concerned with recounting the raw events of revitalization, genocide, and military insurrection than with creating a socialized history in which the violent annihilation of indigenous peoples during the Rubber Boom can be remembered as the beginning of a reempowerment, or an escape from total slavery to partial freedom. Specific historical events, such as Venancio Camico and his followers' collective refusal to participate in the whites' economy in 1858 and Funes's death by rebellious soldiers in 1923, are juxtaposed to create a narrative model of the historical situation of contact during the Rubber Boom and a program for action within the situation of ethnic and class competitions along the Upper Río Negro today. Just as the Kuwái myth cycle serves as a program for ritually producing socialized individuals and reproducing the social order, the narrative about Venancio Camico and Tomas Funes is a prototype for collective actions that socialize alien forms of power and reempower indigenous peoples in the historical present.

Like the narrative about ancestral emergence, the story of Venancio Camico and Tomas Funes must be interpreted in terms of the indigenous view of history as a process of opening up the mythic past of Iñápirríkuli into an expanding world of peoples and places. In a general sense, both narratives are concerned with the creation of a shared historical spacetime that includes both the dominant society of the whites and colonized indigenous peoples of the Upper Río Negro region. The story of mythic emergence explains how the Wakuénai historically adjusted to displacement from their ancestral lands during the late colonial period through forming new relations with Eastern Tukanoan peoples and through an eventual return to the center of mythic power. In the narrative about Venancio Camico and Tomas Funes, the Wakuénai take this process of historical interpretation a step further by showing how the Rubber Boom forced them to take a more active role in opposing and negating the whites' political economy. Surviving the Rubber Boom was more than a simple process of temporary removal from ancestral lands followed by a return; it meant rather that Venancio's warning in 1858 to reject the whites' economy of debt peonage had to be elevated to the status of a sacred cosmological principle. Like the anaconda's rise from the bottom of the river, the Wakuénai reemerged from collective annihilation during the Rubber Boom through doubly reversing the culture of terror.

# 3

# The Genesis of Ritual Power

Wakuénai storytellers explain the genesis of ritual power in a cycle of myths about the transformational space-time of Amáru and Kuwái. The cycle of narratives about Kuwái and Amáru describes the origins of sacred rituals and ceremonies through which men became organized into a ritual hierarchy of specialists and nonspecialists through the acquisition of Kuwái's life-giving powers and after which time they differentiated themselves into a number of distinct peoples by competing for control over Kuwái's sacred flutes and trumpets. These social transformations are integrated into an understanding of the coming-into-being of natural species and specifically human physiological processes of conception, birth, and growth.

The expressive force of Wakuénai narratives about the transformational space-time of Kuwái and Amáru is intimately bound up with another cycle of narratives about Iñápirríkuli, the trickster-creator, and the space-time of mythic beginnings at Hípana. In this more distant, undifferentiated space-time, the world consisted of a single village, a solitary island of terra firma surrounded by rivers and flooded forests. The men of Hípana were engaged in constant warfare against Kunáhwerrim (grandfather of sickness), who was their brother-in-law, or sister's husband. Kunáhwerrim and his animal-human followers succeeded in completely exterminating their affinal foes from Hípana, leaving Kunáhwerrim's wife as the only surviving member of her brother's village. The woman collected the bones from the outer three fingers of her slain brother's right hand and placed them inside a basket that she carried along to her garden each day. One day she forgot to take the basket with her to the manioc garden, and the bones turned into crickets. The name Iñápirríkuli comes from his mythic creation out of bone (*inaápi*). Kunáhwerrim heard the crickets inside the basket, took them out, and threw them on the ground so hard that their stomachs burst open. He left the three crickets for dead, but they sewed up each other's stomachs.

The next three episodes of the myth relate how Kunáhwerrim repeatedly attempted to kill Iñápirríkuli and his two younger brothers, Dzúli and Káali. The three brothers always knew beforehand what their evil uncle was planning, and they invented clever ways of escaping his traps. In the final episode, Iñápirríkuli took revenge on Kunáhwerrim by killing one of his wives and leaving her chopped up body to boil in a pot inside Kunáhwerrim's house. Upon returning home, Kunáhwerrim ate his wife's body, thinking it was game meat.

Other narratives in the cycle describe an unfinished world characterized by unceasing violence and hostility between the group of brothers living at Hípana and their cannibalistic, affinal enemies led by Kunáhwerrim. This state of warfare was chronic and without resolution. Even though Iñápirríkuli eventually killed Kunáhwerrim, the warfare between affines did not cease, and Kunáhwerrim continued to cause death by transforming into malaria and other lethal diseases.

The remote mythic past of Iñápirríkuli was a precultural, presexual space-time in which there was not yet any clear differentiation between human and nonhuman animals and between male and female humans. Iñápirríkuli, his brothers, and their affinal adversaries are portrayed as having animal bodies, and growth is described as a process of transforming through a series of different animal species rather than a series of physiological processes and changes focused on the human body. The animal-humans of the precultural mythic past were created by transforming bones into animals, and even death was merely a transition from one species of animal into another. The animal-humans were always scheming and plotting against their affines. Iñápirríkuli constantly had to devise new strategies to counteract the next conspiracy against him, no matter how ingeniously he had defeated his enemies.

The cycle of narratives about Amáru and Kuwái recounts the biological and social processes that led from the chaotic, undifferentiated mythic past at Hípana to a more recent, specifically human past. The cycle begins prior to the birth of Kuwái with the story of the origin of women's menstruation. This differentiation of male from female beings did not actively transform the space-time of mythic beginnings at Hípana but was an essential precondition for the radical changes that were to follow. The birth of Kuwái and his removal to a remote, isolated house outside of and above the social space of Iñápirríkuli and his brothers at Hípana set in motion processes of cosmic growth and creation. The world opened up as Kuwái flew through the sky, and the landscape became filled with natural species and objects as Kuwái hummed and sang their names. From then on, the musical naming power of Kuwái, or "the powerful sound that opened up the world," became the source of life and death that men and women sought to control.

After Kuwái taught men how to perform the sacred rituals of initiation, Iñápirríkuli pushed him into a bonfire, and the world contracted back to its former size. Out of Kuwái's ashes grew the plant materials for making the flutes and trumpets played in initiation rituals and sacred ceremonies, called *kwépani* (Kuwái-dance). Amáru and the women stole these instruments from Iñápirríkuli, starting a long chase in which the world opened up for a second time as the women played Kuwái's flutes and trumpets throughout the world. Eventually, Iñápirríkuli and the men, disguised as animals, regained control of the flutes. Kuwái, Amáru, and Iñápirríkuli left this world to go live in the various celestial regions from whence they are invoked in rituals.

Ethnologists familiar with the literature on narratives in lowland South America will immediately recognize the second part of the Kuwái myth cycle as a variation upon the theme of women's original possession of sacred male cult items (Villas Boas 1974; Murphy and Murphy 1974). In these myths, women had control of the sacred flutes and trumpets, and men were forbidden to see or play the instruments. A powerful mythic being took the flutes and trumpets away from the women and gave them to men, who have maintained control of them ever since. Despite superficial resemblances to this common Amazonian myth, the struggle between men and women for control of the sacred flutes takes a very different form in the Wakuénai cycle of narratives about Kuwái and Amáru. Amáru and the women were not the original possessors of Kuwái's flutes but, as we have already read, stole them from Iñápirríkuli and the men, who had already mastered Kuwái's musical naming power in a series of earlier myths. The Wakuénai version thus inverts the more widespread Amazonian myth by having women take the sacred flutes away from men, who in turn take them back from women.

The Kuwái myth cycle also inverts the widespread Amazonian myths of the origin of cooking fire. In these narratives, the coming-into-being of a fully human, cultural world is depicted as a process of capturing the prototypical cooking fire from its natural, extrasocial guardians and bringing it into human society (Lévi-Strauss 1969; Turner 1985). For the Wakuénai, the acquisition of fire took place in the distant space-time of mythic beginnings and was not an especially momentous event. The transformational mythic being, Kuwái, was all things in the world except fire, and it was when Iñápirríkuli pushed this being into a bonfire on the village plaza that the first stage of creating a culturally distinct ordering of human society reached completion. Thus, the Kuwái myth cycle inverts the more common Amazonian myths of the origin of cooking fire, since Kuwái represents a synthesis of all worldly elements except fire which must be brought down from a place of banishment in the sky and placed into contact with fire inside the social space of the village at Hípana.

The Kuwái myth cycle not only inverts these common themes of Amazonian mythologies but also integrates them into a complex framework of earlier and later space-times and their transformations. Kuwái opened up the space-time of mythic beginnings at Hípana and brought into being the species and objects of nature through musical naming power. After the fiery death of Kuwái and the closing of the world to its original dimensions, Amáru and the women opened up the world for a second time by playing Kuwái's flutes and trumpets as they fled from Iñápirríkuli. Through controlling these musical transformations of the cosmos in their rituals, men and women construct a hierarchical ordering of ancestors, elders, and descendants out of the chaotic, primal state of warfare between the animal-humans from the space-time of mythic beginnings.

In many respects, the Wakuénai cycle of narratives about Kuwái and Amáru is more comparable to the narrative traditions of peoples living in the sub-Andean *montaña* regions of Peru and Ecuador than to those of indigenous groups inhabiting the vast lowland areas of the Amazon basin and its downstream tributaries. The Amuesha, for example, are a Southern Arawakan people of the Peruvian *montaña* who explain the cosmological origins of their social order in narratives about the acquisition of a genre of sacred vocal music, called *coshamñats*. "Into this world of social chaos and troubled relations with the precocious solar divinity, the Amuesha say that *coshamñats* music and its ritual celebration were introduced, an event that brought with it revolutionary changes in the Amuesha concept of social and cosmic order" (Smith 1984:137). For both the Amuesha and the Wakuénai, the space-time of mythic beginnings was a violent, turbulent world that underwent radical changes with the introduction of a sacred, musical power. However, in contrast to the Wakuénai, Amuesha social and religious organization developed through a long history of direct contact with the Inca Empire and earlier states of the Central Andes (Smith 1977).

Other lowland South American groups with known historical ties to Central Andean state-level societies have also created narratives that are organized into elaborate cycles and that outline a heterogeneous past of earlier and later space-times. The Shipibo, for example, a Panoan group of the Ucayali River Basin in Peru, classify their narratives according to a tripartite chronology: (1) a remote time of mythic beginnings (*moatian icani*), (2) an intermediate past of the time of the Incas (*moatian ica*), and (3) the relatively recent past of the "Grandfathers" (*moatian*) (Roe 1988:111; Gebhart-Sayer 1986:1). In narratives set in the time of mythic beginnings, the Shipibo explain the origins of fire, cultigens, and many other important elements of their culture. However, the remote mythic past was an incomplete creation when animals could speak like people and people could turn into animals. The distinguishing feature of the animal-humans' behavior was their antisocial stinginess with material goods and knowledge (Roe 1988). In narratives about the intermediate time of the Incas, the Shipibo account for the transformation of the remote mythic past into the more recent, historical past of fully social, human beings.

> To paraphrase two variants of the myth, a large village of "Incas" . . . lived there [Cumancayacocha] until one day either a woman shaman or the "Inca" poured flight medicine (*noiarao*) on the ground surrounding the village and it slowly rose. As the village levitated to the sound of drums and flutes, some pots fell to the ground and smashed. The village flew over the Ucayali to descend either upon the mysterious Cerros de Canshahuaya on the lower Ucayali, downriver from Pucallpa, or at Masisea (Roe 1988:106).

Like the Wakuénai cycle of narratives about Kuwái and Amáru, Shipibo narratives set in the time of the Incas are about the transformations that led from a remote, unfinished mythic past of animal-humans to a more recent, historical past in which humans came to be culturally separate from other animals. For the Shipibo as well as the Wakuénai and Amuesha, musical sounds (flutes and drums in the Shipibo case) are described as a powerful force that caused these cosmic transformations to unfold.

Another sub-Andean group whose narratives outline a complex, heterogeneous past are the Canelos Quichua of eastern Ecuador. Canelos Quichua narratives about mythic space-time (*unai*) describe it as an undifferentiated world that existed prior to the separation of humans and animals into distinct categories of being (Reeve 1988; Whitten 1985). Between the present and the mythic past is an intermediate space-time of historical beginnings, called *callari uras*. "The accounts set in beginning times record inter- and intraethnic warfare, migration, the harsh conditions of the rubber boom, and the disappearance, through extermination and transculturation, of two Zaparoan groups" (Reeve 1988: 26). Beginning times culminate in stories about the profound social transformations of the rubber boom (*cauchu uras*), a period which marks the transition to present times. The undifferentiated world of mythic animal-humans continues to exist as a parallel frame of reference for understanding the events of beginning and present times. In their rituals, Canelos Quichua enter into direct relations with the animal-humans of mythic space-time through songs and instrumental music, drug-induced hallucinogenic visions, and pottery making. The Canelos Quichua concept of beginning times differs from the transformational space-times of cosmogenesis among the Wakuénai, Amuesha, and Shipibo insofar as it refers to more recent historical processes of ethnic group formation in the context of European colonial domination rather than more distant historical processes that developed prior to the arrival of Europeans in South America. Nevertheless, the organization of Canelos Quichua narratives follows the same general pattern of a transformational space-time that emerges out of an undifferentiated mythic space-time and that shades into a more recent, human past.

These family resemblances in the organization of narratives into tripartite frameworks of space-time may reflect similar historical processes of interaction between small-scale societies of lowland areas and more powerful state-level societies of the Andes, both pre- and post-Conquest. Alternatively, the resemblances between Wakuénai mythology and narrative discourse in upland, *montaña* regions of the Amazon basin may reflect only the fact that these indigenous societies were all located at the margins of colonial and national systems of power. It is quite possible that other Amazonian peoples living in downstream, more accessible areas had developed complex mythologies prior to the arrival of Western peoples.

## Summary of the Kuwái Myth Cycle

The following version of the Kuwái myth cycle is a synthesis of several myths which Hernan Yusrinu, headman of the Dzáwinai village of Gavilán, narrated to me over a period of several months in 1981. More abbreviated versions were elicited from other men in the village and from the Curripaco-speaking men of Punta Bella. Narrators usually perform only one myth at a time in order to explain the origins of a particular set of ritual or ceremonial activities. However, the entire cycle of narratives is performed as an integral whole during male initiations, and in July 1984 Hernan gave a continuous narration of the total cycle of myths at my request. The cycle consists of nine parts, each of which can be told as a separate narrative.

## Myth 1: The Origin of Women's Menstruation

Amáru, one of Iñápirríkuli's aunts, had a shotgun,[1] and Iñápirríkuli knew that she was planning to shoot him with it. He wanted to steal her shotgun, so he cut a piece of balsa wood and fashioned it into the form of her shotgun. He finished working on the wooden gun in the mid-afternoon.

Amáru kept her shotgun on two pegs against the wall of her house at Mútsipáni, and two macaws perched on the weapon to warn her if Iñápirríkuli came to try to steal it. While she was sitting and talking with a friend in front of the house, Iñápirríkuli came around from behind and snuck inside. He saw the two macaws and realized that he could not take the shotgun without disturbing them. So he gently pushed his balsa wood gun into the place of the shotgun. As he carefully pulled the shotgun out from under the two macaws, one of the birds woke up and yelled, "Gaa." Iñápirríkuli ran out the back door of the house with Amáru's shotgun and fled to his house at Hípana.

Amáru went inside to see what had disturbed the macaws but saw that her shotgun was still in its place. In the late afternoon, Amáru went to Iñápirríkuli's house with the wooden shotgun. She intended to shoot and kill Iñápirríkuli, but he had loaded the wooden shotgun with the fruit of *tsipátsi* (a type of grass). Amáru arrived at Hípana and called Iñápirríkuli outside to the port. She held her shotgun hidden behind her back until he was close enough to shoot. But Iñápirríkuli knew what she was planning and dodged the blast of fruits. Then he shot Amáru in the groin with the shotgun that he had stolen from her earlier that afternoon. Blood trickled down Amáru's legs, and she sat down to hide her condition from men. She had to fast on manioc drinks until the blood stopped running. If Iñápirríkuli had not changed shotguns with Amáru, men would now menstruate instead of women, and women would have penises instead of men.

## Myth 2: The Conception and Birth of Kuwái

Iñápirríkuli secretly made love to Amáru many times until she became pregnant with Kuwái. They were both very afraid to let anyone else know about their incestuous sexual relations.

Amáru became pregnant but could not give birth to the child because she had no birth canal. When the time came for Amáru to give birth to the child, she fell unconscious from the pain. Iñápirríkuli and his brothers sent for the red-beaked dove to try to open up a birth canal. The dove penetrated with only the length of its short, red beak and failed to open a passageway. Next, Iñápirríkuli and his brothers called on the red bo-cachico fish to help. The fish jumped from the water with all its might but only its head penetrated Amáru's body. Finally, Iñápirríkuli called upon the *mataguaru* fish (*ádaru wawím*), which succeeded in penetrating with the full length of its body and opened up a birth canal. Amáru gave birth to Kuwái, a hairy, half-human, monstrous creature.

Iñápirríkuli and his brothers, Dzúli and Dzulíhwerri, took Kuwái away from Amáru immediately after his birth so that no one would know that Iñápirríkuli was the father. When Kuwái was born, the others called him Máhnekánari (no one knows) or Hekwápi ikáina (sperm of this world) be-cause nobody, not even Kuwái, knew the father's identity. Iñápirríkuli and his brothers took Kuwái to live in the corner of the sky (*líwanápu éenu*) because they were ashamed that he had been born of an incestuous sexual relationship and were afraid that Kuwái would cause harm to others.

After leaving Kuwái, Iñápirríkuli and his brothers returned to revive Amáru with tobacco smoke. The placenta and afterbirth had turned into a stingray (*yámaru*), and the three brothers tried to convince Amáru that she had given birth to nothing else. However, Amáru knew that they were lying and had stolen her child from her. She warned them that she would steal Kuwái back someday.

## Myth 3: The Powerful Sound that Opened Up the World

For a long time, no one knew about Kuwái because Iñápirríkuli and his brothers kept him hidden in the sky. The singing and humming of Ku-wái's voice did not reach the others at Hípana, because Iñápirríkuli and Dzúli had muzzled him with a clay pot that muffled his voice. Kuwái grew very rapidly in his house in the sky. Even though he was still young, he appeared to be old.

One day, Iñápirríkuli's youngest brother, Hérri, and three of his nephews were out walking and saw Kuwái flying and singing in the sky. They asked Kuwái to come back to eat with their family, but Kuwái told them that he was fasting. The boys had to start fasting then, too, because they had seen Kuwái. The only food that they could safely eat was a manioc drink made from wild forest fruits. They lied to their parents whenever it came time to eat, saying that they were not hungry and only wanted to drink manioc and beverages made from wild forest fruits.

Iñápirríkuli knew that the boys were lying and that they had seen Kuwái. He went to talk with Kuwái and invited him to come down to his village. There he could stay in a special hut in the forest that Iñápirríkuli would build for him. Kuwái said he would come to visit in the afternoon.

When Kuwái appeared in the sky above the village, the men and four boys greeted him on the village plaza with manioc drinks made by the women. Women and children stayed inside their houses where they could not see Kuwái. The singing and humming of Kuwái was a powerful sound that opened up the world, enlarging it for the first time. Kuwái began by singing the name of the lapa (*Cuniculus paca*), and the world opened up somewhat. Then Kuwái flew to all regions and sang into being the names of all animal, bird, and fish species. He went as far as the Guaviare River to the north and the Vaupés River to the south and west, opening up the world everywhere and filling it with all living creatures. The people listened to Kuwái's voice from far away.

## Myth 4: Kuwái Eats the Three Boys

Kuwái landed in Iñápirríkuli's village and instructed Hérri and the other three boys to continue fasting so that they would grow up strong and healthy. Kuwái led them to the special hut in the forest. For a long time, Kuwái allowed the four boys to eat only manioc and fruit drinks that had been treated with special chants.

When the period of fasting was nearly over and the boys were extremely hungry, Kuwái picked some *awíya* fruits from a tall tree and let them fall into the roofless hut where the boys were fasting. The three nephews of Iñápirríkuli ate some of the *awíya* fruit, but Hérri, Iñápirríkuli's youngest brother, did not eat any. Later Kuwái entered the hut to see which of the boys had eaten the fruit. He opened their mouths to examine their teeth and found that the three nephews of Iñápirríkuli had indeed eaten some of the fruits. Only Hérri's mouth was completely clean, showing that he had not eaten any fruit.

Kuwái caused a storm with heavy rains that fell directly into the boys roofless hut. He came disguised as a rock to give them shelter. The rock shelter was really Kuwái's huge mouth, a room the size of a house. Iñápirríkuli's three nephews all went inside the rock to get out of the rain, but Hérri made a tiny shelter for himself with palm leaves and remained outside. When the rains were about to subside, Kuwái closed his giant mouth, killing and eating the three boys who had entered. Kuwái told Hérri that he would blow smoke and chant for him in three days so that he could end his period of fasting and seclusion.

Kuwái flew over to the rapids along the upper Içana River and vomited up the remains of the three boys. Iñápirríkuli was working in his manioc garden when the rains came, and he knew that Kuwái had killed his three nephews when he caught a handful of rain that was pure blood. He knew that only his youngest brother, Hérri, was strong enough to endure the long period of fasting.

Kuwái came out of the forest where he had eaten the three boys and entered Iñápirríkuli's village at sunset. Iñápirríkuli had prepared four trays of wild fruits. Kuwái returned to the roofless hut in the forest without taking any of the fruits. When Kuwái had left the village, women came out to make manioc drinks from the various fruits that had been put on display. In the forest, Kuwái told Hérri that there were only two days to wait until the end of his fast. Then Kuwái flew up into the sky until going out of sight, because he knew that Iñápirríkuli was planning his death.

## Myth 5: Kálimátu Speaks with Kuwái

Iñápirríkuli went into the seclusion hut and asked Hérri why Kuwái had killed and eaten the three boys. Hérri explained that they had all broken their fast by eating some of the fruits that had fallen into the hut. Then Iñápirríkuli taught Hérri how to create Kuwái's song by putting a bee inside a basket. The buzzing sound was exactly like Kuwái's singing. Iñápirríkuli told Hérri that he could not eat again until Kuwái had returned to blow smoke on the sacred food (*káridzámai*). However, Kuwái had gone back to his corner of the sky, so Iñápirríkuli had to devise a plan to lure him back to the village. With the aid of a coca preparation, Iñápirríkuli made a plan to lure Kuwái back to the village by sending a special messenger with a type of bait.

Iñápirríkuli collected some white palm grubs (*mútsi*) and took them to the village of Kálimátu, a wasp-person. There he persuaded Kálimátu to fly up to Kuwái's house in the sky with the grubs and invite him to come back to Hípana to blow smoke on Hérri's food. On his way up to Kuwái's home, Kálimátu had to pass through a huge doorlike gateway that opened and closed rapidly. The door shut on his body just as he was halfway through and squeezed him very hard on the waist. That is why Kálimátu wasps have such tiny mid-sections today.

Kálimátu arrived at Kuwái's home and found him singing and picking fruits from the grasses and weeds around the house.

"Greetings to you, from Iñápirríkuli. He wants you to come blow smoke on the food of the boys who are fasting."

"No," said Kuwái. "I cannot come because I have already eaten the boys. I might come to blow smoke for Hérri, because he's the only one left. I already ate the others."

"No," said Kálimátu. "The boys are all still alive, all four of them. You know that Iñápirríkuli can bring them back to life. They're alive."

"No, this is not true. The boys are dead. Iñápirríkuli called for me because he wants to kill me," said Kuwái.

"You must come, if only to blow smoke on the food of Hérri. Then you can return here safely," said Kálimátu.

"No, I'm not going," answered Kuwái. "He called for me only so he can kill me. Tell Iñápirríkuli that I'm not coming."

Kálimátu took out the *mútsi* grubs and gave some of them to Kuwái. Kuwái broke open the grubs and held them up to his nose. The intoxicating smell of the grubs had a powerful effect on Kuwái, who would have eaten all of them if Kálimátu had let him.

"OK, Kálimátu. I'll come to Hípana. For this food, I'll come so that Iñápirríkuli can kill me."

"No," said Kálimátu. "Iñápirríkuli won't kill you, because the boys are all still alive. When you arrive there, you'll see that they're still alive."

"Send my greetings to Iñápirríkuli. Tell him that I'll arrive the day after tomorrow. Tell him to order the women to harvest manioc and prepare a strong *yaráki* (liquor). Tell him that I'll come so that he can kill me so he won't have to think about me ever again. Tell him that he cannot kill me with machetes, for my body is made of machetes. My body, it is machetes. Poison, too, is my body. My hair is poison. He cannot kill me with water, for my body is water, and I live in water. He cannot tie me up with vines, for my body is made of vines. Logs and sticks, I am they; they are my body. I am all things, my body is all things. The only thing that my body is not is fire. With fire he can kill me. In fire I cannot live."

"No," said Kálimátu. "He is not calling for you to kill you. He only wants you to blow smoke over the boys' food."

"Tell him that I'm coming the day after tomorrow," said Kuwái. "Have him prepare food made from all the animals, fish, and birds."

Kálimátu started to leave but was afraid of the door of Kuwái's house. He waited for a while until it opened, then went through rapidly so it would not catch his body again as it had on the way up. When Kálimátu returned to Hípana, he spoke with Iñápirríkuli about what Kuwái had told him. Iñápirríkuli and his brothers gathered firewood to make a great bonfire on the village plaza.

## Myth 6: *The First Initiation Ritual*

On the second day, after they had prepared the firewood, liquor, and ritual food (*káridzámai*), the villagers heard Kuwái singing the names of the ancestors.[2] The women went inside a separate house. When Kuwái arrived, the men held ritual whips and formed a line. Iñápirríkuli had fashioned three doll-like effigies from balsa wood to represent the three dead boys. Iñápirríkuli lashed his whip across Hérri's back as Kuwái sang. "When are you going to blow tobacco smoke on the ritual food?" Iñápirríkuli asked Kuwái. "Not for a long time, because I have to name all the different species of animals, fish, birds, and fruits," Kuwái answered.

The men gave each other lashes with their ritual whips outside on the village plaza while the women did the same inside their special house. Kuwái called the men into their house and began to teach them how to chant and blow smoke over ritual food so that young men can end their fasts. Iñápirríkuli sat beside Kuwái, while Dzúli, a younger brother, sat farther away and listened. Kuwái chanted and blew tobacco smoke into the pot of food. Dzúli was silent and listened intently to Kuwái's chants, memorizing them all. Iñápirríkuli left to get liquor and doled some out to each of the men and women. Kuwái grew tired of waiting for Iñápirríkuli's return and started to chant again. When Iñápirríkuli came, Kuwái told him that he could not learn to blow smoke because he had missed part of the chanting. Dzúli sat there listening throughout the night.

Iñápirríkuli left to dole out liquor again, and this time Kuwái did not bother to stop and wait for him. When Iñápirríkuli returned, Kuwái told him that he had missed a lot of the chanting. The rest of the night passed like this. Only Dzúli stayed and listened to all the chants.

Every now and then during the night, Kuwái took Dzúli and Iñápirríkuli outside to teach them how to sing and dance *kápetiápani* (whip-dance). When they returned to the house, Kuwái told Dzúli to continue listening carefully so that he could perform the chants after Iñápirríkuli had killed him in the fire. Since that time, Dzúli has been *málikai limínali* (chant-owner).

When Kuwái had finished the last chant, he drank liquor and told Iñápirríkuli how to conclude Hérri's fast by giving him hot pepper to lick. Then Iñápirríkuli invited Kuwái to dance outside. Kuwái had become very drunk. The two men made circles around the fire, holding each other around the shoulder until Iñápirríkuli pushed Kuwái into the middle of the bonfire. The other men threw armfuls of firewood on top of Kuwái, whose body disappeared in smoke. Iñápirríkuli told his kinsmen to get far away from the fire because it would be dangerous when Kuwái's stomach exploded. Then Iñápirríkuli gave hot pepper to Hérri so that he could eat the ritual food.

## Myth 7: The Sacred Flutes and Trumpets of Kuwái

Iñápirríkuli returned to the site of Kuwái's fiery death to see if anything remained of the body, but he found only some ashes and charcoal. The world contracted until it was no bigger than it had been before the birth of Kuwái.

After a few days, a small sprout of *macanilla* palm started to grow from the ashes where Kuwái had burned. In a single day, the sapling burst forth into a giant tree that grew until touching the sky. Iñápirríkuli was admiring the tree for its smoothness and beauty. He called a squirrel and ordered it to measure the tree. The squirrel ascended the *macanilla* palm, marking the trunk at regular intervals until reaching the sky.

The squirrel returned to tell Iñápirríkuli that the entire tree was marked and asked him to touch the base of the tree with his hand. Iñápirríkuli smoked tobacco and divined that if he were to touch the tree with his hand, it would fall on his head, killing him instantly. For the squirrel had not simply marked the tree with shallow incisions but had cut deeply into the trunk so that the tree would collapse at the slightest touch. To avoid the squirrel's trap, Iñápirríkuli cut a very long log and touched the bottom of the tree from a safe distance. The tree fell in a heap of hollowed out pieces.

Iñápirríkuli gathered up all the pieces of *macanilla* wood. He blew through one of the shortest pieces and heard the voice of a little frog (*molítu*) that sings very beautifully. He blew through the other logs and produced the sounds of the various animal, bird, and fish species that Kuwái had sung when he first came to this world.

A tall hardwood tree (*yebaro*) sprang to life in the same spot where the *macanilla* palm had fallen. Iñápirríkuli ordered the squirrel to cut the bark off the enormous *yebaro* tree. When the squirrel had finished this work, Iñápirríkuli lashed the *molitu* flute tightly inside the *yebaro* bark with *dzámakuápi* vines. When he blew through the flute, the sound that came out was a small bird that flew into all parts of the world. Iñápirríkuli also made the first ritual whips from *dzámakuápi* vines. Since that time, men have fasted for two days whenever playing the flutes and trumpets of Kuwái. Women did not have to fast but were also required to stay inside where they could not see the sacred flutes and trumpets.

## Myth 8: Amáru Steals the Sacred Flutes

Amáru lived at Mútsipáni (palm grub-dance) at the headwaters of Caño Waraná, a stream branching off from the Aiarí River near Hípana. Together with a group of women, Amáru stole the sacred flutes and trumpets of Kuwái from Iñápirríkuli and the men of Hípana. Iñápirríkuli chased after Amáru and tried to corner her near the headwaters of Caño Waraná. But when he had ascended the last rapids on the stream, he heard the sounds of the sacred flutes and trumpets being played far downstream. Iñápirríkuli chased after Amáru until he reached a large village near São Gabriel on the Río Negro. Kuwái's music opened up the world for a second time as the women played the sacred flutes and trumpets in various places. Iñápirríkuli could find no sign of Amáru and the women along the Río Negro and thought that she had probably returned to her home at Mútsipáni on Caño Waraná. He asked some local people if they had seen Amáru, but they had not.

At a stream not far upstream from São Gabriel that forms the mouth of a lake called Amáru, Iñápirríkuli met a crow. He took tiny feathers out of the bird's head and wove them into a long rope. After tying the rope around the bird's neck, he let the bird fly away. The crow flew up the stream and into the lake. Iñápirríkuli followed the rope and repeated this procedure several times until he was close to Amáru and the women. From there he could clearly hear the music of the sacred flutes and trumpets.

When he arrived at the women's camp, Iñápirríkuli greeted Amáru in Yeral (*lingua geral*) in order to disguise his identity. Iñápirríkuli and

Amáru conversed for a while in Yeral, and this is the origin of the Yeral language spoken by people in the area of São Gabriel.

"How are you?" asked Iñápirríkuli.

"I'm fine. You haven't seen Iñápirríkuli, have you?" asked Amáru.

"No, not any sign of him," answered Iñápirríkuli.

"I just want to know, since he is chasing after me and wants to kill me. What is it you want, Grandson?" asked Amáru.

"Grandmother, I want to know what this woman is doing?" asked Iñápirríkuli.

"She is fasting. Tonight, my grandson, I am going to blow tobacco smoke over her food so that she can end her fast," Amáru informed him.

"I'd like to come and watch," said Iñápirríkuli.

"No, you can't watch because you're a man. You can eat with us, but you can't come to where we're holding the sacred rites," Amáru told him.

Then Amáru instructed Iñápirríkuli to stay inside a special house filled only with men. The women went into another house with the young woman who was fasting.

Amáru went to find a large gourd-dipper of manioc beer to give to Iñápirríkuli. He took the gourd but drank only a mouthful. Then he gave it back to Amáru. The gourd was almost full, so Amáru asked him to drink some more. "No, I'm not used to drinking much," said Iñápirríkuli. "That bastard, Iñápirríkuli, always drinks a whole gourdful of beer and then asks for more," said Amáru. Thus she was convinced that the grandson was not Iñápirríkuli in disguise.

Iñápirríkuli and the men went walking in search of Amáru's ceremonial house. Amáru and the women had gone to the forest to make ritual whips. The men could hear the sound of the sacred flutes and trumpets coming toward them and ran ahead until reaching the ceremonial house. Iñápirríkuli and the men went inside the house while Amáru and the women danced in a circle around the house, carrying ritual whips and playing the sacred instruments.

In the evening, the women hid the sacred flutes and trumpets, and Amáru began to chant for the sacred food of the girl-initiate. Iñápirríkuli came outside and watched the women dance *kápetiápani* (whip-dance) around a large bonfire. At midnight, Iñápirríkuli picked a fruit (*pikáka*) and put it into the women's manioc beer. The women danced and became very drunk during the night, but they did not grow tired. By the end of the night, the women were very drunk, and one of them started a general brawl by striking another woman with her whip. Iñápirríkuli jumped into the middle of the group of women and tried to kill Amáru with a machete. But Amáru knew already that Iñápirríkuli would come to try to kill her, and she fled with the sacred flutes and trumpets into a hole inside her ceremonial house. From there she traveled underground to Mútsipáni, her house on Caño Waraná. Iñápirríkuli looked unsuccessfully for the instruments. Finally, he found the hole where Amáru had escaped with the flutes and trumpets. He knew then that Amáru had gone back up the Içana and Aiarí to Mútsipáni.

Iñápirríkuli went up to the headwaters of Caño Waraná again, closing the river on his way by making rapids and waterfalls. Again he heard the sound of the flutes and trumpets being played far downstream. He hurried down to the last rapids on the Vaupés, called Camanão, and closed the river. But again he heard the flutes and trumpets downstream. Amáru had fled to where the sky begins, a place where the river runs in a full circle.

## Myth 9: Iñápirríkuli and the Men Regain the Sacred Instruments

Iñápirríkuli did not want Amáru and the women to keep Kuwái's sacred flutes and trumpets, so he fomented a revolt of the men against the women. He led the men from Hípana to Amáru's village of women at Mútsipáni. The men disguised themselves as *molítu* frogs.

Upon arriving at Mútsipáni, Iñápirríkuli asked Amáru to show him the sacred flutes and trumpets, but she refused. Iñápirríkuli sent a lightning bolt down on the village of women, who all fell unconscious. He and the men ran into the village and took Kuwái's sacred instruments. When the men had hidden all the instruments, Iñápirríkuli blew tobacco smoke over Amáru and the women, who revived and got up.

"What happened to my things?" asked Amáru.

"I don't know. We were all knocked out by the lightning," replied Iñápirríkuli. "Kuwái's sacred flutes and trumpets all turned into animals and ran away into the forests and rivers."

Amáru did not really believe Iñápirríkuli. He told her that from then on, he and the other men would own Kuwái's flutes and trumpets, since they had all turned into animals, fish, and birds.

The men returned to Hípana with Kuwái's flutes and trumpets and held a sacred ceremonial exchange, called *kwépani* (Kuwái-dance). Amáru and the women also came to Hípana, where they had to stay inside a separate house during the ceremony. The men played the sacred instruments outside on the village plaza all night long. Anticipating Amáru's skepticism, Iñápirríkuli had gathered fur from each different species of forest animal, feathers from each species of bird, and skin from each species of fish. Iñápirríkuli went inside the women's house while men played the flutes down at the port. As the men came closer to the house and started to dance circles around it, Amáru asked him the name of the animal that was singing outside. Iñápirríkuli told her the name of each animal and gave her a stick to push through a small hole in the wall of the house. The end of the stick was covered with *pendari*, which was very sticky. Outside, the men put a little piece of fur on the end of the stick. Amáru drew it back inside the house and, seeing the piece of fur on its end, was tricked into believing that Kuwái's flutes and trumpets had indeed turned into animals. Iñápirríkuli and the men did the same thing for every species of animal, bird, and fish until Amáru was convinced that Iñápirríkuli was telling her the truth. Since then, Kuwái's flutes and trumpets have belonged to Iñápirríkuli and the men.

Iñápirríkuli showed the men how to insert *molítu* flutes into resonators made of *yebaro* bark with vines so that they could make the ancestor trumpets of Kuwái. He instructed them how to carry and hold these enormous trumpets during male initiation rituals. Then Iñápirríkuli left this world to go live in the celestial paradise (*likáremi*), the place of eternal sunlight. Amáru returned to *Eenutánhi* in the eastern sky, and Kuwái went back up to his house in the corner of the sky.

## Analysis of the Kuwái Myth Cycle, Part I

The Kuwái myth cycle contains a wealth of sexual, psychological, and religious symbolism that bridges the transition from the space-time of mythic beginnings at Hípana to a proto-human space-time in which ritual actions define the social boundaries between humans and other animate life forms and between male and female humans. At the most general level, the Kuwái myth cycle consists of two parts, or stages, of creation, the division of which is clearly marked by the fiery death of Kuwái at the first initiation ritual (Myth 6) and the contraction of the world back to its former size. Part I (Myths 1–6) of the cycle is concerned with psychosocial processes of development that unfold in parallel with a cumulative series of transformations in the spatial and temporal structure of the cosmos. Part II of the cycle (Myths 7–9) focuses on the working out of the politics of gender relations in a patrilineal, patrilocal social order and the emergence of a horizontal structure of separate peoples and places in the world.

In part I of the myth cycle, Kuwái is initially removed from Amáru's womb to "a corner of the sky," a place that is *above* and *outside* of the social space of the village at Hípana. The opposition between the "above and outside" and the "down on the ground and inside" is gradually mediated through a series of transformations in which the childlike, musical creativity of Kuwái is lured into revealing the secrets of its life-giving and life-taking powers and coaxed into coming "down and inside" the social space of the village at Hípana.[3] When the secrets of Kuwái's musical naming power have been fully memorized by Dzúli, they become an infinitely self-replicating principle for socially reproducing a ritual hierarchy of elders and ritual specialists who mediate between the life-giving powers of the ancestors and the life cycle transitions of a younger generation of male initiates. The first stage in Kuwái's musical creation of the world reaches completion when the original movement "up-above and outside" is transformed into the reverse movement "down-into and inside."

The reversal of spatial movements through the external structure of the cosmos in Part I of the narrative cycle runs parallel to the reversal of externalizing and internalizing movements of bodies and foods across the boundaries of the human body. The imagery of giving birth, or of one body passing from inside to outside of another body, is cumulatively transformed into the symbolism of food and eating as an internalization, or the passage of bodies from outside to inside the body. At birth, Kuwái is stuck inside Amáru's womb (Myth 2), and it is the intervention of a male sibling group that allows Kuwái to escape from death inside the maternal body to life outside of it. This process of externalization at birth is completely reversed in the myth of the first initiation ritual (Myth 6) into processes of internalization whereby Hérri, the first male initiate, ingests the life-giving powers of the sacred food and Dzúli, the first chant-owner, memorizes (i.e., cognitively "ingests") the secrets of Kuwái's musical naming power. By eating the sacred food, the first initiate escapes death by starvation and being stuck in the liminal space-time of the isolated forest hut outside the village. Kuwái's eating and vomiting of the three boys in Myth 4 and the accompanying contrast of this reversible action with Hérri's refusals to eat and be eaten provide the mediating symbols between the opposing processes of externalization through giving birth (Myth 2) and internalization through eating foods (Myth 6). Myth 4 dramatically portrays the premature ingestion of food and return of the body to the inside of the body as deadly mistakes that preempt the culturally prescribed methods for reversing the inside-to-outside direction of giving birth through fasting, chanting, and other ritual activities that safely mediate the passage of nonhuman bodies into the human body.

The reversal of bodily and cosmic processes in part I of the Kuwái myth cycle is also concerned with negating the incestuous, animal-like sexuality of Iñápirríkuli and Amáru. "There were no other people" (*karrú pakápa padáwa náiki*). Incestuous sexual relations are cited as the principal motive for removing Kuwái to an isolated celestial abode and as the reason for Kuwái's potential harmfulness to the residents of Hípana. The series of cumulative transformations in myths 2–6 outlines a process of transforming this initially harmful, incestuous sexuality into its opposite. Beginning with Hérri's refusal to accept Kuwái's offerings of food and shelter (Myth 4), the tokens of childhood dependency and incestuous longings to return to the maternal womb, these negations culminate in the fiery death of Kuwái and subsequent destruction of the expanding space-time of the first stage of creation.

In Myths 2–6, the theme of incestuous sexuality is submerged, or repressed, into the symbolism of eating versus fasting and the closely related communicative process of chanting and blowing tobacco smoke. Food taboos, obligatory fasting, and the eating of the sacred food are ways of defining the shared substance of a patrilineal descent group (*náiki*) as a hierarchical ordering of ancestors, elders, and descendants and for requiring that the infantile, incestuous sexuality of childhood be negated and directed outward to socially appropriate others. As Part I of the narrative cycle demonstrates, the conversion of incestuous sexuality into ritually controlled restrictions on food and eating is not a simple negation but a complex, multiple-phase process of mediating between opposing life-giving and life-taking powers.

In the beginning of the narrative cycle, creative and destructive dimensions of Kuwái's powers conflict with one another as polar opposites. Amáru's womb threatens to deny life to the child inside until it is opened up, with the help of animal intermediaries, by Iñápirríkuli and his brothers. In the next myth (Myth 3), the same opposition between life-taking and life-giving powers is juxtaposed, or "embedded" (Turner 1985:76), in the relationship between the three fathers (Iñápirríkuli, the father, and his two brothers) and Kuwái (the son or brother's son). By attempting to confine and hide Kuwái in an isolated celestial abode, Iñápirríkuli and his brothers have come to embody a transformed manifestation of the life-denying power of the maternal womb in Myth 2. To complete the image of life-denial, Iñápirríkuli and his brothers muffle the sound of Kuwái's voice by placing a clay pot over his mouth. However, the artificial womb constructed by the three fathers is not as life-threatening as the maternal womb, since Kuwái manages to break out of it by himself and to establish contact, albeit remotely, with the world below at Hípana. Kuwái becomes a self-propelled life force that brings into being the various species of animals, fish, and birds, and opens up the world. This first creation of the world marks the beginning of Kuwái's self-transformation from the initial situation of opposing, conflicting powers of creation and destruction into a single being that synthesizes both life-giving and life-taking powers.

Kuwái's first creation of the world in Myth 3 transforms the polar opposition between creative and destructive powers in Myth 2 but does not reverse their basic spatial orientation from inside (death) to outside (life). As long as Kuwái is confined inside the "corner of the sky," he remains unseen and unheard in the world below. Kuwái's escape to the outside makes him visible to Hérri and the three nephews, and the sound of his voice is audible from far away as he flies about the sky. The contrast, on the one hand, between those who see Kuwái and must fast and, on the other hand, those who can only hear Kuwái but not see him becomes a prominent theme in defining male-female relations throughout the narrative cycle. Parallel to Kuwái's movement from inside to outside in the sky is the terrestrial movement of Hérri and the three boys from inside the social space of the village at Hípana to a seclusion hut in the forest which is outside the village. Food imagery also supports the basic spatial orientation of inside-to-outside motion inasmuch as Kuwái and the boys who see him are all required to fast on drinks made from manioc and wild fruits. Kuwái now begins to embody the initially opposing creative and destructive powers within himself, since he has created animal, fish, and bird species while at the same time denying the possiblity of eating these new species.

In Myth 3, Kuwái's first creation of the world unfolds in the skies above Hípana rather than on the ground. As Turner pointed out in his analysis of a Kayapó creation myth, the vertical dimension of mythic space-time "is essentially a metaphor for developmental time, the time of growth and of passage from stage to stage or cycle to cycle of repetitive social processes. Vertical removal from the lower (ground) level is invariably associated with childhood. . . . The ground, as the lower extremity of vertical space, is conversely identified with adults" (1985: 65). In the Wakuénai cycle of narratives about Kuwái and Amáru, the vertical dimension is a metaphor not only for developmental time but also for generational time between ancestors and descendants. The process of bringing Kuwái down to earth at Hípana is at one and the same time a metaphor for the (male) child's attainment of early adulthood at puberty and the transmission of Kuwái's powers from ancestors to descendants.

The first clue of the passage of generational time comes in the beginning of Myth 3, when Kuwái is still confined inside an isolated corner of the sky. "Kuwái grew very rapidly in his house in the sky. Even though he was still young, he appeared to be old." This curious juxtaposition of childhood growth and old age hints at the simultaneous elapsing of developmental and generational time as the vertical dimension of space becomes mediated in later myths through the movements of Kuwái from up in the sky to down on the ground. The first clear indication of the passage of generational time comes in the transition from Myth 3 to Myth 4, when Kuwái comes down to the ground at Hípana and removes Hérri and the other three boys to a seclusion hut in the forest. The movement of Kuwái down to the ground and outside the social space of the village adds a generation of time depth. In Myth 4, Kuwái has replaced the senior generation of father and father's brothers in the role of confining the younger generation of male initiates. The food and shelter that Kuwái offers to Hérri and the three nephews are tokens of the parental nurturing and sheltering of children, only now the relationship of parental protection and childhood dependency must be reversed and severed through stoic resistance. The three nephews' eating of the fruits and entry into the "cave," or the mouth of Kuwái, lead back inside the belly of Kuwái, or the womb of Amáru, rather than forward into the social space of the village. Kuwái's killing and eating of the three boys is an inversion, or an upside down mirror image, of his earlier negation of the artificial womb constructed for him by his father and father's brothers (Myths 2–3).

In Myth 4, the process of reversing the initial removal of Kuwái to a place above and outside the social space of the village at Hípana reaches the half-way point. Kuwái has come down to the ground but only in the extrasocial space of the forest hut. Furthermore, the vertical descent of Kuwái from the sky is only half-finished, since he still remains vertically above Hérri and the three other initiates. When Kuwái drops the fruits into the boys' hut, he is neither down on the ground nor up in the sky but in the intermediary vertical zone of the forest canopy. Kuwái cannot yet share the same vertical space with the male initiates without disasterous consequences: the eating and killing of the three boys who had eaten the fallen fruits.

In a similar manner, the reversal of bodily processes of externalization is only half complete in Myth 4. The three boys who ingest the fallen fruits are themselves ingested by Kuwái, who then vomits their remains on the rocks beside the Içana River. In other words, the myth describes a stalemate between internalization and externalization: two acts of eating are negated by a subsequent act of vomiting. This stalemate is concretely embodied in a petroglyph at Raudal Kuwái, which shows the putrid remains of the three boys complete with the partially digested fruits inside their stomachs. The situation of the three boys who go inside Kuwái's mouth is a double bind from which there is no escape. Like the fruits dropped to the ground that tempted the boys to their death, the rain that falls on the manioc gardens has become a macabre flow of blood.

In contrast with this mythic stalemate of life and death, one boy, Hérri, refuses to eat the forbidden fruits and to take shelter from the rains by going inside Kuwái's mouth. These actions are pivotal in the cumulative transformation of bodily and cosmic processes in Part I of the narrative cycle. The first stage in reversing the initial inside-to-outside movement takes place through Hérri's decision to remain motionless by staying on the outside rather than moving from outside-to-inside (i.e., the fate of the other three boys). In contrast with the vicious circle of eating, being eaten, and being vomited suffered by the other three boys, Hérri's actions are a model of the individual's self-empowerment through taking control over his own biological needs.[4] He is hungry and needs food but can delay gratification of this basic need in favor of a more powerful, culturally defined process of eating the sacred food of the ancestors.[5] When he needs protection from the rains, he builds his own shelter from the palm-leaf materials at hand. The pattern of expectation is clear: the way forward, or down-into the social space of the village at Hípana, is through demonstrating self-control and autonomy by rejecting parental nurturance and protection. Although these actions foreshadow an eventual resolution, the horizontal situation of Hérri on the ground is analogous to the vertical situation of Kuwái in the intermediary vertical zone of the treetops. Hérri is half-way back to the village from the forest, since Kuwái tells him that he must wait only two more days until the end of his fast.

In Myth 5, the expectation of Hérri's return into the social space of the village at Hípana is blocked by Kuwái's return to the sky. The reversal of the inside-to-outside direction of spatial movements is imminent, even though not yet accomplished. Hérri is now stuck outside the village and can only be allowed to come inside after Kuwái has returned to the ground inside the village. Meanwhile, back up in his corner of the sky, Kuwái eats some of the *mútsi* grubs that Iñápirríkuli has sent up with Kálimátu. This event marks the first successful reversal of the inside-to-outside direction of spatial movement and anticipates the ending of

Hérri's fast through eating the sacred food at the end of Myth 6. The *mútsi* grubs emit a smell that intoxicates Kuwái and lures him into revealing the secret of his powers to Kálimátu.

*Mútsi* grubs are an especially well-suited species for serving as the food substance that reverses mythic space-time in Myth 5. The oily, white grubs are harvested from the soft, inner pith of felled palm trees and are considered a delicacy when fried in their own fat over an open fire. The life cycle of *mútsi* grubs is what makes them so appropriate as symbols of mythic reversal. Through metamorphosis, the white grubs mature into large, shiny black weevils, called *déetu*. These insects have enormously long proboscises used for sucking the sweet sap of felled or damaged palm trees.[6] At the same time as they extract sap from the palm trunk, the mature *déetu* weevils deposit hundreds of minute eggs into the pith, where the larvae grow into large grubs after about two months. The life cycle of *mútsi* grubs thus collapses the processes of eating and reproducing into a single ambiguous totality, for the mature insects eat from the same place as they lay eggs. The felled palm is both "womb" and food source. The relevance of this natural process as a metaphor for the reversal of space-time in the Kuwái myth cycle is obvious: the *mútsi* grubs represent the final stage of transforming the themes of incestuous sexuality and giving birth into the symbolism of food and eating. The name of Amáru's terrestrial home, Mútsipáni (palm grub dance), provides an additional semantic linkage between these insects and the theme of incestuous sexual relations.

Kuwái's eating of the *mútsi* grubs in Myth 5 takes place in the context of an extended dialogue between him and Kálimátu, the wasp-person messenger sent by Iñápirríkuli to lure Kuwái back to the ground at Hípana. This dialogue marks an important change in the progressive embedding, or juxtaposition, of Kuwái's life-giving and life-taking powers from an initial opposition toward an ultimate synthesis that encompasses both creative and destructive powers. The spatial orientation of Kuwái's creative powers has now shifted to the internal composition of his body rather than the creation of animal, fish, and bird species in the external world. "My body, it is everything" (*phiúmi kwákada, nudáketsa*), Kuwái explains to Kálimátu, thereby revealing the source of his creative, life-giving powers and the reason why he is so difficult to kill, or negate. From then on, human beings and the world of objects with which they interact through eating, touching, seeing, hearing, and other sensuous contact are to have a double existence as generic categories of being coupled with specific individual beings. The poetic mediation of these two complementary dimensions of the cosmos, its "everything-ness" and its "oneness," becomes the basis of ritual power in human society. In Kuwái's dialogue with Kálimátu, he also reveals that fire is the only element that can negate the creative principle of the One in the Many. The way to effect a total synthesis of Kuwái's creative and destructive powers is now clear: Kuwái, the One in the Many, must be pushed into an enormous fire.

The dialogue between Kuwái and Kálimátu in Myth 5 also marks an important change in the form through which Kuwái expresses his powers. Earlier in the cycle of narratives, Kuwái's power manifested itself as a raw, biological life force that hummed and sang into being the various natural species of animals, fish, and birds through musical naming power. This powerful, world-opening sound was an unsocialized, explosive force that broke out of the corner of the sky to which it had been confined by Iñápirríkuli and his brothers. The dialogue between Kuwái and Kálimátu in Myth 5 transforms the unsocialized, monological, musical naming power of Kuwái in Myth 3 into a socialized, dialogical conversation that takes place inside the corner of the sky and that is subsequently transmitted by Kálimátu to Iñápirríkuli down on the ground at Hípana.

The vertical spatial dimension, or developmental/generational time, is transformed in Myth 5 into a fully differentiated, reversible space-time. Kálimátu goes from the ground at Hípana up to Kuwái's corner of the sky and returns to the ground. Thus, within the narrative framework of a single myth, Kálimátu has replicated the entire structure of action in Myths 2–4, the removal of Kuwái up to the sky and his return to the ground. Kálimátu's actions in Myth 5 demonstrate that the vertical dimension of space-time is now reversible, a necessary precondition for Kuwái's second, and final, descent from the sky to the ground in Myth 6 (as well as for the reversal of horizontal space on the ground so that Hérri can go from outside to inside social space).

Kálimátu's ascent and descent also show that the vertical dimension of space-time has become differentiated into distinct upper and lower worlds. The threshhold between these two vertical zones is no longer a static barrier to be broken open by explosive forces but an ongoing process of opening and closing "doors." This new manifestation of the mouth of Kuwái closes down upon Kálimátu as he travels upward with his cargo of *mútsi* grubs. Unlike the cave, or mouth of Kuwái, in Myth 4, the new door does not bring death but merely constricts the middle section of Kálimátu's body. The crimped body of Kálimátu becomes a metaphor for the new vertical structure of the cosmos and the means of passing between vertical zones. Like Kálimátu's body, the cosmos now consists of upper and lower parts connected by a narrow, middle passage. And like the squeezing action that painfully crimps the middle of Káli-mátu's body, the passage between vertical zones (i.e., developmental stages or generations) requires people to endure hunger in their guts, a pain that permanently reshapes them but that does not destroy them.

In the final narrative of Part I of the cycle, Myth 6, Kuwái's return from the sky to the ground at Hípana leads to the realization of all the expectations that were established in the series of transformations in Myths 2 through 5. Kuwái descends to the plaza of the village and calls for Iñápirríkuli and his brothers to come inside the ceremonial house where he will teach them the sacred *málikai* songs and chants of initiation. The reversal of the initial movement of Kuwái up and out in Myth 2 is now complete, for Kuwái sits down on the ground inside the house of Iñápirríkuli and the other adult men.

The vertical movement of Kuwái from up-above to down-inside in Myth 6 also brings about the passage of another generation of time depth. In this case, generational time is not merely alluded to by implication but openly specified through reference to Kuwái's singing the names of the ancestors, or jaguars. These animals represent the culmination of Kuwái's musical creation of animal species and are considered to be the most humanlike of all natural species. In male initiation rituals, groups of men play enormous, four-meter long wooden trumpets to create the sounds of the jaguar-ancestors in front of male initiates. These trumpets are called "great jaguar bones" (*dzáwiñápa íhwerrúti*). The word *íhwerrúti* is an adjective meaning "ancient" or "great" (i.e., extremely large) and derives from the noun *ihwérrim*, which means "grandfather" (any male relative in the second or higher ascending generation). Thus, Kuwái's singing-into-being of the jaguar-ancestors at the beginning of Myth 6 transforms the previously two-generational structure of mythic social relations into a three-generational ordering of grandfathers, adult men (father and father's brothers), and pre-adolescent males (grandsons, sons, and brother's sons).[7]

After Kuwái has sung the names of the jaguar-ancestors and come down to the ground at Hípana, his main concern becomes the teaching of sacred *málikai* songs and chants to Iñápirríkuli and his brothers. Iñápirríkuli, who busies himself with doling out liquor to everyone in the village, misses the opportunity to learn all the chants and songs. Only Dzúli, a younger brother of the trickster-creator, has the patience to sit in one place all night long and listen to the entire set of chants.

Kuwái's mythic teaching of *málikai* songs and chants to Dzúli is the crucial remaining action that must take place before men can transform the cosmos through uniting the life-creating power of Kuwái with its ne-gation, the life-taking fire. By listening to and memorizing all of Kuwái's chants and songs, Dzúli becomes the first chant-owner and embodies the process of accurately communicating the secrets of Kuwái's life-giving powers across generational time. The supremely socialized form of com-munication is not the dialogical conversation carried through intermedi-ary messengers but the direct, monological transmission and reception of powerful genres of chanting and singing between elders and adult men. "Becoming socialized, in other words, implies acquiring the power to replicate the process one has undergone, which is to socialize others" (Turner 1985: 97). The teaching of *málikai* is the most socialized form of communication because it imparts the ability to socialize others and, through replication, to pass that ability on to other descending genera-tions of men ad infinitum.

Once Dzúli has memorized the songs and chants of initiation, Kuwái's creative and transformative powers have not only been brought inside social space but also implanted inside human social consciousness. At the same time, this internalization of Kuwái's powers transforms mythic social relations from a simple, three-generational structure of grandpar-ents, parents, and children into a ritual hierarchy of specialists, or chant-owners, who substitute for parents as mediators between the younger generation's passage from childhood to adulthood and the life-giving powers of the jaguar-ancestors. The younger generation, represented in myth by Hérri, remains stuck outside the social space of the village until the parental generation has internally differentiated itself into specialists, or the keepers of the sacred chants, who control the ancestral powers over life and death, and nonspecialists who merely serve these powers.

Once the ancestral powers have been fully transferred from Kuwái to the keepers of the sacred chants, the way is open for the negation of the father's parental role of provider and protector for the son. When the father (Iñápirríkuli) kills his son (Kuwái) by pushing him into a great bonfire, he terminates the son's relation of childhood dependency and, at the same time, brings to completion the synthesis of ancestral life-giving and life-taking powers into a powerful conflagration that transforms the entire cosmos.

Finally, the transformational power of Kuwái's fiery death is passed from outside-to-inside the body through the first initiate's licking of hot pepper and eating the sacred food (*káridzámai*). The simultaneous im-plosion of the external world of animals, fish, and birds, and internaliza-

tion of this newly miniature world in the form of *káridzámai* into the
body of the first initiate marks the completion of the series of transformations leading to a reversal of the initial movement from inside-to-
outside Amáru's womb (Myth 2). Part I of the Kuwái myth cycle ends
with an act of internalization that is diametrically opposed to the opening
story of Kuwái's birth as a process of escaping from death inside the
womb to life outside of it. In the end, the first initiate escapes from death
in the exterior, extrasocial space of the forest (i.e., the fate of the three
boys eaten and vomited by Kuwái in Myth 4) to life inside the village by
eating the sacred food, which is in turn a transformation of the external
world of animals, fish, and birds created by Kuwái's musical naming
power.

## Analysis of the Kuwái Myth Cycle, Part II

Through a series of embedded transformations, Part I of the Kuwái myth
cycle (Myths 1–6) outlines the processes leading from an undifferentiated mythic space-time of animal-humans to a world of socialized human beings who are culturally separate from nonhuman animal species
and who control and define humanness through activities of chanting (or
learning to chant), fasting, and eating. The primary axis of bodily, social,
and cosmic transformation in Part I of the myth cycle is the vertical dimension of space-time. These transformations along the vertical axis simultaneously unfold as developmental processes of bodily growth and
self-empowerment, generational processes of aging and transmitting
forms of power to the young, and cosmological processes of the coming-
into-being of nonhuman species and the forming of a differentiated structure of upper and lower worlds. These powerful forces of change in the
vertical dimension of mythic space-time tower over the still microcosmic
horizontal dimension of space-time, which consists of only a single, prototypical human village and the extrasocial space of the forest. The movements of bodies and foods across the boundaries of the human body
connect, both metonymically and metaphorically, the powerful, macrocosmic transformations of vertical space-time with microcosmic changes
in the horizontal dimension of the forest and the village. Giving birth,
fasting, vomiting, and eating form the processual matter through which
an evolving structure of vertical space-time is inscribed into the body,
which in turn serves as a metaphor for the transformations of vertical
and horizontal space-time.

    In Part II of the Kuwái myth cycle, the primary axis of cosmic transformation is the horizontal dimension of space-time, or the opening up of a sociogeographic world of places through movements between "this place here" and "those places there." These changes in horizontal space-time determine changes in the vertical dimension. The mediation of vertical space is no longer problematic, since its structure is self-generated at the beginning of Myth 7 through Kuwái's resurrection in the form of enormous trees and vines. Kuwái has now transformed into an external object in the world, and the power of this object is no longer an independently creative force but one that must be actualized by male and female human beings who move across the horizontal dimension of forests and rivers. In Part I of the narrative cycle, Kuwái's body consisted of a gravity-defying synthesis of all worldly elements that had to be coaxed down to earth through a series of complex events. Kuwái's body in Part II of the cycle becomes a natural plant species that can be chopped down like any other plant. No coaxing is needed to bring Kuwái back down to earth in Myth 7: his body is now so heavy that its falling weight threatens to kill Iñápirríkuli by crushing him under a pile of logs.

What has happened in the transition from Myth 6 to Myth 7 is a total pivoting of mythic space-time that results in the turning inside-out and upside-down of bodily, social, and cosmic processes. The "up-above and outside" is now the "down on the ground and inside," and the transformations of space-time in Myths 7–9 outline a process of reversing this initial tumbling down to the ground into its opposite, or the final departure of Kuwái from the ground at Hípana to the sky world. The inversion of internal and external space results in a shifting of focus from processes of internalization and externalization across the boundaries of the human body to processes of going from one place to another, or here to there, in the external world. Whereas Part I of the narrative cycle can be understood as the use of human bodily processes as metaphors for the opening and closing of vertical relations of descent between adjacent generations, Part II of the cycle is concerned with the complementary process of using movements across social and geographic space as metaphors for the opening and closing of horizontal relations of exchange between descent groups.

In Myth 7, most of the action takes place in Hípana at the site of Kuwái's fiery transformation, but the opening up of horizontal space-time is foreshadowed in the final episode of the myth when Iñápirríkuli blows through the newly constructed sacred trumpet and creates a small bird that flies into all parts of the world. The sacred flutes and trumpets are multivocal symbols of Kuwái's creative powers. Most directly, each type of flute or trumpet has an animal namesake, such as the *molítu* frog, the white heron (*máari*), the toucan (*dzáate*), the paca (*dápa*), and numerous other species. When played as an ensemble of male-dancers in sacred rituals and ceremonies, called *kwépani* (Kuwái-dance), the sounds of these flutes and trumpets constitute a musical, zoomorphic representation of the mythic being of Kuwái as the creator whose voice sang-into-being all nonhuman animal species. At the same time, each kind of sacred flute or trumpet is associated with a particular part of the body of Kuwái. The two white heron flutes (*máario*), for example, represent the thumb and index finger of Kuwái's hand. Conversely, the thumb and index finger, when straightened and pressed together, are said to resemble the long-necked body of a white heron in flight. In *kwépani* ceremonies, pairs of men play *máario* flutes together with trios of men playing the three *waliáduwa* (newlike) trumpets, which represent the outer three fingers of Kuwái's hand. Taken together, the five musicians form a quintet of "fingers" that makes up a complete hand of Kuwái.[8]

On an even grander scale, a large ensemble of male musician-dancers creates an image of the entire mythic body of Kuwái by uniting all the different body parts. Thus, in the newly transformed cosmos of Myth 7, men link together zoomorphic and anthropomorphic images of the mythic being of Kuwái through constructing musical instruments out of plant materials.

The flutes and trumpets of Kuwái also embody concepts of gender and sexuality. Gender meanings are attributed to instruments that come in pairs according to the principle that shorter, thinner flutes are "male" and longer, thicker flutes are "female." The *molítu* flute is more directly associated with sexual power, since it represents the penis of Kuwái. The *molítu* frog is perhaps the most significant animal symbol in the second part of the Kuwái myth cycle, since the men eventually regain control of the sacred flutes and trumpets from Amáru and the women by disguising themselves as *molítu* frogs. The *molítu* flute is the quintessential symbol of adult male sexualilty and procreativity. In Myth 7, it is the sound-producing mechanism that creates new life when wrapped into the womblike cavities of resonators made from the bark of *yebaro* trees and securely fastened into place with *dzámakuápi* vines.

In *kwépani* ceremonies, the *molítu* flutes are the only instruments that allow male dancers to communicate with women who are enclosed inside a ceremonial house. By holding one hand over the opening of the short, thick flutes, the men produce semi-distinct syllables and words. Releasing their hands quickly at each word, the men shape words with their mouths

---

Women: *Molítu?*

*Molitu*: Mu.

Women: Kwáka lipítana limínali?
(What is the name of your owner?)

*Molitu*: Juan, Mu, Juan, Mu.

Women: *Kwámi?*
(What?)

*Molitu*: Juan, Mu.

Women: *Óh-hon.*
(Yes, OK.)

Women: *Molítu, kwáka ruénipe sruátaha kewédani?*
(Molítu, what sex will her unborn child have?)

*Molitu*: *Ínarruátsa, ínarruátsa, mu.*
(Female, female.)

Women: *Kwámi?*

*Molitu*: *Ínarruátsa.*
(Female.)

Women: *Pímaka píra turúru, molítu?*
(Do you want to drink liquor, molítu?)

*Molitu*: *Óh-hon, mu, óh-hon.*
(Yes, yes.)

---

3.1   *Transcription of dialogues between* molítu *flute player and women*

without voicing any of the syllables, which might give away their identities to the women. Once the *molítu* players have passed the test of disguising their identities from the women, they become a sort of musical oracle to which pregnant women can address the question of whether their unborn children will turn out to be male or female (see Figure 3.1).[9] In the *molítu* flutes, men condense zoomorphic, anthropomorphic, and sexual dimensions of Kuwái's mythic powers into a single ritual object.

Outside of ritual and ceremonial contexts, *molíti* frogs are linked, both symbolically and pragmatically, with the annual cycle of horticultural activities. *Molítu* frogs are said to be Káaliéni, or the children of Káali.

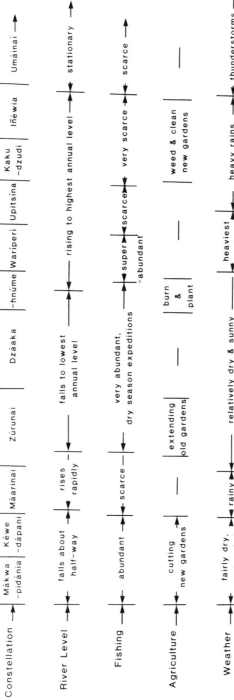
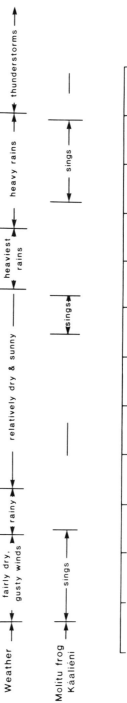

3.2  *Annual cycle of fishing and horticultural activities; seasonal changes of important natural phenomena (reprinted by permission from the American Ethnologist 1984)*

Men and women listen for the *molítu* frogs' singing to begin during the month of *Mákwapidánia* at the start of the short, September-to-November dry season. The frogs' singing is interpreted as a sign of Káali telling people when to start a new annual cycle of gardening activities by selecting and cutting down sections of forest to make new gardens.[10] Later, at the very end of the long dry season, men and women listen for the *molítu* frogs' singing to determine when to burn the felled vegetation and plant new gardens in the month called *Wáripérihnúme,* or "the mouth of the Pleiades" (i.e., the period in late March-to-early-April immediately preceding the time of the Pleiades; see Figure 3.2). The general concept guiding interpretations of the *molítu* frogs' singing is that people who work in synchrony with the frogs' singing find their labor in the gardens to be less difficult and safer. In particular, the men's dangerous activity of cutting down tall forest trees by notching a row of trees and pushing them over like dominoes is believed to proceed more safely when they work in harmony with the *molítu* frogs' mythic, ecological clock.

The dual association of *molítu* frogs with male sexuality and male horticultural activities of cutting and planting new gardens is a crucial piece of cultural knowledge for understanding how social processes are encoded in the myth of the origins of Kuwái's sacred flutes and trumpets. The *molítu* frog as both the prototypic human penis and the ecological clock for slash-and-burn gardening is subtly alluded to in Myth 7 through the tree that threatens to kill Iñápirríkuli by falling on top of him and that becomes the source of the first *molítu* flute. Mythic allusion to the annual cycle of horticultural activities receives further expression in the last episode, when Kuwái transforms into an enormous *yebaro* tree, a hardwood species (*Epurea purpurea*) that is commonly used in the selection of new garden lands.

The linkage of male sexuality to the cutting and planting of gardens in myth encodes an important message about Wakuénai social reality. Adult male social identity is largely defined through demonstrating competence as cutters and planters of manioc gardens (the latter activity is jointly carried out by men and women). After initiation, young men enter a transitional status, called *wálitáki* (newly fasted), in which they are responsible for felling and planting a portion of their fathers' manioc gardens each year. Prior to recent missionary interventions, the transition between young adulthood and fatherhood was accomplished by sending young men to live in their wives' communities, where they were obligated to cut and plant manioc gardens for their wives' kin group. The bride-service was a period of great tension for young men because their fathers-in-law observed their skills in gardening and other productive activities, such as house-building, in order to judge whether or not they were worthy of marriage. Young men who were deemed lazy or incompetent in their performance of gardening activities were sent away without their brides.[11] Although brideservice has largely ceased to be practiced due to sustained pressures from the New Tribes missionaries, adult men are still judged by their ability to select the best lands for gardening and their willingness to clear areas large enough to enable their wives to process more manioc than is needed for domestic consumption. Women whose husbands are lazy gardeners lack sufficient manioc to make breads, drinks, and other products for sharing with other households of the village and with visitors from other villages. Lazy, or stingy, husbands become targets of social irony: "He really made a hu-u-u-ge garden for his wife this year."

In the myth of the origin of Kuwái's sacred flutes and trumpets, the connections between gardening and the formation of adult male sociality are neatly finessed through the images of the falling tree, the *molítu* flute, and the movement of the flute's sound (in the form of a small bird) away from Hípana to other places. The sound of the *molítu* flute traveling outward, away from the center in the form of a small bird hints at the forthcoming reshaping of the cosmos as Amáru and the women play the sacred flutes and trumpets in different places. However, the *molítu* flute's departure from Hípana in Myth 7 is an unfinished process, since only the sound (or bird) travels to other places, not the flute itself. Furthermore, the bird-sound does not travel on the ground but flies through the sky, and there is not yet any opening up of the horizontal dimension of space-time. This mythic imagery of a vertically elevated horizontal journey is a metaphor for the development of horizontal relations of exchange between husbands' and wives' kin groups. The departure of young men from their natal villages to perform brideservice for their wives' kin in other villages is the first stage in the development, or opening up, of an affinal relationship between two descent groups. Like the mythic journey of the *molítu* flute's bird-sound "up-over across the world," the departing young men are at the beginning of a process leading to full adulthood. They are no longer children but have yet to demonstrate fully adult male social abilities of providing food and shelter for wives and children.

In Myth 8, Amáru and the women steal Kuwái's flutes and trumpets from Iñápirríkuli, and the horizontal dimension of space-time opens up as the women play the sacred instruments in different places. The women's first spatial movement is away from the center and across the world

to a downstream location near the present town of São Gabriel. Iñápirríkuli chases after Amáru and the women and succeeds in locating them
with the help of a crow. The string made of the bird's "hairs," or feathers,
becomes a new metaphor for the evolving horizontal structure of the
cosmos, which now consists of people living at the center and peoples
living in other places that are connected to the center by long, narrow
pathways, or rivers. However, the male pursuit of female others is an
unfinished project, since the bird's string is still an "up-over across" form
of motion.

Contrasting with the incomplete quality of the male departure from
Hípana to other places downstream, Amáru and the women move across
the surface of the world and powerfully transform its structure with Kuwái's sacred flutes and trumpets. When Iñápirríkuli finally catches up
with Amáru, he disguises his identity by speaking to her in a new language, Yeral (*lingua geral*), and the ensuing dialogue between mythic
man and woman becomes the origin of this new form of communication.[12] Here, mythic imagery depicts the emergence of historical consciousness in men and women as a process of becoming aware of their
own social agency, or the capacity to participate in the social creation of
meaning. Amáru and Iñápirríkuli create a new language in the newly
opened world of spatially distinct peoples and places. In the context of
patrilineal, patrilocal social relations, women are inextricably associated
with change and otherness, and gender consciousness becomes the seed
of a historical consciousness of changing relations between "we people
here" and "those peoples there."

The social situation in Myth 8 is highly dynamic and creative at the
same time as it is highly unstable and contradictory. Amáru and the
women are firmly in control of Kuwái's creative powers and can order
men to stay inside a ceremonial house as if they are young, uninitiated
children. Amáru expresses this inversion of generational time by repeatedly addressing Iñápirríkuli as "Grandson" (to which he reciprocates by
addressing her as "Grandmother") and informing him that he cannot be
present at the first ritual of female initiation. However, as the long night
of dancing and drinking wears on, the women's orderly exchange of
blows with ritual whips degenerates into a drunken brawl, allowing the
opportunistic trickster-creator to escape from the ceremonial house and
make an effort to regain control over Kuwái's flutes and trumpets. The
situation of Amáru and the women in Myth 8 is internally contradictory:
they have control of Kuwái's life-giving powers but cannot successfully
reproduce these powers. Although Amáru has taken the sacred flutes and

trumpets, the secret of making these instruments of power still belongs to Iñápirríkuli.

The mythic situation of Amáru and the women metaphorically expresses the social situation of young women undergoing the transition from childhood to young adulthood. The paradoxical situation of pubescent girls in a world of patrilineal, patrilocal social relations is that of being simultaneously included into the space-time of adult social relations in their natal communities so that they can then be excluded from this same social space to become wives and mothers in some other peoples' villages. In myth, Amáru and the women can take control of Kuwái's flutes and trumpets only by going away from Hípana to other places far downstream where they become, in a sense, other peoples. In other words, female developmental time is only partially integrated into the vertical, or generational, dimension of space-time but is firmly attached to the opening up of horizontal relations of competition, trade, and intermarriage between descent groups from different places.

The ambivalent, inclusive/exclusive situation of the newly initiated girl (*wálimerú*) has an individual dimension that becomes the focus of prolonged post-initiation rituals. Unlike male initiations, female initiation rituals are more individualized events in which each girl goes through a process of fasting, ritual advising, and eating the sacred food shortly after the time of reaching her first menses. For several years after this rite of passage, a newly initiated girl remains in a situation of ritual danger and works alongside her mother in cultivating and processing manioc. Each new species of animal and plant food that enters her diet during this period of time must be chanted over to protect her from excessive loss of menstrual blood. Blood loss of any kind is considered to be the loss of part of the human body-shaped soul (*likáriwa*), a weakening of health that places individuals in danger of being attacked by witches and spirits of the dead. The Wakuénai abhor violent deaths involving extensive blood loss because the souls of such unfortunate people linger for a long time in the dark netherworld as recently deceased persons (*lidánam,* or "shadows") who can return to the world of living people to make them sick.[13] The ambiguous social situation of newly initiated girls is thus connected to the ambiguous situation of recently deceased persons through the shared symbolism of blood loss. Since the girl's menstruation, or blood loss, is interpreted as a potential loss of physical and spiritual strength, special ritual chants are performed over her food so that she can acquire the strength needed to gradually take on the workload of a fully adult woman.

The mythic corollary of these ritual connections between female initiation and death is expressed in the form of Amáru's escape from Iñápirríkuli during the women's drunken brawl at the first ritual of female initiation. Anticipating Iñápirríkuli's attack, Amáru flees with Kuwái's flutes and trumpets through a hole in the ground that leads back to Mútsipáni. This movement establishes the reversibility of the newly opened horizontal dimension of space-time and creates a new, underground region in the vertical dimension. Amáru's return to Mútsipáni is a movement "down-under and across" the world from "over there" to "back here," an inversion of Iñápirríkuli's earlier movement "up-over and across" the world from here to there. The reversible, underground journey of Amáru mythically creates the ritual space-time of the shaman (*malírri*), whose curing activities are understood as the bringing back of lost souls from the houses of the dead in *íyarudáti* to the world of living people (*hekwápiríko*).

Like the social situation of Amáru and the women at the first female initiation ritual, *íyarudáti* is described as a place where the social order of living people is inverted. Unlike living people who must hunt for game meat and cook it prior to consumption, the shadow-spirits in *íyarudáti* control the forest animals and birds like domesticated species and consume rotten meat. The *lidánam* shadows are still partially in this world and can return to cause sickness to the living by transforming themselves into forest animals or birds that people eat or by revealing themselves to humans as evil omens (*hinimái*), or signs of unavoidable bodily cosmic destruction. Thus, the *lidánam* spirits are simultaneously inside and outside the world of living people, exactly as young, adolescent women are both included in the local patrisib by ritually fasting and eating the sacred food of the ancestors and excluded from the local kin group by going to live in their husbands' villages upon reaching full adulthood. Both recently deceased persons and newly initiated females are in a temporary double-bind that is eventually resolved through movements into a new space-time: the *lidánam* spirits through transmigration to the celestial paradise of the ancestor spirits and the girl-initiate through post-marital residence in her husband's village and gradual acceptance into the social order of his local patrisib.

In the final episode of Myth 8, Iñápirríkuli returns to the center of the world only to find that Amáru has again escaped across the world with Kuwái's flutes and trumpets to a place far downstream. The second movement of Amáru away from the center of the world establishes the new horizontal structure of the cosmos as a world differentiated into "we people here" and a plurality of "those peoples/places there" rather than a simple opposition between two peoples.

The reversibility of horizontal space-time in Myth 8 becomes its actual reversal in Myth 9 through the movement of Iñápirríkuli and the men away from Hípana to Mútsipáni and their return with Kuwái's sacred instruments to *Hípana*. There are two major differences between the men's journey to Mútsipáni in Myth 9 and Iñápirríkuli's chasing after Amáru and the women in Myth 8. First, Iñápirríkuli and the men travel together as a group in Myth 9. And second, the group of men transform themselves into animals, or *molítu* frogs, in their journey to Mútsipáni. The transformation of Iñápirríkuli's individual male quest into a collective male reversal of the horizontal dimension mythically encodes the social processes whereby individual men return to their natal villages after completing brideservice for their wives' kin groups and are reintegrated into the collective order of adult male members of the local patrisib. The mythic return of men as *molítu* frogs cements this social imagery by multivocally evoking the adult men's capacity to become fathers through sexual relations with women from other places and their competence as cutters and planters of manioc gardens.[14]

The collectivization and desocialization, or naturalization, of men into *molítu* frogs in Myth 9 is accompanied by a dramatic turn of events: a bolt of lightning sent by Iñápirríkuli causes Amáru and the women to fall down on the ground. The women's temporary loss of consciousness allows Iñápirríkuli and his army of frog-men to permanently regain control of Kuwái's flutes and trumpets. Through this imagery, Myth 9 transforms the ambivalent situation of the individual female initiate's simultaneous inclusion in and exclusion from her patrisib into a collective process of "death," or loss. The individual "death," or loss of menstrual blood, by a newly initated girl is ultimately experienced as a collective loss of female blood-relatives by wives' kin groups to husbands' kin groups. The myth portrays this collective loss as a simple gender opposition between adult men and women. Analysis, however, reveals that the horizontal dimension of exchange is actually a more complex social confrontation between descent groups whose members include both male and female descendants of the local ancestor spirits. One group's gain is experienced as another people's loss, or death.

In the next episode of Myth 9, Iñápirríkuli and the men hold a sacred Kuwái-dance (*kwépani*) ceremony in order to convince Amáru and the women that Kuwái's instruments have indeed turned into forest animals and birds during their temporary "death," or loss of consciousness, at Mútsipáni. This episode completes the process of reversing the initial movement of Amáru and Kuwái's flutes outward from Hípana across the surface of the world. Kuwái's flutes and trumpets are taken back from the other peoples' places to the center of the world at *Hípani,* and Amáru and the women are confined inside a ceremonial house within the village where they can hear but not see the men's dancing on the plaza outside.

The myth of the first *kwépani* ceremony signals the men's successful reversal of the horizontal dimension of space-time. The men have now collectively absorbed other people's women into their village-"house," or social order.[15] However, the apparent stability of this mythic situation is contradicted by the progressive desocialization of Kuwái. Through the use of fur, feathers, and skins to convince Amáru of the reality of Kuwái's transformation from plant materials into animal bodies, the men transpose their own transformation into animals (e.g., *molítu* frogs) to the desocialization of the mythic body of Kuwái. In doing so, the male musician-dancers in *kwépani* ceremonies become like the *lidánam* spirits in *íyarudáti,* since they take symbolic control over feral animal species. In effecting the collective "death" of Amáru and the women and bringing them inside their social world, Iñápirríkuli and the men have internalized the ambivalent inclusivity *and* exclusivity of the horizontal dimension of exchange relations between descent groups. The women who are contained inside a ceremonial house by men in *kwépani* encompass both the inclusion of other peoples' female kin and the eventual exclusion of their own people's female kin. By internalizing the simultaneous gain and loss of female blood relatives through exchange, the men, disguised as animals, embody an alienated consciousness of themselves as other peoples' others. Thus, the men's control over Kuwái in *kwépani* ceremonies comes to resemble the *lidánam* spirits' domestication of forest animals and birds in the houses of the dead. Like the *lidánam* spirits, male musician-dancers in *kwépani* are both outside and inside the social world of living people.

The contradictory situation of male musician-dancers in *kwépani* is well illustrated in the *molítu* flute performances described in an earlier section. The *molítu* players must disguise their voices so that women inside the ceremonial house are unable to identify them. The *molítu* performances thus express the alienated, semi-social status of men in *kwépani* ceremonies by masking their individuality and their humanness. They communicate in a nonhuman voice in semi-human "words" and "syllables" (actually stress patterns).

In the culmination of *kwépani* ceremonies, groups of men perform *tsépani*, a dance consisting of two *máario* (white heron) flute-players and three *wáliáduwa* trumpets. *Tsépani* musical-dances commemorate the mythic event in which Kuwái ate the three boys who had eaten the fallen fruits and taken refuge from the rains by going inside the cave, or mouth of Kuwái (Myth 4). By collectively evoking the half-finished space-time of Kuwái at the end of *kwépani* ceremonies, men construct a ritual frame within which the vertical dimension of space-time is partially reversed. The goal of collective ceremonial action is to move Kuwái up from the ground into the sky, from "down here" to "up there."

In the final episode of the Kuwái myth cycle, Iñápirríkuli leaves Hípana to go live in the celestial paradise (*likáremi*) of the ancestor spirits after teaching men how to construct the sacred, *dzáwinápa* (jaguar-bone) trumpets of the ancestors. The mythic ascent of Amáru and Kuwái from the ground at Hípana to the sky world completes the reversal of the vertical dimension from the initial movement of Kuwái as a tree falling to the ground in Myth 7. The reversal of vertical space takes place after the reversal of horizontal space in Myth 9 and brings an end to the men's ambiguous situation of inclusivity and exclusivity during the first *kwépani* ceremony. Just as the *lidánam* shadows, or the alienated consciousness of living people of themselves as victims of "no longer living beings," transmigrate into ancestor spirits in the celestial paradise of Iñápirríkuli, Kuwái as the alienated consciousness of people as "other peoples' others" is sent up to the sky world after the first *kwépani* ceremony.

In the two parts of the Kuwái myth cycle, the Wakuénai narratively construct two contrasting views of their social world and its relations to the inner world of bodily experiences and the outer world of nonhuman animal nature. The first perspective on human social relations is that of the child's internal, bodily experiences of birth, separation from the parents, and self-empowerment through internalization of socialized animal nature. The socialization of individual, bodily processes in children is a process of mediating and constructing a vertical dimension of space-time, or the opening up of a cosmic structure of upper and lower worlds and a power structure of ancestors, ritual specialists, and descendants. In this internal view of the social world, the child's experience of socialization is also defined along the vertical dimension of space-time as a movement down from the initially natural status of newly born infant (*kérramu*), through the various intermediary transformations of the semi-socialized child (*yénpiti*), and down to the ground as a fully socialized, initiated young adult (*wálitáki*, or "newly fasted"). With the internalization of socialized nature, or the sacred food (*káridzámai*), the child's internal perspective of social reality has reached completion, and not a single reference to the first initiate is made throughout the entire second part of the narrative cycle.

The social processes of exchange, or inclusion and exclusion, that open up along the horizontal dimension of space-time in Part II of the Kuwái myth cycle are inherently collective processes of integration and separation among peoples, or descent groups, from different places and cannot be reduced to the level of the individual's socialization. The disappearance of Hérri, the first socialized individual, from the sequence of narratives in Part II of the myth cycle concretely expresses the irrelevance of the individual level of experience for the development of collective institutions, such as brideservice, exogamy, and patrilocal residence. As Turner noted in his analysis of a Kayapo creation myth, the story of the proto-human individual's socialization sets in motion another story about the coming-into-being of the family structures into which the individual has been socialized: "namely, how the collective form of human society arose from the dispersal of an individual domestic family, and how the collective institutions in turn established the pattern for the reproduction of all future families" (1985: 95). For the Wakuénai, Part II of the Kuwái myth cycle answers these questions by showing how the individual experiences of young, newly initiated men and women are transformed into collective processes of inclusion and exclusion among a plurality of intermarrying descent groups, or peoples. Part II of the myth cycle demonstrates how a single descent group was opened up to produce a world consisting of a collectivity of "we people here" and a contrasting plurality of social others, or "those peoples there." In doing so, the second part of the Kuwái myth cycle also establishes the pattern for reproducing the plurality of social others through the negation of a people's alienated consciousness of themselves as "other peoples' others."

The child's internal view of social reality as a process of becoming human and the adult's external view of it as the collective reproduction of descent groups form two contrasting perspectives that are defined relative to one another in the Kuwái myth cycle and yet cannot be reduced to mere reflections of each other. In the final analysis, to control social reproduction, or the formation of descent groups through exogamous exchanges of male labor and female blood relatives, is a more dynamic and powerful process than the intra-descent group process of the individual's socialization. However, these two hierarchical levels of power relations are mutually defining, since the more dynamic processes of social reproduction embodied in Part II of the narrative cycle are themselves a product of the transformation, through turning upside-down and inside-out, of the socialization of Kuwái and the first initiate in Part I of the myth cycle. This double perspective upon Kuwái's two openings of the world constitutes the highest level of mythic meaning, or the symbolic mediation of the social contradiction between the individual's socialization and the collective reproduction of descent groups. This level of mythic meaning cannot be integrated into the collective consciousness of ordinary human beings but is instead condensed into the tri-fold imagery of Kuwái's *super*socialized transmission of *málikai* songs and chants to the first chant-owner, the father's (Iñápirríkuli's) *over*-socialization of the son (Kuwái) by pushing him into a bonfire, and the first initiate's eating of the *super*-naturalized, imploded external world of animal species in the form of the sacred food (*káridzámai*).

As Turner has argued, the narrative business of myth is, in part, to construct higher levels of structural meaning that represent "aspects of human society that are rendered inaccessible to social consciousness as a result of their incompatibility with the dominant framework of social relations" (1985: 105). As I will demonstrate in the following chapters, the ritual business of *málikai* and *málirríkairi* singing and chanting is to use the musicality of human speech and Kuwái's naming power to explore *poetically* the hierarchical levels of mythic meaning.

# 4

# Birth and the Art of Microtonal Rising

Shortly after the birth of a child, the parents of the newly born infant go through a rite of passage that allows them to resume everyday economic and social activities. This rite of passage follows a period of seclusion and fasting. Two different sets of *málikai* chants are performed in childbirth rituals, one for the tools, weapons, and objects of the father's work activities and the other for the food (*káridzámai*) that marks both parents' return to a normal diet of fish, game, garden products, and wild plants. These two sets of chants consist of taxonomies of spirit-names transposed into horizontal lines of spoken, chanted, and sung speech. Wakuénai chant-owners regard the spirit-names of Kuwái as the main source of mythic power in their performances of *málikai,* since each name embodies the life-giving principle of Kuwái as the One in the Many through its internal composition as a generic category united with a specific name. In addition, the specific ways in which chant-owners manipulate the taxonomies of spirit-names link the social situation of childbirth to the coming into being of a vertically differentiated world in Part I of the Kuwái myth cycle.

As a verbal art form, *málikai* embodies a process of generic classification in which each specific object, species, or person is categorized in one or more generic classes of nouns. Memorizing the basic categories of nouns and the rules for allocating nouns into classes is the first step in learning *málikai* and reflects the importance of memorization in the mythic episode that recounts how Kuwái taught *málikai* to Dzúli, the first chant-owner. After memorizing the basic taxonomies of spirit-names, an apprentice is expected to learn the art of interpreting the more powerful, esoteric names through asking his teacher questions. The most powerful spirit-names, for example, are assigned to a special class called *dzáwi-ñápirríkuli* ("jaguar of Iñápirríkuli," or "jaguar made from bone"). These spirit-names refer to different episodes of mythic creation or to ritually powerful materials and substances. Other powerful names are verbally marked by shifting a species to a different classifier set than that to which it would intuitively belong in order to signify a mythic episode of transformation. For example, a bird that transformed itself into an anaconda in myth is classified in *málikai* along with fish and other aquatic animals in the *umáwari* ("anaconda," or "water animal spirit") set of spirit-names. Finally, the names of powerful mythic beings, such as Amáru and Hérri, can be combined with specific names or adjectives to create sets of powerful names. The process of becoming a chant-owner thus requires the apprentice to develop skills at interpreting the nuances of mythic meaning and ritual power embodied in the spirit-names of Kuwái before going on to learn how the taxonomies of spirit-names can be transposed into the lines of spoken, chanted, and sung speech.

In a broader sense, the entire series of spirit-names invoked in each performance of *málikai* constitutes a complex, multivocal verbal image of the mythic being of Kuwái and the mythic processes of transforming body, society, and cosmos. Ritual uses of generic classification in *málikai* are based on generative semantic principles that result in open-ended, polythetic sets of nouns rather than closed semantic sets. The principle of generic classification enables chant-owners to express profoundly con-tradictory images of the mythical figure of Kuwái. On the one hand, chant-owners can enact Kuwái's vertical creation of the world by placing emphasis on generic categories that include many distinct individuals, species, and objects in a single compound entity. This process, called "heaping up the names in one single place" (*wakéetaka nakúna papí-nirítsa*), is a relatively simple technique of naming a generic class of spirits and then filling it up (*wakámtaka nakúna*) with specific names. On the other hand, the chant-owner can juxtapose a variety of different generic names, each with a complementary, specific name, to enact Kuwái's sec-ond, horizontal creation of the world. The result of this process, called "chasing after the names" (*wapinétaka wátsani nakúna*), or "going in search of the names" (*wapinétaka wadzúhiakaw nakúna*), is a dynamic montage of unique metaphors highlighting the uniqueness of specific spirit-names that exclude all but a single individual, species, or object on the basis of distinctive qualities.

The two processes of spirit-naming in *málikai*, "heaping up" and "searching for the names," are semantic expressions of a relative hierarchy of structural levels that pervade Wakuénai sacred myths and rituals. "Heaping up the names," or categorizing specific objects, species, and individuals into generic classes, is a taxonomic principle that defines a lower-level pattern of relations. "Heaping up the names" is a classificatory operation in which the natural, social, and mythical worlds are organized into relatively discrete, bounded semantic classes, each of which is analogously constituted to all the other classes through the generic-to-specific relationship. The more dynamic process of "searching for the names" operates against the relatively static taxonomic principle of "heaping up the names" into discrete categories. "Searching for the names" is a series of rapid, abrupt movements among different categories of spirit-names (see Figure 1.1).

In any given performance of *málikai*, chant-owners make use of both naming processes, but one or the other of the two principles is dominant. In childbirth rituals, the more dynamic process of "searching for the names" is dominant in the first set of chants, which are conceived of as a search inside the infant's body for male and female tobacco spirits of the mythic, patrilineal ancestors. In the second set of chants, the taxonomic principle of "heaping up the names" preponderates in the naming of edible animal species. Thus, the two naming processes, and the mythic processes of vertical and horizontal transformation which they embody, are both given active expression within the same ritual context.

## Childbirth Rituals

For the Wakuénai and other Arawakan peoples of the Upper Río Negro region, childbirth is a highly significant process in which newborn infants and their parents are ritually marked off from the rest of society through the use of special terms of reference, withdrawal from social relations, fasting, and abstention from subsistence activities. For the first week of life, the identities of newborn infants are totally merged with those of their parents. The father's activities are especially dangerous to the newborn's health during the week of seclusion, and both parents must avoid eating any "strong" foods, such as fish or game meat. The parents' absence from communal meals, withdrawal from social life, and abstention from economic chores cannot fail to be noticed by the other families in the village. Accentuating the ritual separateness of the newborn infant and its parents are special terms of reference: the father is called *kinénerri* instead of the usual *hnunírri*, the mother is called *kinédua* instead of *hnúdua*, and the newborn infant is called *kérramu*.

The following description of ritual activities is based on a childbirth ritual held on October 12, 1981, for a family from the village of Sebucan, a few miles upstream from Gavilán. The father, a Baniwa man, and his Guarequena wife brought their eighth child, a son, to Gavilán because there was no longer any practicing chant-owner in Sebucan. These three ritual participants arrived in the early afternoon in a large dugout canoe, accompanied by a number of children and an elderly, maternal grandfather. Hernan, the headman of Gavilán and chant-owner, invited the visitors to stay overnight in a guest house, and he dressed himself the next morning in the white shirt and pants that he almost always wore when performing *málikai*. Aside from Hernan's white clothing, there were very few visual indications that an important ritual act was about to be performed: the shotgun and machete of the newborn's father that were conspicuously set out on the floor of the guest house, the inactivity and fasting of the parents, and the pack of PielRoja ("Red-Skin") from which Hernan calmly took out one of the unfiltered cigarettes as he sat down, straddling the low-lying hammock a few feet away from another hammock where the mother was nursing her newborn son. By their very commonness and simplicity, the shotgun, the machete, the tobacco, and the nursing mother set in relief the complex web of mythic meanings and vocal, musical sounds that slowly began to fill the silent house.

The chant-owner embarked on his search for the tobacco spirits of the newborn infant with four soft, low-pitched sounds (hmm-hmm-hmm-hmm). The first words emerged slowly and almost inaudibly out of these humming sounds, and the phrase ended with a slight elongation of syllables before a short rest for breathing. Each subsequent phrase had the same general pattern: (1) an aspirated /hmmm/ sound, (2) a rapid succession of syllables with minimal voicing of vowel sounds, and (3) a slight ritardando prior to a short breathing rest. In the course of the first chant, Hernan raised the intonation of his voice through a series of microtonal intervals until he had gone a full major third higher than the deep bass tone on which he had started. The volume of his voice and the tempo of his speech also increased by small gradations throughout the first chant. Short pauses for breaths of air punctuated at irregular intervals the otherwise constant, and increasingly tense flow of chanted and spoken speech.

Toward the end of the first chant, Hernan continued to increase the volume and tempo of his voice without elevating the pitch any higher. Suddenly he reached a point of repose and let his voice trail off, sliding back down over the series of microtonal intervals upon which he had interwoven his chanting and speaking. Lighting up another cigarette, he squatted over the shotgun and machete of the newborn's father and exhaled a thick veil of smoke over each of the two objects. Seconds later, he sat down again in his hammock, blew smoke into his package of cigarettes, and began to hum the same tone on which he had finished the last chant.

Hernan chanted louder than before and at about the same speed, his breaths continuing to mark off irregular phrase lengths. This time he only raised the tone of his chanting by a single chromatic half-step before letting his voice fade out. Again he lit a cigarette and blew clouds of smoke over the shotgun and machete of the newborn's father. The third and last chant was much shorter than the first two and resumed the microtonal raising of pitch by another half-step from where the second chant had ended. After blowing smoke on the shotgun and machete, Hernan stood up and walked over to the hammock where the mother was nursing her baby. There he blew tobacco smoke twice on each of their heads. Turning to the father, he explained that he could now return to his everyday activities.

The father left to go hunting and returned to the village with a small rodent (*píci*, or *Dasyprocta aguti lunaris*) in the late afternoon. The newborn's mother boiled a small pot of the meat in hot peppers. Hernan took the pot of meat, walked across the village plaza, and set the pot of meat on the floor of his house. I was the only person present when Hernan lit up a cigarette and started to chant the names of all edible animal species over the pot of hot-peppered, boiled game meat. Some women sat outside the house within hearing range, weaving baskets and talking among themselves. The father and mother of the newborn infant stayed inside their house across the village plaza throughout the hour-long performance for the *káridzámai* with which they would end their week of fasting on manioc drinks.

Hernan performed six chants over the *káridzámai*, stopping at the end of each one to blow tobacco smoke into the pot of food. These chants had a very regular phrase structure, and each word of the text was bisected into two parts of equal duration. Instead of a dynamic synthesis of chanted and spoken speech, the six chants for *káridzámai* consisted entirely of chanted speech with no changes in tempo or loudness. The pitch rose only minimally, or about one half-step between the beginning and end of the six chants. At the end of the sixth and last chant, Hernan blew tobacco smoke one more time into the pot of boiled meat, covered it with a lid, and carried it back across the village plaza to the guest house where the newborn's parents awaited him. Upon eating the *káridzámai*, the parents ceased to be *kinénerri* and *kinédua* and returned to their everyday statuses as father and mother. The newborn infant (*kérramu*), receiving the effect of the food through his mother's milk, had become a human child (*yénpiti*).

## Spirit-Naming in the First Set of Childbirth Chants

Spirit-naming in the first set of *málikai* chants performed in childbirth rituals is primarily concerned with protecting the newborn infant against potentially harmful effects of the father's resumption of everyday work activities. Every action that the father takes upon the material world of natural objects and species is supercharged with powerful effects, or danger (*línupána*), for the newborn infant. Cutting plants, digging the soil, paddling a canoe, fishing, and hunting can cause harm to the infant, since they act upon Kuwái's musically created world of spirit-names (*nakúna*) and, by implication, upon the raw, biological, and unsocialized life force embodied in the newborn infant. For the first week of life, a short black stub of dried umbilical cord covers the infant's navel, a visible reminder of the biological transition from inside the maternal womb to outside in the external world. After this vestige of the umbilical cord falls off is the proper time to ask a chant-owner to begin the childbirth ritual. The biological ambiguity of the newborn infant is matched by its socially marginal status as an individual who has not yet been connected to the tobacco spirits of its mythic ancestors and who is therefore extremely vulnerable to the harmful effects of powerful spirits. As a form of verbal art, the first set of *málikai* chants consists of an exploration of the newborn's biologically and socially ambiguous status, a poetic search for the names of ancestral tobacco spirits to protect the infant's health against powerful, dangerous spirits.

The navel is the spiritual center of the infant's body, since it is both the point through which dangerous spirits can enter the body to cause harm and the place where the chant-owner can bring to bear the life-giving, protective powers of the ancestral tobacco spirits and other helpful spirit-names. An internal, spiritual umbilical cord connects the newborn child's navel to its spine and feet, and the chant-owner calls upon various kinds of tobacco to make this invisible cord strong and to prevent the infant

from damaging the cord by kicking with its feet, pushing its head backwards, crying, or becoming frightened.

*Ménopánan dzéema,*
That-has-no-danger tobacco,

*Hmépule íwatsákan dzéema,*
That-the-navel-does-not-come-out tobacco,

*Mákaliápi ihyúkan dzéema,*
That-he-does-not-become-frightened tobacco,

*Mékwa hyématákan dzéema,*
That-he-does-not-cry tobacco,

*Madáki hitsuádan dzéema,*
That-he-does-not-push-his-body tobacco,

*Núakáwa lidákiwa mánupánali dzéema.*
I give for his body that-has-no-danger tobacco.

For the remaining years of childhood, the health, growth, and emotional security of the individual depend upon the strength of the internal
umbilical cord that connects the child to the life-giving powers of the
patrilineal, mythic ancestors just as it anchors the soft flesh of the belly
and navel to the bones of the feet and back. If a child becomes seriously
ill, a chant-owner must perform the first set of chants for childbirth rituals before he can treat the patient with counterwitchcraft songs or ask
for the help of a shaman (*malírri*).

The order of dangerous spirit-names invoked in the first set of chants
can vary from one performance to the next, depending upon situational
factors such as the season of the year and the father's social identity. I
recorded two performances of the chants, one during a childbirth ritual
in 1981 and the other during a curing ritual in 1984. In addition, Hernan
and his son, Siderio, recorded a spoken version of the chants in early
1985. Variations in the order of dangerous spirit-names arise primarily
in the middle section of the chants during the naming of useful plant
species. In all three performances, steel tools and weapons belonging to
the category of Amáru spirit-names were the first class of dangerous spirits to be invoked. Similarly, jaguars and other species of large, feline
predators were invoked near the end of the last chant in all three performances. This progression from Amáru to jaguar categories of spirit-

names makes sense in terms of Part I of the Kuwái myth cycle, which commences with Amáru's loss of the shotgun to Iñápirríkuli and concludes after Kuwái has sung the name of the jaguar-ancestors in the skies above Hípana, the "navel" of the world.

The category of Amáru's spirit-names are considered to be especially powerful and dangerous to newborn infants by virtue of their heat. Shotguns, machetes, and motors are made from metal that must be melted and molded at extremely high temperatures. The spirit-names of these metal objects convey the idea of heat through the prefix *tsímu-*, a morpheme related to the word for hot (*hlímukani*) in everyday speech. Thus, machetes receive the name *tsímukáita srú Amáru*, shotguns the name *tsímukápi srú Amáru*, and motors the name *tsímukáda srú Amáru*. The category of Amáru spirit-names is a set of variations on the theme of hot (*tsímu-* or *hlímukani*). The heat of these metal objects, when placed in contact with the father's hands, can be transmitted to the newborn infant in the form of fever.

> *Wadéemta línakúka líkanúpa límidzáka likérramuléna,*
> So that no harm comes to the newborn infant,
>
> *Likáiteri rúmawénukápika srú Amáru,*
> The name of Amáru's shotgun is spoken,
>
> *Likáiteri tsímukápi sru Amáru.*
> The name of Amáru's hot thing is spoken.
>
> *Rukáiteri híkuka lipálakápiríko.*
> She speaks the name of the place where iron is made.
>
> *Nénirri, rukáiteka, kámukánaka liakúna.*
> There, she says, it is very hot, this place-name.
>
> *Núakáwa lidákiwa dzéema,*
> I give for his body tobacco,
>
> *Madáki-hímukánami dzéema,*
> That-the-body-does-not-have-fever tobacco,
>
> *Maihnápi-ítukwákan dzéema,*
> That-the-bones-do-not-break tobacco,
>
> *Mákaliápi-ihliúkan dzéema.*
> That-the-body-does-not-frighten tobacco.[1]

The term *liakúna*, or spirit-name, can also be translated as "place." The place of Amáru in myth is called Eenutánhi, or the place where the sun rises on the eastern horizon, giving it a natural association with solar heat. In this context, the chant-owner does not name places in the external world but "places" within the human body. By implication, the "hot place" in Amáru's body is her genital region, the place where she was struck by a shotgun blast fired by Iñápirríkuli and the locus of mythic acts of incestuous copulation and insemination. The association between Amáru's heat and sickness is also important in counterwitchcraft songs (*málikai*), where the spirit-name of exogenous diseases brought by Europeans is *rupápera srú Amáru*, "the paper of Amáru." In both childbirth and curing rituals, chant-owners call upon tobacco spirits to counteract the fever-producing effects of Amáru's spirit-names.

Closely related to the concept of hot objects that can transmit fever to the newborn infant is the idea that the father's use of sharp, pointed objects and sharp-edged blades can puncture or sever the child's internal, spiritual umbilical cord. The general spirit-name for sharp, pointed objects is *tsímukéwikáni srú Amáru*, "the hot-sharp-pointed things" of Amáru. The name for fishhooks, *likápiwanáunka hítiwánakáli*, is an exception that means "hand-finger hook," a reference to the hand and finger of Kuwái. The piercing, jerking movement of the father as he sets a hook in the mouth of a fish is considered to have a similar effect on the newborn infant's internal umbilical cord. In the same manner, the father's use of cutting tools, such as machetes and axes, is believed to act directly upon the infant's interior cord if not properly named in *málikai* chants. Beliefs in the transmission of disease through sharp objects are also important in shamanistic curing, the goal of which is to suck sharp-pointed splinters from the bodies of patients.

The category of Amáru's spirit-names implicitly forms a semantic domain for classifying the technologies and diseases introduced into the Upper Río Negro region by European peoples during the colonial era and the more recent past. Steel tools and firearms are tokens of the Europeans' technological superiority and their power to coercively transform autonomous indigenous populations into dominated populations of slave laborers and debt peons. The introduction of manufactured tools undoubtedly had profound effects on social relations within local groups (see Landaburu and Pineda 1984). By invoking the spirit-names of metal tools and weapons at the very beginning of the human life cycle, the chant-owner connects each child's identity to the history of interethnic relations as well as to the autochthonous emergence of mythic ancestors. The use of Amáru's hot things as a category for naming these historically transforming objects coheres with the mythic significance of Amáru as an agent of historical change and consciousness in Part II of the Kuwái myth cycle.

The invocation of Amáru's spirit-names at the beginning of the first chant also establishes a connection between loud sounds and the newborn infants' emotional, bodily health. If the father fires his shotgun, the loud sound of the explosion frightens the newborn infant so that it begins to cry and kick with its feet, tearing the internal umbilical cord and causing the navel to swell and bleed. The percussive sounds of metal tools striking against wood or other materials are also transmitted to the newborn infant and cause fear or sickness. The last spirit-name belonging to Amáru, *tsímukáda srú Amáru*, covers all types of motors and machinery that contain sharp, moving pieces (e.g., gears, fans, and pistons) and that make loud noises. The Wakuénai of Venezuela have access to several types of machines, such as the outboard motors, gasoline-powered manioc graters, and diesel electric generators that the Venezuelan government donated in the 1970s. In the childbirth ritual held in October 1981 the naming of Amáru's motor was considered especially important because the newborn's father was the operator of the electric power generator in his village.

The power of Amáru's spirit-names to spread fear and disease to newborn infants through sounds is continued in later chants in a variety of other categories of spirit-names. The spirit-name of garden soil, *lipwuik-wáleka Káali*, is invoked so that the sound of the father's digging in the garden will not frighten his child. *Pwáapwa*, a palmwood species that men use for weaving baskets and other products, is named *límutukéku éenu*, or "the ripping sound of the sky," referring to the ripping, tearing sound produced when the outer bark of the tree is peeled off to make thin strips of weaving material. *Eenu* means "sky" in everyday speech, but in *málikai* chants *éenu* is a category of spirit-names that includes various species of wild palms that are sources of useful material and/or edible fruits. Palm trees have a broader mythic significance as the reincarnation of Kuwái after his fiery "death." As the vertical pathway between the celestial world of mythic ancestors and the social world of human descendants on the ground, palm trees form a cosmic umbilical cord that nourishes humanity with life-giving ancestral powers. This connotation of the term *éenu* is expressed in the spirit-naming of *pwáapwa* palms which, like other important species or objects, receives more than one spirit-name in *málikai.*

*Wádewátsa liákan, likáiteri límutukéku éenu,*
So that no harm is done, the name of the ripping-sound sky-spirit is spoken,

*Likáiteri litiékuka éenu,*
The name of the cutting smooth sky-spirit is spoken,

*Likápani hliépulepukúke éenu,*
The navel of the sky, the manioc sieve, is looked upon,

*Wádewátsa línakúka líkanúpa límidzáka ikérramuléna,*
So that no harm is done to the newborn infant,

*Núawa lidákiwa mánupánam dzéema.*
I give for his body that-has-no-danger tobacco.

Like the spirit-names for sharp, cutting tools, the second spirit-name for *pwáapwa, lítiekúka éenu,* associates the smooth, thin strips of weaving material with cutting and loss of blood. The third name relates *pwáapwa,* the material for making manioc sieves, to an anthropomorphic image of the cosmos as a "body" linked to the celestial world of ancestor spirits through a "navel" at the center of the world, or Hípana. Thus, in the space of one short stanza, the chant-owner synaesthetically interweaves auditory, tactile, and visual images of mythic power to verbally construct the *pwáapwa* palm as a ripping-sound, cutting-smooth, cosmic navel of the human universe.

Auditory images are prevalent in spirit-naming throughout the remaining chants. Like the *pwáapwa* palm, the species of palm called *etípa* must be named because of the loud, ripping sound that is produced when its bark is stripped to make backpacks for hauling manioc tubers.[2] Sounds resulting from the father's work activities are transmitted directly to the newborn infant. In addition, the father can indirectly spread fear and sickness to the newborn child by experiencing the natural sounds produced by large animal species. Through onomatopoeia, the low, grunting sounds made by herds of white-lipped peccaries are rendered as *nabíribírikere éenunai,* or "grunting forest animal." The most dangerous of all natural, animal sounds is the loud, water-spouting breathing of freshwater dolphins as they break the river's surface to come up for air.

*Wadéemta piákani pía éenuka páranaliánikáapi,*
So that you, the dolphin that makes a splashing sound, do not come,

*Wadéemta piáka kématáka yúmahniúka límidzáka lidákina,*
So that you do not come to make him cry, to frighten his body,

*Núaka lidákiwa dzéema.*
I give for his body tobacco.

*Wadéemta piákan pía Hérri idánam,*
So that you, the shadow-soul of Hérri, do not come here,

*Wadéemta híakan hía yamúanai,*
So that you forest monsters do not come here,

*Wadéemta hiákan hía kémakánri líwakánitákani,*
So that you that live in the forest do not come here,

*Wadéemta hiákan hiéeku ipwámi límidzáka idákina kerrámu*
    *himénawátsa,*
So that they do not come running to harm the body of the infant who
    is listening,

*Nupjíaka lidzéemanáwa dzéema.*
I blow tobacco smoke.

In these two stanzas, the chant-owner uses auditory images of the dolphins' sneezelike breathing sounds and the infant's activity of listening (*hímenawátsa*) as a frame for invoking a variety of powerful spirit-names. The most important of these names is *Hérri idánam*, or the dead soul of Hérri. In a myth about the origins of shamanistic curing practices, the owner of hallucinogenic snuff (*dzáato*) gave some of the drug to six "people": the jaguar, the dolphin, the tapir, the forest monster (*áwaka-rúna*), a medicinal plant (*uwína*), and Hérri, the first initiate and youngest brother of Iñápirríkuli. The first five recipients of *dzáato* snuff all went crazy and turned into animals and plants, but Hérri controlled himself and went on to become the first master-shaman (*dzáwináitairi,* or "snuff-jaguar"). By using the name *Hérri idánam* in association with spirit-names for dolphins and forest monsters, the chant-owner alludes to another context in which the power of sounds to transmit fear and sickness is a prevalent theme.

The production and perception of sounds is the first and most powerful sense mode, and the chant-owner's search for tobacco spirits is in the first place a verbal process of socializing the aural sense mode. Just as Kuwái's mythic creation of a vertically differentiated cosmos began as a "powerful sound that opened the world" (*kémakáni hliméetaka hekwápi*), the newborn infant is most directly and powerfully influenced by the sounds that its father produces or experiences. As the same time, tactile and visual images of the monstrous, hairy mythic body of Kuwái enrich the underlying process of naming powerful sounding objects and species.

These visual-tactile images include several spirit-names of long-thin plant species that are metaphors for the infant's internal, spiritual umbilical cord. The spirit-names of vines, for example, are all considered to be highly powerful parts of Kuwái's mythic body, because Iñápirríkuli and his brothers used vines (*kadápu*) to make the first ritual whips for initiation and to tie up the body of Kuwái.

*Wádewátsa liákani, likáiteri litiakákani Hérri*
So that no harm is done, the name of Hérri's whip is spoken,

*Likáiteri lítulékaka líkapjénipída lipápiwe Máhnekánari.*[3]
The name of the vine used to tie up Kuwái is spoken.

*Néni, likáiteka, kánupánaka liakúna.*
There, it is said, is the most dangerous name/place.

*Núhwa, hnuenéeta ínupána liúdza.*
I sit, I cast out the danger from him.

"Tying up Kuwái with vines" is a metaphor for the construction of *dzáwiñapa* trumpets, which are made by lashing sections of *yebaro* bark to a framework of poles with *dzámakuapi* (two snakes) vine. In addition to their significance in myth and ritual, vines are used for a multitude of practical purposes in everyday contexts. The mythic power of vines is linguistically marked in the system of numeral classifiers in everyday speech dialects by placing them into the same category as the anaconda (*umáwari*), other snakes, large catfish species, and nylon fishing lines.

The visual-tactile metaphor of long-thin plants is also connected to snakes and the hairiness of Kuwái's mythic body in two other spirit-names. The snakelike hairiness of *chique-chique* palms is directly expressed in the spirit-name *umáwari pátsikulénali* or "anaconda hair-covered." *Moriche* palms also have long, hairlike fibers that liken them to forest monsters, Kuwái, and the infant's internal umbilical cord. Both *chique-chique* and *moriche* palms are placed into the category of *umá-*

*wari* or "water-animal spirit-names," because their appearance of hairiness gives them mythic and ritual power that overrides their classification as plant species. Hair is treated as a dangerous, disease-causing object in shamanistic curing rituals and in a variety of narratives, including the Kuwái myth cycle.

In another variation on the long-thin metaphor, the chant-owner names two species of useful plants that when cut exude sap and fibers resembling guts hanging outside a body. The grass species, *duhéepa* and *plantanilla* trees are both named for this reason. The leaves of *plantanilla* trees have the same broad, rounded shape as the leaves of cultivated plantain and banana trees but also have a waxy coating that makes them ideal for use as a plate for cutting open pineapples and other fruits while working in the manioc gardens or walking through the forest. Sticky fibers that ooze from the stems of the *plantanilla* leaves are said to resemble the stub of a newborn infant's umbilical cord that remains on the navel for about a week.[4] The spirit-name of *plantanilla* trees, *lihnakárupjémi Hérri,* or "the plate on which Hérri ate," simultaneously refers to the practical value of the leaves as plates and to the first initiate's mythically powerful act of eating the sacred *káridzámai* food.

Visual imagery becomes increasingly prevalent in the spirit-naming of animal species in the third and last chant. Unlike the auditory and tactile, or shape, images discussed above, the visual qualities of animal species do not have the power to directly cause harm to the newborn infant but can only be indirectly transmitted from the father to the child. If the father encounters a jaguar or puma while hunting in the forest, the fear that he experiences can be passed on to the infant and cause fever. The spotted jaguar is named *táwarinúma iénipe* or "the starch-white mouthed one's children," since the sight of a jaguar's white beard can terrify the father. *Dérripénari íduwári,* the spirit-name of the puma, relates the animal's even, yellowish-brown coloring to the color of *plantanilla* leaves (*derrípje*) after they have been cut. *Náduhénari éenunai,* the spirit-name of tapirs, refers to the shiny red spots on the animal's sides. These markings resemble the small, polished stones (*dúhe*) that master shamans (*dzáwináitairi* or "snuff-jaguars") use for killing sorcerors (*máhnetímnali,* or "poison-owners"). The tapir's spots, the jaguar's beard, and the puma's coloring are visual images of fear-inspiring powers that can indirectly cause fear and sickness to the newborn infant.

The relative paucity of visual imagery in the chant-owner's search for ancestral tobacco spirits is consistent with the way Kuwái's first creation of the world is described in narratives. In myth, Kuwái was taken away to live in a corner of the sky so that he could not be seen by people on the ground at Hípana, and his musical naming-into-being of natural species was a process that people could hear but not see. The chant-owner invokes the invisibility of Kuwái at this early stage of creation immediately before giving ancestral tobacco spirits to the newborn infant.

*Núaka lidzéemanáwa kádzuwátsa, líkadzudzuéka, Wámidzáka*
    *Ipérrikána,*
I give tobacco thus, like him, the one who is like our older brother,

*Kátsapídaliéka mánupalítsa ikápaka límidzáka idákinawa,*
He who did not have any danger in his body,

*Néni mákapákanáka límidzáka idákina imáli mánupanáka liakúna.*
Whose body could not be seen and had no danger.

*Núhwa nuenéeta linúpa liúdza, núakáwa lídakíwa dzéema.*
I sit, I cast out the danger from him, I give for his body tobacco.

The spirit-name of Kuwái is Wámidzáka Ipérrikána, or "the one who is like our older brother," because Kuwái was the first human being to be born and is thus like an older brother to all living people. However, Kuwái was invisible to his parents after he was born, and for this reason his body did not contain any harmful or dangerous elements.

Immediately after naming Kuwái, the chant-owner gives male and female tobacco spirits of the child's patrilineal ancestors. The tobacco spirits of children descended from Baré, Baniwa, Guarequena, and Yeral ancestors are collectively called "The Cigar of Hérri and the White Men's Children" (*nádzamána Hérri halépiwánai iénipe*) because these peoples do not have sib names (*nanáikika*) like those of the Wakuénai. In the Wakuénai myth of the emergence of sib ancestors, Iñápirríkuli gave each ancestor a pair of male and female grandparents who guarded the sacred tobacco used for curing and other ritual purposes by their living human descendants. After he had finished searching for the powerful sib names and tobacco spirits of Wakuénai phratries and sibs, Iñápirríkuli searched for sib names to give to the Eastern Tukano-speaking Cubeo, Desana, and Uanano. In some versions of the myth, when Iñápirríkuli got to the ancestors of the Arawak-speaking neighbors of the Wakuénai he had run out of sib names and tobacco spirits, so he heaped them all into the same "place" as the whites.

After completing the search for the newborn infant's tobacco spirits, the chant-owner also calls upon two species of animal-helpers, the tapir and the tortoise. Tapirs, like jaguars, are a fundamentally ambiguous species that simultaneously embodies the life-giving and life-taking powers of Kuwái and the mythic ancestors. Although the tapir's red spots evoke fear of death by supernatural execution, the tapir is also an ancestor of the Waríperídakéna phratry and the spiritual owner of their house (*héemapána*) in the dark netherworld of the dead. In this context, the chant-owner enlists the spirit-names of the tapir and the tortoise to press down the newborn infant's navel so that the internal, spiritual umbilical cord is securely fastened to the spine.

> *Matsiákaruwátsa pjiékuka nudésre,*
> It is good that you run to my house,
>
> *Pjía nuhwérri máwekúipali,*
> You, my grandfather, the tapir,
>
> *Piékatsa pípua liakúna límidzáka hiépulena límidzáka líkerrámuléna*
> That you tread upon the spirit-name of the infant's navel
>
> *Tapáami líakunatán límidzáka ihnápinanákule.*
> So it enters until the spine of his back.
>
> *Néniwátsa núhwa núpatúita liakúna,*
> From there, I sit, I press upon the spirit-name,
>
> *"Aaan," piawátsa pjía néwakadápida hnáa éenunai, "Aaan,"*
> you arrive, tortoise animal-spirit,
>
> *nádzawítipálepída hnáa éenunai.*
> invisible-headed animal-spirit.
>
> *Matsiénawa piékuka pitíkuta liakúna*
> It is good that you touch the spirit-name with your nose,
>
> *Matsiákarru piékuka píwidátekáni liakúna.*
> It is good that you touch the spirit-name with your head.
>
> *Hnuéetaka tapáam liakúna hliéwakáli jérri,*
> I make the spirit-name enter to the place where the sun falls,
>
> *Tap-jáan límidzáka ihnápinanákule.*
> En-ter like this to the spine of the back.

In this stanza, the chant-owner evokes the weight of the tapir and the tortoise's ability to make its head invisible as metaphors for pushing the child's navel inside the body until it reaches the spine. The spine of the back is also "the place where the sun falls," a phrase that shamans use to designate *íyarudáti*, the space-time of recently deceased persons. The importance of this name is underscored by the emphatic tone of the chant-owner's voice as he pronounces the word *tap-jáan* (en-ter!) for the final time. His search for the infant's ancestral tobacco spirits has traveled along an invisible umbilical cord through the entire microcosmos, from Amáru's "hot place" where the sun rises, inside the womb, the source of new life; to the cold, dark netherworld where the sun falls, at the spine of the back, the remains of the old life.

## Spirit-Naming in the Second Set of Childbirth Chants

The dynamic montage of powerful spirit-names in the chant-owner's search for the infant's tobacco spirits gives way in the second set of chants to a more orderly, gradual process of heaping up the spirit-names of edible animal species. The Wakuénai rely upon fish and other aquatic animal species for their daily protein intake, and their subsistence economy is oriented to a combination of fishing and horticulture along the banks of major rivers in the Içana-Guainía drainage area. Hunting and gathering of wild forest products are important, secondary activities that are integrated into the underlying pattern of fishing and gardening activities. This essentially riverine orientation of Wakuénai social and economic life is concretely expressed in the set of six chants performed for the sacred food (*káridzámai*) of a newborn infant and its parents. The first three chants are entirely devoted to the naming of fish and other aquatic animal species. The spirit-names of these aquatic species are all considered to be "children" (i.e., to belong in the category) of the mythic anaconda (*umáwari*). As a category of spirit-names, the term *umáwari* can best be translated as "prototypic water-animal spirit."

Other edible animal species are "heaped up" into two broad categories, called *éenunai* and *képinai* or "prototypic forest animal-spirit" and "prototypic bird-spirit," respectively. In the most literal sense, the term *éenunai* means "sky-owner," but in the mythically powerful, poetic language of *málikai* the term *éenu* is a category of spirit-names that includes useful and edible species of wild palms. Forest animals, and to a lesser extent birds, are mythic owners of wild palm species in two senses. First, the palm trees used to make the sacred flutes and trumpets of Kuwái have animal namesakes, such as *dápa* (*páca*), *tsítsi* (a species of monkey), and *dzáate* (toucan). Second, the fruits of wild palms are an important food source for forest animal and bird species, and the local availability of game animals is closely tied to the seasonal flowering and fruiting of wild palm species. When the palm trees fail to bear fruit in the usual season, a shaman must travel to *máliwéku,* the house of *éenunai* and *képinai* spirits in *íyarudáti,* musically open the door with his songs (*málirríkairi*), and entice the animals outside with offerings of *guaco* (the bean-shaped fruits eaten by the three nephews of Iñápirríkuli in the Kuwái myth cycle), *uúri* and other species of wild palm fruits. The ecological, trophic relationship between forest animal and bird species, on the one hand, and the fruits of wild palm species, on the other, is closely observed by Wak-uénai hunters and becomes an object of symbolic elaboration in *kwépani* ceremonies, where men determine which "species" of animal and bird instruments to make by the species of wild palm fruits harvested for cere-monial exchange. In childbirth rituals, the chant-owner devotes the fourth and fifth chants for *káridzámai* to heaping up the spirit-names of forest animals (*éenunai*) and the final, sixth chant to the spirit-names of bird (*képinai*) species.

When the three main categories of spirit-names for edible animal spe-cies are understood as parts of an integral whole, or the mythic body of Kuwái, they constitute a classification of edible animal nature into three types of habitat: aquatic, sylvan, and avian. The principle of "habitat taxonomy" forms the basic, lower-level pattern of mythic meaning for the chant-owner's verbal activity of "heaping up the names" (*wakéetaka nakúna*) throughout the six chants. Although there are important excep-tions to this simple classification by habitat, the principle accounts for forty-eight out of sixty-two, or over three-fourths, of the species named in the six chants.

At a deeper level, the principle of habitat taxonomy asserts the close affinity between people and their riverine habitat. Human beings are de-scended from mythic ancestors who emerged from a hole in the earth beneath the rapids of the Aiarí River beside Hípana, the Center of the World. The aquatic origin of humanity is reestablished in the chanting of animal spirit-names through the belief that the *umáwari,* or aquatic ani-mal-spirits, reside in the world of living human beings (*hekwápiríko*). In contrast, *éenunai* ("forest animal-spirits") and *képinai* ("bird-spirits") do not live in the space-time of living people but in *íyarudáti,* the dark neth-erworld of *lidánam* (shadow) spirits of recently deceased persons.

The unique, quasi-humanness of the *umáwari* category of spirit-names is marked by making it the first and largest category in the set of six chants. Thirty-three out of sixty-two, or over half, of the spirit-names belong to the category of *umáwari* spirits. Furthermore, the categorical name of *umáwari* always precedes the specific spirit-name, whereas the categorical names of *éenunai* and *képinai* are placed after the specific spirit-names in all but three instances (see Figure 4.1). This seemingly minor contrast in the ordering of generic and specific components of spirit-names in *málikai* actually forms part of a more broadly significant cultural distinction between living human beings and the spirits of recently deceased persons (*lidánam*). When people fall seriously ill, their specific, human body-shaped souls (*likáriwa*) separate from the collective, animal-shaped souls (*líwarúna,* or the soul of the mythic ancestors). The lost souls of sick persons travel to the houses of the dead in *íyarudáti* until they can be brought back to *hekwápiríko* in shamanistic rituals. Failing that, the body-shaped souls are transformed into shadows (*lidánam*) that must remain in the netherworld of the dead until their eventual transmigration into ancestor spirits in the celestial paradise of Iñápirríkuli. *Iyarudáti,* in other words, is a place where the specific, individual souls of people are alienated from their collective, ancestral souls. By placing the specific spirit-names of forest animal and bird species prior to the categorical names (*éenunai* and *képinai*), the chant-owner verbally constructs an image of these species as inhabitants of the dark netherworld.

All the edible animal species named in the six chants are considered to have mythic power (*línupána*) to cause harm to the newborn infant, who receives the effect of the mother's diet through breastfeeding. The purpose of the chants is to allow the parents to return to a normal diet of fish and game meat without harming their infant child. By "heaping up the names" of edible animal species, the chant-owner attaches a series of specific names to their generic category and verbally constructs the wholeness of Kuwái's mythic body by uniting the two sides of his creation, its "oneness" and its "everything-ness." In addition, the lines of the opening refrain of each chant repeatedly establish the intention of purifying the various species of animal meat before they enter the parents' diet. Four basic actions are mentioned in the opening refrain: (1) licking the hot pepper, (2) the falling off of all harmful qualities, (3) killing rawness, and (4) calling the generic spirits of aquatic, sylvan, and avian animals to cut off the heads of the specific names in each category (see Figure 4.2).

"Licking the hot pepper" evokes the mythic episode in which Hérri, the first initiate, was given hot pepper to lick before he received the sacred food. Hot pepper (*áati*) is regarded as a purifying substance that com-

4.1 *List of spirit-names for edible animal species in order of incantation in second set of* málikai *chants performed in childbirth rituals*

| Spirit-name in chants | Everyday name | Spanish name | Scientific name |
|---|---|---|---|
| *Chant 1:* | | | |
| umáwari kámarinúma ienípe | táari | bocachico blanco | *Leporinus sp.* |
| umáwari daruítepérri ienípe | dúpari | bocachico rabo colorado | *Leporinus sp.* |
| umáwari duísinúma ienípe | dúme | bocachico pintado | *Leporinus sp.* |
| umáwari máriapinúma | tírri | chanqletta | *Brachyplatysoma sp.* |
| hlípa ñákim dzáwi-ñápirríkuli | wétsuri | payara | *Hydrolicus pectoralis* |
| umáwari yámutsiáduwa ienípe | yamúti | bocón | *Brycon whitei* |
| umáwari úwirritána ienípe | hnúkurri | laulau | *Brachyplatysoma sp.* |
| umáwari kwáyačáduwa ienípe | uhwí | machete | ? |
| umáwari yámatéwirri ienípe | ínirri | guabine | *Hoplias malabaricus* |
| káduičípa dzáwi-ñápirríkuli | čípa | anchoa | ? |
| kerráipenúma dzáwi-ñápirríkuli | kérrapúkurri | anchoa grande | ? |
| umáwari púrutáinuma ienípe | káatama | anchoa mediano | ? |
| umáwari mákaruáduwa ienípe | tsípa | palometa | *Mylossoma duriventris* |
| umáwari perrékua ienípe | dakáta | temblador negro, medio amarillo | *Electrophorus electricu* |
| umáwari wawiáduwa ienípe | dakáta | | |
| liápam máhnekánari ienípe | yámaru | raya | *Potamotrygon hystrix* |
| umáwari wítawitáduwa ienípe | dawáki | bagre liso | *Brachyplatysoma sp.* |
| hépulekáda oráinainái | háyo | vieja loura | *Cichlasoma sp.* |
| umáwari kúlikuliáduwa ienípe | ikúli | cabezón | ? |
| umáwari túmukiáduwa ienípe | tamáki | morocoto | *Colossoma macropomus* |
| *Chant 2:* | | | |
| umáwari oráinainái náturúda | érritu | viejita pintada | *Cichlasoma sp.* |
| umáwari duírripánari mólituáduwa | dzawírra | viejita propria | *Cichlasoma sp.* |
| umáwari tímahéwerri ienípe | pára | algojón | ? |
| umáwari hwarrúi | ukírra | sal* | ? |
| umáwari lipáramarétem OR lipáramarétem dzáwi-ñápirríkuli | káači | cangreja | ? |
| líkerérripírri itádam dzáwi-ñápirríkuli | dzáaka | camarón | ? |

*Salt is an important material for preserving fish. The mythical owner of salt is said to be an anaconda that had large teeth like people do today but that took them out and buried them in the ground.

| Spirit-name in chants | Everyday name | Spanish name | Scientific name |
|---|---|---|---|
| **Chant 3:** | | | |
| máwari kudzáinuma ienípe | dzápa | pavón | *Cichla ocellaris* |
| máwari holáduwa | hóla | caribe grande | *Serrasalmus rhombeus* |
| máwari bebéduwa ienípe | kaimána | caimán | *Cocodrylus intermedius* |
| máwari kamáwa kutíye enípe | katsírri | babilla | *Caiman sclerops* |
| máwari límalídali iñákim záwi-ñápirríkuli | katsírri | babilla, cabeza roja | *Caiman sclerops* |
| máwari áapituáduwa ienípe | kulírri | rayado | *Brachyplatysoma* sp. |
| **Chant 4:** | | | |
| áwibírrikírri éenunai | apídza | báquira | *Tayassu pecari* |
| apúruikáda éenunai ienípe | dzámurítu | cháchaaro | *Pecari tajacu* |
| érramána éenunai | néeri | venado colorado | *Mazama americana* |
| áhipiánuali éenunai ienípe | táaru | osso palmero | *Myrmecophaga tridactyla* |
| áduhénari éenunai ienípe | héema | danta | *Tapirus terrestris* |
| asraínida éenunai | dápa | lapa | *Cuniculus paca* |
| adáparéda éenunai | dápa | lapa | *Cuniculus paca* |
| wadanápale dzáwi-ñápirríkuli | píči | picure del monte | *Dasyprocta* sp. |
| tíyen pánare iñákim dzáwi-ápirríkuli | píči | picure de la sabana | *Dasyprocta* sp. |
| **Chant 5:** | | | |
| áturuápa éenunai | kapíti | guachi | *Nasua nasua* |
| áturúda éenunai | arídali | armadillo pequeno | *Dasypus* sp. |
| keráruli iñéni dzáwi-ápirríkuli | ádzana | armadillo del monte | *Pridontes giganteus* |
| álekáda éenunai | áate | osso hormiguero | *Tamandua tridactyla* |
| étakána éenunai | dzówi | guachi pequeno | *Potos flavus* |
| ápuikáita éenunai | káparu | mono caparro | ? |
| nawíha-kánari éenunai | púwi | mono machin | *Aotus trivirgatus* |
| álekáita éenunai | háaru | mono blanco | *Cebus albifrons unicolor* |
| ékakáda éenunai | tsítsi | monochicoto | *Cacajao melanocephalus* |
| ákumhakáita éenunai | wáaki | mono negro chiquito | ? |
| ámaréna éenunai | ítči | mono araguato | *Alouatta seniculus* |

continued

4.1    *List of spirit-names for edible animal species in order of incantation in second set of* málikai *chants performed in childbirth rituals* (cont.)

| Spirit-name in chants | Everyday name | Spanish name | Scientific name |
| --- | --- | --- | --- |
| *Chant 6:* | | | |
| líkulimáparae líkhwatépe iñákim dzáwi-ñápirríkuli | máare | úquirra | ? |
| nápuruikápa képinai | itsírri | úquirra pedrero | ? |
| néturéda képinai pérrumánare ienípe | atíne | grúa | ? |
| nétakápa képinai umáwari** iñániperrí ienípe | kwíči | paují amarillo | |
| natewapa kepinai ienipe | dzate | piapoco | *Rhamphastidae* sp. |
| képináika bolánerri | ádaru | guacamaya | *Ara* spp. |
| éenunai pepírri nakáuli | paíči | rana | ? |
| képinai dzámutsináre ienipe | kwíči | paují blanco | |
| lípalitákerri ñákim dzáwi-ñápirríkuli | *** | *** | |
| limáitakérri ñákim dzáwi-ñápirríkuli | *** | *** | |

** In this spirit-name, the use of *umáwari* violates the distinction between fish and bird species because in myth the pauji (*kwíči*) turned itself into a dangerous anaconda.
*** These two names come from *hípalitakau* (to cover with earth) and *himátakau* (to burn) and refer to baking and roasting, respectively.

pletes the cooking of meat, and in both initiation rituals and mythic narratives hot pepper metaphorically transfers Kuwái's fiery transformation of the external world to the inside of initiates' bodies, preparing the way for the ritual internalization of socialized animal nature. The "falling off of harmful qualities" and "killing of rawness" metaphorically relate the six chants to processes of purification.[5] The cooking metaphor is repeated at various points later in the chanting by invoking the ritual whips of initiation (*líwanápu éenu*, also the name of Kuwái's mythic home in the sky) to "beat the rawness out" of the animal meat. The invocation of generic spirit-names to "cut off the heads" of specific names is done to neutralize the strong associations between animals (especially forest animals and birds) and spirits of the dead. In an important narrative about the origin of evil omens (*hínimai*), Iñápirríkuli cut off the heads of two monkeys/brothers-in-law that he had previously killed with poisoned darts from his blowgun. The two severed heads sprang up overnight into enormous fruit trees, a metaphor for the transmigration of dead souls up to the celestial paradise. Thus, in a mythic sense, the verbal act of de-

4.2    *Refrain section from second set of chants in childbirth ritual*

capitating animal species in *málikai* chants is a way of killing them for a second time so that their souls are reunited with the ancestors rather than left to wander about the living to cause illness.

The various metaphorical activities of licking hot pepper, purifying, cooking, and decapitating that make up the refrain stanzas of the six chants are all subsumed by the more global metaphorical process of "heaping up the names," or classifying edible animal species according to the principle of habitat taxonomy. The general movement of spirit-names in the six chants outlines a progression from *umáwari*, or aquatic species, that are somewhat less powerful and closer to human beings to *éenunai* (sylvan) and *képinai* (avian) species that are relatively more powerful and distant from human beings due to their association with death, illness, and shamanistic journeying.

Like this general progression, the ordering of spirit-names within each of the three major habitat categories is not only a reflection of mythic, cosmological beliefs but also expresses practical, ecological concerns. The first species to be named in each category of habitat is also the most frequently captured and eaten species in everyday activities of fishing and hunting. The first species of fish named in the opening chant are the white, red-tailed, and spotted *Leporinus* (*táari, dúpari* and *dúme*), and these species are captured in great quantities during the annual spawning migrations at the beginning of the long wet season. These species migrate into newly flooded forests during Wáripérihnúme (the "Mouth," or beginning of the Pleiades), and men capture them in large quantities by blocking off the mouths of streams as the fish return to the rivers' main channel.[6] The next species of fish to be named in the first chant is *tírri,* a species of small catfish that becomes very important in the local diet at the height of the long wet season when fishing becomes underproductive. The first animal species named in the fourth chant are white-lipped and white-collared peccaries, two of the most important sources of game meat in the diet. Herds of white-lipped peccaries are frequently killed in August and September when they come down to the banks of streams and rivers to forage on newly exposed vegetation. A feast of peccary meat is greatly relished at this time of year, since it brings to an end the long period of eking out a living on the extremely meager fishing and hunting yields of the long wet season. By naming the spirits of the most frequently captured fish and animal species before the less frequently captured animal species, the chant-owner fine-tunes the mythic, cosmological pantheon of spirits to the undeniable ecological reality of a scarcity of fish and game meat that people experience in long wet seasons.[7]

Aside from the general classificatory process and the ecological importance of certain fish and game animal species, the ordering of spirit-names in the six chants is not prescribed. Nearly one fourth of the spirit-names break out of the tripartite classification due to their significance in sacred myths and rituals. The great majority of these extraordinarily powerful names are placed into the category of *dzáwi-ñápirríkuli* ("out of the jaguar's bones"). These names systematically cross-cut the three classes of edible animal species by appearing at least once in each of the six chants. Each *dzáwi-ñápirríkuli* name refers to a specific act of mythic creation. As Hernan, the chant-owner, put it, these are names about which one must "tell a long story" (*padámawátaka*). In most cases, the story comes from an episode within one of the narratives about Kuwái and Amáru. The two species of squirrel (*píci*), for example, belong in the *dzáwi-ñápirríkuli* category because of the squirrel's role in marking off and cutting up the *macanilla* palm that grew out of Kuwái's ashes and that was to be made into the animal flutes and trumpets of Kuwái. The crab (*káaci*) originated when Iñápirríkuli and his brothers threw away their crowns of *seje* palm fronds at the end of the first *kwépani* ceremony. Other names in the *dzáwi-ñápirríkuli* category are regarded as extraordinarily powerful due to their association with heat and fire, the only element capable of transforming the mythic body of Kuwái. The red-headed cayman (*katsírri*), for example, is the mythic source of cooking fire. Baking and roasting are classified as *dzáwi-ñápirríkuli* names because they bring animal meat into direct contact with fire and are considered more likely to cause sickness than boiling, the most common method of cooking meat in everyday social life and the only form of cooking used to prepare *káridzámai* in ritual contexts.

Two of the more powerful spirit-names in chants for aquatic species are related to Amáru. *Liápam máhnekánari* or "the children of nobody knows whose placenta," refers to Kuwái's name at birth (*Máhnekánari,* or "Nobody Knows") and the mythic episode in which Iñápirríkuli and Dzúli showed Amáru her afterbirth in the form of a stingray. The stingray is greatly feared for its extremely painful sting, and its everyday name, *yámaru*, is very nearly a homonym for Amáru. The spirit-name for salt, *umáwari hwárrui*, is also related to Amáru through mythic narratives. In mythic times, the anaconda named *hwárrui* had large, humanlike teeth that he took out and buried in the ground. The anaconda's teeth transformed into salt that looked like white sand. When Amáru approached the anaconda *hwárrui* to ask him for salt, he showed her where to dig it from the ground. As a substance produced by the mythic meeting of two powerful beings, *umáwari* and Amáru, salt is capable of causing sickness to a newborn infant if the parents eat salted foods without the proper naming of the mythic owner of salt.[8]

Finally, a few spirit-names override the lower-level principle of habitat taxonomy by their unusual placement. The spirit-name for *páici* frogs, for example, is invoked in the middle of a chant otherwise devoted entirely to bird-spirits (*képinai*). In this case, *páici* frogs are an aquatic animal species that is shifted to the category of bird-spirits in *íyarudáti* because the species is the spiritual owner of the house (*Páicipána*) of recently deceased persons of the chant-owner's patrisib (the second-to-highest ranked sib in the Dzáwinai, or "Jaguar-Owner" phratry). A similar logic is at work in producing the unusual placement of the bird species called *kwíči* into both *képinai* and *umáwari* categories. *Kwíči,* or the yellow currassow, is the mythic ancestor of a lower-ranked sib in the Dzáwinai phratry, the *Kwíčidakéna* ("Currassow-Grandchildren"). Also, in mythic times, the yellow currassow transformed itself into an anaconda, so its spirit-name belongs to both avian and aquatic habitats.

Spirit-naming in *málikai* demonstrates a ludic, play element in which semantic meanings are used to poetically explore the hierarchical levels of mythic meaning and ritual power. In some cases, the principle of generic classification is extended to include the specific, adjectival modifiers of generic spirit-names and results in the creation of a novel semantic category. A number of white-colored species, for example, receive spirit-names derived from the everyday word for the color white (*halédali*). *Hálekáda éenunai* is a species of small white anteater (*áate*), *hálekáita éenunai* is a species of white monkey (*háaru*), and *hálekápa képinai* is a species of white heron (*máari*). In all three spirit-names, the prefix *hále-* is taken from the everyday word for white and combined with suffixes that are not used with the adjective for white in everyday speech. The naming process here is identical to the naming of steel tools and weapons as a set of variations on the theme of "hot" (*hlímukáani* or *tsímukáni*). In other cases, spirit-names consist of unique metaphors that juxtapose natural species usually not found in the same semantic domain. The spirit-name for cabezon turtles, for example, is a poetic metaphor that plays upon the similarity between the bright yellow-green color of parakeets and that of the underside of cabezon turtles. In the language of *málikai,* the common turtle becomes *umáwari kúlikúliáduwa iénipe* or the "parakeet-like anaconda's children."

In performances of *málikai,* the chant-owner uses the diversity of natural species, objects, and elements as a palette of colors, shapes, sounds, textures, and temperatures to verbally paint a mythically and ritually powerful portrait of natural and social worlds. Through word play, classificatory logic, and the construction of overriding relations of mythic power, the chant-owner transforms everyday language into a multivocal, semantically enriched, poetic, enchanted language of Kuwái and the jaguar-ancestors.

## The Elementary Forms of Poetic Speech

In comparison to the chant-owner's search for tobacco spirits in the first set of chants, the "heaping up" of spirit-names in the set of chants for *káridzámai* is a relatively static process of gradual movements between semantic domains. The more dynamic process of "searching for the names" is embodied in the set of more powerful *dzáwi-ñápirríkuli* names and a few other examples, but the principle of habitat taxonomy accounts for the great majority of spirit-names and mutes the effect of more powerful, cross-cutting names in the six chants for *káridzámai*. In the first set of chants, the relationship between the two naming processes is exactly the opposite: almost all the spirit-names refer to exceptionally powerful beings, and the chant-owner moves rapidly among many distinct categories of spirit-names. The more static, gradual process of "heaping up the names" is weakly represented in the use of Amáru as a category of "hot things," but the rapid movement among categories in search of the tobacco spirits is clearly the dominant semantic principle in the first set of chants.

This same relationship of more-to-less dynamic processes is extended into the preverbal realm of language music. In the first set of chants for the tools, weapons, and objects of the newborn's father, the chant-owner moves his voice through a series of microtonal intervals, vocal timbres, tempos, phrase lengths, and levels of volume to carry out musically a journey through the microcosmos of the infant's body and its emergence from the maternal womb into an external world of mythically powerful sounds. Each phrase of the three chants is composed of a dynamic inter-weaving of chanted and spoken speech. The length of phrases varies widely, from a minimum of slightly less than three seconds to a maximum of more than fifteen seconds. In the opening chant, for example, the first twenty phrases have durations of approximately three, six, six, five, six, five, six, eight, six, seven, six, five, six, thirteen, six, four, six, four, six, and six seconds, respectively. The constant alternation between chanted and spoken vocal timbres and variation between shorter and longer phrase lengths creates a musical sound-image of zig-zagging movements that are somewhat uncoordinated and faltering. Like the first steps of a child learning to walk or the utterances of a child first attempting to speak, the language music in the chant-owner's search for tobacco spirits is an unsteady, erratic form of motion.

While vocal timbre and phrase length continue to outline a multi-directional alternation and variation throughout the set of three chants, pitch, tempo, and volume are all steadily increased to produce a musical sound-pattern of progressive growth. The opening pitch is G-sharp in the second octave below middle C. By the fourth phrase, when the chant-owner has begun to invoke the powerful Amáru category of hot spirit-names, the pitch has sharpened slightly. By the eighth and ninth phrases, the pitch is moving closer to A-natural than to G-sharp. In the tenth through the eighteenth phrases, the pitch reaches A-natural and slowly ascends to a raised A. By the twenty-fifth phrase, the pitch has risen to B-flat. This process of microtonal rising continues throughout the first chant and reaches a level slightly above C-natural, one octave below middle C (see Figure 4.3). Using the number of phrases between each chromatic interval as an estimate of the number of intermediate pitches of less than one hundred cents (one cent equals one one-hundreth of a chromatic half-step), the number of microtonal intervals per chromatic half-step is between ten and twenty. Thus, the chant-owner's microtonal rising consists of movements between intervals of five-to-ten cents.

In the last three minutes of the first chant, the pitch rises only a fraction of a half-step to a raised C-natural. Pitch rises much more gradually in the last two chants of the first set, and the total span of microtonal rising is approximately one half-step in each chant. Thus, after rising at a rate of nearly one half-step per minute throughout the first five-and-a-half minutes of chanting, the rate of microtonal rising slows down consider-ably in the remaining three minutes of the first chant and in each of the last two chants. In parallel to the more rapid microtonal rising in the opening part of the first chant, the level of volume and acceleration of tempo also increases most noticeably in this section. Within each phrase of the chanting, volume is highest in the initial /hm/ sound, falls consid-erably in the rapid succession of syllables in the middle part of the phrase, and increases slightly during the final, elongated syllables at the end of each phrase. In short, the chant-owner's search for tobacco spirits begins as a musical process in which pitch, tempo, and volume increase at an exponential rate and gradually tapers off until the rate of increase ap-proaches zero.

In the second set of chants, the "heaping up" of names inside a pot of hot-peppered meat, the musical processes of microtonal rising, increasing levels of volume, and rhythmical acceleration are almost totally absent.

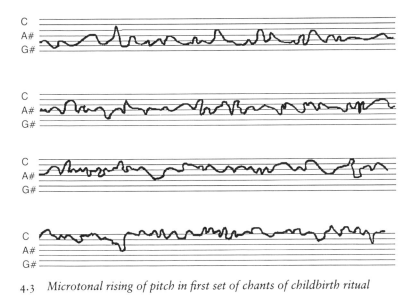

4.3  *Microtonal rising of pitch in first set of chants of childbirth ritual*

The six chants for *káridzámai* last for nearly one hour and display the following musical characteristics: (1) a binary rhythmic structure in which each word of the text is bisected into two parts of equal duration, (2) an unchanging tempo of 110 beats per minute, (3) minimal changes of pitch, and (4) no changes in the volume level. Aside from a slight rising of pitch spanning an interval of less than one half-step, the six chants contain no discernible changes in the organization of musical sounds from beginning to end. The length of phrases does not vary, and volume and tempo remain constant at all points within each phrase. Even the rests for breathing and the characteristic /hm/ sounds of *málikai* are constrained within the binary meter (see Figure 4.2).

My attempts to elicit indigenous terminology and concepts about the musical structuring of vocal sounds in *málikai* have not been met with the same spontaneous outpouring of explanations as my questions about spirit-naming. The chant-owner teaches *málikai* and explains it primarily in terms of its mythic meanings and the verbal processes of "heaping up" and "searching for" the spirit-names of people, species, and objects. Nevertheless, *málikai* is clearly more than a purely spoken genre of verbal art and requires the performer to make poetic uses of the volume, tempo, rhythm, pitch, and timbre of spoken, chanted, and sung speech. Just as the chant-owner moves abruptly among categories of mythic being in his search for tobacco spirits, he moves his voice through many different tonal and rhythmic variations and progressions. And in his gradual "heaping up" of the spirit-names of edible animal species, the relatively steady pitch, rhythm, tempo, volume, and timbre of the chant-owner's voice extend the semantics of spirit-naming into a parallel language music.

The relative lack of indigenous terms for describing musical sounds in *málikai* can be interpreted as an indirect way of underscoring the central importance of musical sound as an embodiment of sacred ritual power.[9] The extension of semantic principles of spirit-naming into parallel speech-music is an attempt to make language transcend its grounding in social semiosis, or the attribution of meaning to objects and activities, by attaching it to pre- or nonverbal, more and less musical ways of speaking. The more musical process of "searching for the names" is a musicalization of mythic speech, a concrete expression of sheer ritual power, and a virtuoso display of poetic imagination. In "searching for the names," the dynamic montage of mythically powerful spirit-names is subsumed by processes of musicalizing speech that are still more powerful and dynamic. The less musical process of "heaping up the names" is a mythification of musical sound and an embodiment of the power of language as a process of mythic classification to facilitate the arts of memory and transmitting knowledge across the generations. In "heaping up the names," the relatively tidy organization of animal species into habitats is imposed upon the musicality of language to create a steady pulse of chanted speech.

Thick clouds of tobacco smoke transfer the chant-owner's poetic vocal sounds into the sensual realms of vision, touch, taste, and smell. The art of performing *málikai* is called *ínyapakáati* or *ínyapakáati dzéema*. Bilingual informants translate the term for chant-owner (*málikai limínali*) as *soplador* ("blower"). Although this translation is interesting because it calls attention to the importance of breathing or exhaling in indigenous conceptualizations of *málikai*, a great deal of the original meaning of *ínyapakáati dzéema* is lost in the translation into Spanish, probably as a way of providing a "gloss" for outsiders. At the very least, the term *ínyapakáati* specifies an aspirated, voiced exhaling of the breath, a sort of humming with an additional loud exhaling sound (/hm-m-m-p-f-f-h-h/) released with a thick veil of tobacco smoke over the ritual participants, onto the father's tools and weapons, and into the pot of sacred food. The breath is given visual substance in the form of tobacco smoke and acoustical substance by closing the lips (/hm/). As if the musical tones are stuck inside the chant-owner's speech organs, they are forcefully pushed out as a burst of air, smoke, and chanted sounds through a mouth that is reluctant to open. This inchoate, primordial human vocal sound is the elementary poetic material from which the chant-owner weaves distinctive patterns of spoken and chanted sounds in *málikai*.

## The Mythification of Musical Sound

The childbirth ritual is a poetic exploration of the subtle shadings and hierarchical levels of meaning in Kuwái's mythic creation of a vertically differentiated cosmos of upper and lower worlds. Like Part I of the Kuwái myth cycle, the childbirth ritual begins in the microcosmic space-time of the body and the spatial movement from inside the social space of a village of people out to a surrounding, extra-social space of forests teeming with powerful-sounding, fear-inspiring plant and animal species. The chant-owner's search for tobacco spirits is a poetic journey into the dangerous world of the forest that clears a pathway for the newborn's father, who must actually search the forests for game animals at the conclusion of the first set of chants. The father's return to the village with game meat reverses the initial movement from inside to outside of social space and provides the raw material for constructing the vertical dimension of mythic space-time through the mother's cooking of game meat and the chant-owner's "heaping up" (i.e., socializing) of edible animal nature. In the second half of the ritual, the mother's actual cooking of game meat through boiling it in hot pepper precedes the chant-owner's metaphorical cooking of animal species in his chants for *káridzámai*. Thus, the overall sequence of ritual activities outlines a chiasmalike process: metaphorical searching precedes actual searching, and actual cooking precedes metaphorical cooking.

Like the first creation of the world in Part I of the Kuwái myth cycle, childbirth rituals outline the two-fold process of an initial movement from inside to outside social space followed by a gradual reversal into an opposite movement from outside to inside. This reversal is not limited to the father's return from the forest with game meat but is also expressed in the chant-owner's removal of the pot of cooked game meat from the guest house where the ritual participants were lodging to the floor of his extended family household. Relations of ritual power and kinship are mirrored in the spatial layout of households within the village of Gavilán. The guest house is situated near the southern, downstream end of a row of houses, away from the households of Hernan, his brother, and their sons at the upstream tip of the island village (see Figures 4.4 and 4.5).

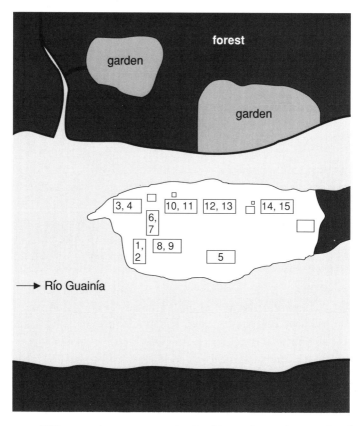

4.4    *Village settlement pattern in Gavilán, 1981–1985; patrilocal core of village kinship formed by Hernan (1), his brother (3), and their adult sons, Siderio (8) and Juan (10) (adapted from Hill and Moran 1983: 128)*

Hernan's household is the center of social and ritual space in Gavilán. Newly arrived visitors are escorted into the large front room of his house to converse and share manioc drinks, and the floor of the room becomes a gathering place for adult men and women each evening as they squat in separate circles around bowls of fish and game meat to partake in communal meals. In initiation rituals, the pot of sacred food is set on the floor in the same spot where men usually gather at communal meals. Removing the sacred food from the guests' house to the floor of Hernan's house in childbirth rituals is thus highly charged with social and ritual significance. In addition, moving from the periphery to the center of the village reproduces the mythic movement of Kuwái from up-above and

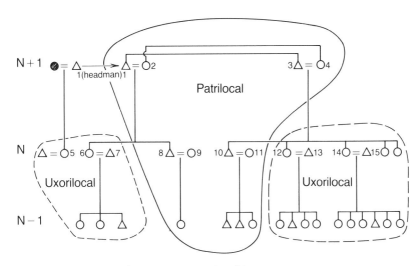

4.5    *Kinship and residence patterns in Gavilán, 1981–1985*

outside social space to down on the ground and inside social space.

Hernan's movement of the food from the guests' house to his own house also crosses a generational line between the space inhabited by the two village elders at the upstream tip of the island and the downstream row of houses inhabited by their children and grandchildren. By moving to the upstream area of village elders, the chant-owner evokes the creation of vertical, generational time in Part I of the Kuwái myth cycle.

The transformation of bodily processes and sexual relations into the symbolism of food and eating is another major theme of the Kuwái myth cycle that is explored in the two parts of childbirth rituals. Whereas the first set of chants centers around bodily images of birth and the newborn infant's attachment to its parents, the second set of chants transforms these bodily images into the metaphors of purifying and cooking the sacred food, which becomes the shared substance linking the infant and its parents into a vertically defined group of people descended from the same mythic ancestors. As in Part I of the Kuwái myth cycle, childbirth rituals make use of bodily processes of externalization and internalization, or giving birth and eating, to inscribe the pattern of movements through external social and natural worlds into the microcosm of the human body.

The chant-owner's performances of *málikai* in childbirth rituals also draw upon the fundamentally musical, poetic qualities of Kuwái's first creation of the world. What is perhaps most striking about childbirth rituals is the relative simplicity and brevity of ritual activities in comparison to the complexity and duration of the chant-owner's performances of *málikai*. In essence, childbirth rituals consist of a core of musico-poetic performances around which a few simple, yet highly meaningful, objects and actions are integrated. Similarly, the social, spatial, and bodily imagery developed in Part I of the Kuwái myth cycle was overshadowed by the explosive creativity of Kuwái's musical naming power, or "the powerful sound that opened up the world," and the gradual transformations of this raw, unsocialized, musico-poetic force into the source of humanly controlled ritual power. In myth, the trickster-creator's attempts to bring Kuwái's musical naming power down to earth inside the center of social space at Hípana could not move forward until Kuwái's power had been socialized into the form of mythic, dialogical speech (i.e., the conversation between Kuwái and Kálimátu in Myth 5). Only after this transformation of musical sound into mythic speech did Kuwái return to the ground at Hípana and directly, monologically implant the poetic forms of ancestral power into men's consciousness.

Childbirth rituals embody the same transformation of musical sounds into mythic speech. In the first set of chants, the search for tobacco spirits is a poetic instantiation of Kuwái's musical, world-opening creation of the world. Through alternation across the spectrum of spoken to chanted vocal timbres, variation of phrase lengths, and progressive increases in tempo, volume, and pitch, the chant-owner musicalizes mythic speech. In this musicalization of speech, the nuances of mythic meaning are transposed into the musicality of spoken and chanted speech. In the interlude between the first and second sets of chants, the musicality of spoken and chanted speech is replaced by a dialogical exchange of words between the chant-owner and the newborn's parents. Like the mythic dialogue between Kuwái and Kálimátu, the brief conversation between ritual specialist and participants takes place outside the center of social space, and an exchange of food substances immediately foreshadows the final movement from the outside to the inside of social space. In the second set of chants, the "heaping up" of names of edible animal species embodies the ritual transformation of musical sounds into mythic speech. Mythic principles of order, or habitat taxonomy, constrain the musicality of language into a steady flow of chanted speech that moves slowly through the three basic categories of edible animal species. In ritual as in myth, the mythification of musical sounds constructs a vertically differentiated space-time in which keepers of the sacred chants poetically mediate the transmission of power from mythic ancestors to their human descendants.

# 5

# Initiation into the Cult of Kuwái and the Musicalization of Mythic Speech

Male and female initiation rituals are complex, highly elaborate social gatherings at which performances of *málikai* songs and chants are embellished with a variety of instrumental music, dances, sacred artifacts, and collective activities. As in childbirth rituals, the sacred food (*káridzámai*) of Kuwái and the jaguar-ancestors is a focal object of ritual transformation through *ínyapakáati*, or smoke-blowing. However, in initiation rituals the food becomes a concrete embodiment of Kuwái's second opening up of the world and the chant-owner's search for an initiate's soul (*líwarúna* or *rúarúna*) in the external, horizontal dimension of peoples and places. The microcosmic searching of the individual's body along an internal umbilical cord becomes transformed in initiation rituals into the collective singing and playing-into-being of a celestial umbilical cord (*hliépule-kwá éenu*) that connects Kuwái and other mythic beings to the world of human beings at Hípana, the place of collective mythic emergence. From there, the chant-owner musically searches across the known world of living peoples and their houses of the dead in *íyarudáti* before returning to Hípana and the celestial umbilical cord. At the end of each song or chant, he stops to blow tobacco smoke into the covered pot of sacred food. In short, initiation rituals evoke the cosmic turning inside-out of the world after the fiery "death," or transformation, of Kuwái in myth. The mythic transformation of Kuwái from a monstrous, world-opening being into an enormous palm tree and other plant materials is paralleled in the ritual transformation of spoken and chanted speech into sung and chanted speech. The chant-owner's vocal movements between vertically distinct tones create a musical pathway for the descent of Kuwái from the sky-world to the ground at Hípana along the celestial umbilical cord. At the same time, the transformation of Kuwái into an external object is collectively evoked by groups of men through dancing and playing the sacred flutes and trumpets. In bringing together the various parts, or natural species, making up Kuwái's mythic body, male musicians dance and play into being the sacred palm tree connecting the sky-world of mythic ancestors to the terrestrial world of human beings. The collective objectification of Kuwái's life-giving powers is extended to include women in performances called *kápetiápani*, or "whip-dance," where groups of men are joined by female dance partners as they sing and mark time by pounding the handles of ceremonial whips (*kapéti*) against the ground in unison. Kuwái is no longer an independent being whose musical naming power spontaneously generates the cosmic opening of the world but a set of objects that must be created and empowered through human activities of singing, dancing, making musical instruments, and using instruments to produce musical sounds.

In the context of initiation rituals and the evocation of a stable, macrocosmic connection between vertical regions, the long series of *málikai* chants for an initiate's sacred food takes on new form and meaning. The chant-owner's naming of edible animal species is interwoven with the spirit-naming of places in performances of sung and chanted speech that musicalize the mythic journeys of Amáru with the sacred flutes and trumpets of Kuwái. In parallel with the dynamic, verbally constructed movements to places far downstream and upstream from the center of the world at Hípana, the chants for an initiate's food employ musically dynamic processes of microtonal rising, acceleration of tempo, and the use of different starting pitches to embody the world-opening, horizontal movements of Amáru and Kuwái. In sum, *málikai* chants for the initiate's food are not an internalizing process of movement down and inside but an externalization of Kuwái's mythic powers away and across the world from center to periphery and back again.

The most powerful material symbol of the turning inside-out of mythic space-time in initiation rituals is the sacred *kadápu* whip. In the language of *málikai*, the spirit-name of *kadápu* whips is also the name of Kuwái's mythic home, *líwanápu éenu*, or "the corner of the sky." *Kadápu* whips are made from a species of vine called *dzámakuápi* ("two snakes"), one of the plant species that grew from the ashes of Kuwái in myth and the material used for lashing treebark around long poles to make *dzáwiñápa* ("jaguar-bone") trumpets in male initiation rituals. *Kadápu* whips are never used in ceremonial dances (*kápetiápani*) but only for tapping out the rhythm of *málikai* chants for an initiate's food, lifting a morsel of hot peppers and meat to the initiate's mouth, and striking the initiate across the back at the conclusion of the ritual. The use of *kadápu* whips to accompany *málikai* chants adds a layer of sharp, percussive sound to the binary division of spirit-names and other words in the chants' texts. The shift from purely vocal performances of *málikai* in childbirth rituals to vocal performances accompanied by percussive instruments in initiation rituals is another ritual expression of the mythic transformation of Kuwái from an independent being into an external object.

In both male and female initiation rituals, groups of adult, initiated men play the sacred flutes and trumpets of Kuwái on the village plaza while women and children remain secluded inside a ceremonial house. These performances are much shorter in duration in female initiation rituals and do not include the playing of enormous, jaguar-bone trumpets. The greater importance of Kuwái's musical instruments in male initiation rituals is reflected in the name *wakapétaka iénpitipé*, or "we show our children," referring to the climactic moment when adult men show the *dzáwiñápa* trumpets to male initiates. In addition to learning how to construct and play Kuwái's sacred instruments, male initiates are made to reflect upon the instruments' meanings through listening to the elders' narrations of the Kuwái myth cycle and other important myths. The young men also receive instruction in a variety of practical skills, such as weaving baskets, making fish traps, and building houses. Throughout the period of training, the elders frequently exhort the initiates to work hard. Female initiation rituals are less concerned with passing down practical and mythic knowledge than with attaching a sacred, mythic significance to the girl's menstruation. Because girls have already begun helping their mothers with child-rearing, gardening, and other adult tasks by the time they reach puberty, they need less practical instruction than boys, who are allowed to roam about in play-packs until their initiation. The name for female initiation rituals is *wakáitaka iénpiti*, or "we speak to our child," referring to the ritual advice that the girl receives from the chant-owner and other elders.

Males are initiated in groups representing more than one phratry, whereas females are individually initiated shortly after the onset of their first menstrual bleeding. Male initiation rituals are relatively large events in which three or more villages of people gather at the household of a renowned chant-owner during the entire four-week period of the boys' seclusion and training. Separate bowls of *káridzámai* food are prepared for each of the boys by their mothers and offered to the chant-owner by their fathers. Chanting, singing, dancing, and other ritual activities marking the transition back to secular reality last for three consecutive days and nights, and neither the boys nor their adult male kin are allowed to sleep or eat during the entire time. The ritual advising of male initiates is carried out in plural style, with each father giving advice to his own son in addition to collective speeches made by ritual specialists and senior women. In contrast to the prolonged series of performances in male initiation rituals, the entire sequence of dances, songs, chants, and advice making up female initiation rituals are compacted into a two-day period of activities. Collective attention is more sharply focused upon the individual girl-initiate (*wálimerú*), the sacred food, and the chant-owner's performance of ritual advice.

Due to the size and complexity of male initiation rituals, they are held far less frequently than the smaller, single-community initiations of females. Although external pressures from missionaries and merchants have undoubtedly contributed to a recent decline in male initiation rituals, they have probably always been held at wider intervals than female initiation rituals because of the practice of initiating age sets of males ranging from eight-year-old boys up to fifteen-year-old adolescents. Female initiation rituals are not postponed in this manner and can be held more than once in the same village within a few months' time, depending on the coming of age of young women. In Gavilán, people celebrated female initiation rituals in September of 1980, July and October of 1981, and February of 1985. In the same five-year interval, they held only one male initiation ritual in early 1985.

The following description and analysis of initiation rituals focuses primarily upon performances of *málikai* and ritual advice in female initiation rituals. Although there can be variations in the details of spirit-naming depending upon situational factors such as the social identity of the female initiate and the time of year when her initiation is held, the general processes of spirit-naming as a dynamic, musicalized search for the girl's mythic ancestors remain the same in all female initiation rituals. A girl's loss of blood at the onset of menarche places her into an ambiguous, potentially dangerous social category. Because of the strong associations between blood loss, soul loss, and spirits of the dead in *íyarudáti*, the pubescent girl is immediately placed into seclusion in a special compartment within her natal household and required to fast on drinks made from wild fruits and manioc flour. The flow of blood down from the body to the ground alienates her human body-shaped soul (*rukáriwa*) from the collective, animal-shaped soul (*rúarúna*) of her mythic ancestors. Along with the spilling of blood down into the ground, the girl's soul enters the ground and must be actively searched out in the chant-owner's performances of *málikai* songs and chants for her sacred food.

## *Female Initiation* (Wakáitaka Iénpiti)
### The Opening Song-Chant

Early on the morning of the girl's ritual coming out of seclusion, her mother cooked some of the freshly killed game meat in a pot of hot peppers. Other women gathered to make juices from wild palm fruits mixed with manioc flour. Around mid-morning, the mother came to offer the pot of boiled game meat and hot peppers to the chant-owner by placing it on the floor in front of his bench. Hernan and his brother stood up to accept the food in a formal conversation, called *yáphikai*, and instructed the girl's mother to bring white *yagrumo* (*Cecropia sp.*) leaves and a wide, shallow basket to cover the pot of food. They folded and wrapped the *yagrumo* leaves tightly over the food, leaving a tiny opening in one corner as a passageway for tobacco smoke. The overturned basket was then placed over the pot of food, and the two singer-chanters sat down with sacred *kadápu* whips in their right hands.

The opening performance of *málikai* for the female initiate's sacred food began with a few seconds of rapid percussive sounds as the chant-owner and his brother tapped on the overturned basket with their *kadápu* whips. The name of Dzúli, the first chant-owner, was forcefully sung out in a high baritone-to-low tenor range.

Dzo-re   Dzore  Dzore   Dzo-re Dzore-Dzore,   Dzo-re Dzore-Dzore

Using two lower, passing notes at the start of each phrase, the chant-owner proceeded to sing the names of Kuwái's ritual whips (*líwanápa éenu*), the dangerous jaguar-bone spirit-names (*dzáwi-ñápirríkuli*), and the celestial umbilical cord that connects these powerful mythic beings to the ground at Hípana, the center of the world. He returned several times to sing the name of Dzúli on higher notes, calling for Kuwái to come down to the ground at Hípana.[1] The opening performance of *málikai* was a breakthrough into the realm of sung speech. Movements between vertically separate pitches poetically constructed the vertical dimension of Kuwái's mythic creation. The extremely rapid tapping of whips added a parallel dimension of percussive sound to the poetic transformation of mythic speech into musical sound.

In the middle of the opening performance, Hernan simultaneously shifted from sung to chanted speech and slowed the tempo of his rhythmic tapping to a tempo of about ninety-eight beats per minute. After repeating the name of Dzúli several times on the same pitch, Hernan transformed his song into a steady pulse of chanted speech that strongly resembled the chants for *káridzámai* in childbirth rituals.

Dzo-re  Dzore-Dzore    Dzo-re  Dzore-Dzore

*Ménua-dám mápuru-kanám hlíakawa-nám káridza-mái wádza-wá*
So that the sickness does not fall into the sacred food, we go

*hnánua-dám hliépule-kwá ée-nú.*
to look for the umbilical cord-place in the sky.

*Hlínua-kárremi líaku-nám dzá-wí nápirri-kulí.*
It is killed, the name of the jaguar made from bone.

*Mátsia-karrú hnítsia-kám, rúperru-kanám rúmidza-ká*
So that no harm comes from the poison-sickness, she licks like this

*liáti-tenám, wárikani-rú iéni-pé.*
the hot peppers, the new female child.

*Hlíunawa-dám líwana-pú ée-nú.*
The name of *kadápu* whips, the corner of the sky, is called.

The transition from sung to chanted speech marked the completion of Kuwái's descent to the ground and the transformation of the vertical dimension of mythic power into a horizontal process of opening up the world.

The refrain verses of the opening song-chant use many of the same expressions as the verses for heaping up the names of edible animal species in the chants for the food of newborn infants and their parents. General categories of sickness, or of powerful beings that can cause disease, are named in order to negate their harmfulness through the purifying effects of licking hot peppers. The *kadápu* whip, both as a spirit-name and a musical instrument, embodies the chant-owner's power to transform sickness, death, and fear into a renewal of life, health, and happiness.

The naming of places in the remainder of the song-chant proceeds from Hípana to other sacred locations along the lower Aiarí River. The chant-owner does not stop at any of these places to heap up the names of fish and animal species, nor does he ascend the stream called Dzukwárri to name the place of Amáru's mythic home. The first place named after Hípana is *lidziúhaka-kwá dzákare*, a whirlpool near Hípana where Iñá-pirríkuli raised the mythic ancestors and gave sib names and tobacco spirits to each of them. The concern for chthonian, underground (or underwater) spiritual beings is a major theme throughout the chants for female initiation and evokes the mythic journeys of Amáru from place to place via subterranean passageways. Beneath the world of living people lies a shadow-world of deceased humans and the spirits of forest animal and bird species, and the chants for female initiation outline a subterranean journey that parallels the naming of rivers, villages, and other places in the surface world.

Other place-names along the lower Aiarí River connect the shamanistic search through the underworld to the celestial world of Kuwái and the ancestor spirits. *Máapari-kwá dzákare*, or "honey village-place," is one of the mythic homes of bee spirits, called *Kuwáiñai* (Kuwái-People). Bees are considered to be sacred animals, in part because their buzzing, humming sounds are similar to the musical humming of Kuwái in myth. Also, the ability of bees to make honey from the nectar of flowers associates them with immortality, since honey is both a prototypic curing substance and the sacred food of ancestor spirits in the celestial paradise of Iñápir-ríkuli. The chant-owner's evocation of honey and Kuwáinai spirits in this context forms part of a more general attempt to protect the female initiate by transforming images of bodily, cosmic danger into contrasting images of purity. Two other place-names along the lower Aiarí River that follow the same line of reasoning are *Dzáateri-kwá dzákare* (Toucan village-place) and *Dúkurepe-kwá dzákare* (White Cecropia leaf village-place). The toucan is named as a protective species because it feeds upon *seje* and other species of wild palm fruit that are the only safe food for initiates. The toucan (*dzáate*) is also the namesake for pairs of sacred flutes that represent the shoulder and arm of Kuwái's mythic body. White *yagrumo* leaves (*dúkurepe*) are wrapped over the female initiate's sacred food to keep harmful spirits from entering and to hold in the benevolent effects of the chant-owner's tobacco smoke.

The parallel musical journey through subterranean space begins at *Wapína-kwá dzákare*, the place where female initiates' souls (*rúarúna*) enter the shadow-world and disappear to other regions far downstream along the Río Negro. The opening song-chant ends at Wapína-kwá, the jumping-off point for a prolonged search for the initiate's wandering soul. The chant-owner leans forward, planting his knees and elbows on the clay floor of his house, and slowly lifts up one side of the overturned basket. A soft "Hm-m-m-p-p-f-f-f" and a rush of air and tobacco smoke emerge from his mouth and disappear into the pot of hot-peppered food.

## Málikai *Chants for Female Initiation*

The chants for female initiation continued for an entire day. Everyone in the village gathered to witness the elders' acceptance of the initiate's food and to hear the opening song-chant. The beginning of the female initiate's coming out of seclusion was an important moment for the entire community, since it marked the first stage in the dispersal of her natal family and a step toward her eventual departure to reside in her husband's village after marriage. Nevertheless, the formality of these initial performances was punctuated by periods of relaxation, drinking, and other festivities. Interludes between chants were filled with laughter and gaiety. For the rest of the day, men and women came and went, falling silent when Hernan was performing but sharing jokes and drinks with him between chants. In the day-long series of *málikai* chants for female initiation, the chant-owner outlined a complex series of movements along the Upper Río Negro and throughout the Içana-Guainía drainage area. In all, the twenty-one chants encompassed an encyclopaedic array of spirit-names and place-names that in one way or another touched upon nearly every major domain of indigenous social experience. Ecological knowledge about plant and animal species was integrated with historical, social, and geographic details into the general framework of Amáru's musical opening up of Kuwái's mythic creation. Along the way, the names of a myriad of spirits and places alluded to a correspondingly diverse set of mythic episodes. In short, the chants for female initiation did not construct a neat, tightly organized classification of edible plant and animal species but a heterogeneous mixture of species, objects, and places, all in perpetual motion.

In his search for the female initiate's soul, the chant-owner filled in the world of forests and rivers with an intricate mosaic of specific places. In a general sense, the naming of places mapped out four subregions centered around the ancestral lands of the Dzáwinai phratry, or the middle Içana River.

1. The center of mythic space-time along the Aiarí River and its tributaries, including the stream called Dzukwárri (curved) that flows from Mútsipáni.

2. Downstream places along the Río Negro, the lower Içana, Xié, Tomo, and lower Guainía rivers. This area includes São Gabriel, a city on the Upper Río Negro and important focus of interethnic relations between indigenous and European peoples in the colonial period.

3. A northern triangle of territories along the Aki, middle and upper Guainía, and Cuyarí rivers.

4. Upstream locations along the Içana River, centering around the rapids called *Inhída-kwá dzákare*, or the place where Kuwái vomited up the remains of the three boys who ate *guaco* fruits.

For convenience and clarity, the set of chants are numbered one through twenty-three, where "1" refers to the opening song-chant, "2–22" to the series of twenty-one chants, and "23" to the closing song. The chant-owner devotes six or seven performances of *málikai* to the naming of places and species in the first (1, 18–23), second (2–8), and fourth (12–17) of these subregions but only one chant (11) for the third subregion. Two chants (8, 9) near the middle of the series focus upon the ancestral Dzáwinai territory along the middle Içana River (see Figure 5.1).

The dominant principle of spirit-naming throughout the set of chants is that of "searching for the names," but the principle of "heaping up the names" is also important at major points of transition in the naming of places. The two naming processes are combined to create images of a cumulative expansion of species and places. After naming plant and animal species along the Río Negro, for example, the chant-owner names *Amáru-kwá dzákare*, or "the place of Amáru," a lake where she attempted to hide from Iñápirríkuli in myth. Once there, he names all the approximately sixty plant and animal species that he had previously named in earlier chants so that he can take them up the Içana and over to the Xié and Tomo rivers. Each movement, in other words, is an expan-

5.1    *Spatial movements in* málikai *chants for female initiates' food*

sion of the plant and animal species that make up Kuwái's mythic body
as well as an opening up of horizontal, social, and geographic space.
When he reaches a new region, the chant-owner begins by asserting that
the fish spirit-names from the other river, or downstream, have arrived
and mixed (*natsíkiakau*) with the fish spirit-names in the new, upstream
location. The total number of fish and other natural species continues to
increase, so that by the time the chant-owner has completed naming
places in the first, or downstream, subregion, he has named over one
hundred species of plants and animals.

From this point on, the principle of "heaping up the names" becomes
a means for abridging the process of naming edible species, a sort of
ritual shorthand that allows the chant-owner to quickly gather up all the
spirit-names in an area before taking them to be mixed with those in a
different area. To speed up his journey, the chant-owner needs only to
name major categories of spirits, such as *áati* (hot peppers), *umáwari*

(aquatic animal species), *éenunai* (forest animal species), and *képinai* (bird species), without taking time to fill up each category with individual names. This accelerated version of heaping up the names is performed at three places: Tonowí (*Dúduahípani-kwá dzákare*), the Guainía River (*Wapádzawídza*), and the upper Içana River (*Iniárri*). Tonowí is a large Dzáwinai village situated near a relatively high stone outcropping with a small pond at its summit. In a narrative about Uliámali, the anaconda child, a cosmic flood caused the world to shrink in size until only the top of the hill at Tonowí remained. With all the natural species of Kuwái's creation crowded into this small space, Dzúli, the first chant-owner, invented the practice of heaping up the names.[2]

In *málikai* chants for female initiation, "heaping up the names" and "searching for the names" are woven together to form a macrosemantic, snowballing process of accelerating growth and expansion. The chant-owner's metaphorical bringing of fish and other species from one subregion to another is related to indigenous cycles of ceremonial exchange, called *pudáli*. *Irápaka*, the verb used to describe dancing in *pudáli*, is also the term used to denote the spawning activities of fish species, and the names of fish species are applied to instruments, melodies, and dances. In short, *pudáli* ceremonial cycles were contexts in which exchanges of fish and other food products formed part of a broader process of signification that compared human social interaction to the natural reproductive behaviors of fish species and that blurred the boundaries of cultural separateness between human beings and fishes.

The metaphorical comparison of fishes and peoples that becomes dramatically and explicitly constructed in musical-dances of *pudáli* is only implicitly alluded to in *málikai* chants for female initiation. Although *málikai* chants for initiation are about the mythic opening up of a horizontal dimension of exchange relations between distinct peoples, the language used in *málikai* chants does not explicitly refer to human social groups but to fish species. Nevertheless, the interpretation of *málikai* chants for female initiation as a metaphorical expression of the mixing of fishes and peoples from different areas is not totally beyond the range of indigenous discourse, at least at the level of specialists who perform *málikai*. In July 1984, when Hernan and I were listening to tape recordings of the October 1981 female initiation ritual, he commented that fish species from the middle Içana River mixed with those at Tonowí in the same way that the Máuliwéni and other peoples from the lower Içana 'mixed,' or intermarried, with the people living at Tonowí. In a more general sense, the overall pattern of place-naming in *málikai* chants from downstream to upstream locations symbolically replicates the migratory routes of fish species from downstream locations along the Río Negro in dry seasons to the headwaters of the Içana and Guainía rivers in wet seasons. Early in the long wet season, vast schools of *Leporinus* fish are captured in traps as they seek to return to the rivers' main channels after spawning in newly flooded areas. In the past, the brief superabundance of *Leporinus* fish at the beginning of long wet seasons was the ideal time for initiating ceremonial cycles, so it is probable that the downsteam-to-upstream orientation of *málikai* chants paralleled not only the ecology of fish spawning runs but also the sociopolitical process of food exchange and intermarriage among phratries.[3]

Both *málikai* chants for female initiation and the musical-dances of *pudáli* share a common sociological grounding in the dispersal of patrilineal kin groups through musically opening up a horizontal dimension of mythic, social space. In this sense, *málikai* chants for female initiation symbolically produce affinal exchange relations that are in turn reproduced through symbolic activities of giving, eating, drinking, dancing, and making music together in *pudáli*. In both performative genres, musical sounds act as the principal medium for transforming affinal Others from potentially hostile enemies who are culturally and spatially distant into allies who share the same naturalized social space.

The use of natural species as metaphors for constructing human processes of social reproduction is closely interrelated with indigenous conceptions of the afterlife as a place where semi-human, semi-animal beings mingle with each other and ambiguously straddle the boundary between living and dead beings. Shadow-spirits of the dead are said to pass the time by performing the musical-dances of *pudáli*.[4] In female initiation rituals, the girl-initiate's losses of menstrual blood and ancestral soul are counteracted through the chant-owner's search across the world of forests and rivers and a parallel, subterranean journey through the houses of the dead belonging to different patrilineal descent groups. *Máliwéko*, the general term for the place of forest animal (*éenunai*) and bird (*képinai*) spirits in *íyarudáti*, is named in the tenth chant, followed by the naming of various forest animal species. Later, the chant-owner invokes several houses of the dead in *íyarudáti: ádaru-kwá dzákare* (the house of a lower-ranked Dzáwinai sib), *Páicipána-kwá dzákare* (the house of Hernan's group, a highly ranked Dzáwinai sib), *Pámari-kwá dzákare* (the house of a lower-ranked Waríperídakéna sib), and *Héemapána-kwá dzákare* (the house of the highest-ranked Waríperídakéna sib). Like the naming and metaphorical mixing of fish spirits, the naming of *Máliwéko*, houses of the dead, and associated forest animal and bird spirits provides a discourse for speaking about the relations among living peoples in an implicit, indirect manner. The only group of living human beings named in the course of the chants is the Dzáwinai phratry of the middle Içana River, the social group of which both Hernan and the girl-initiate, his brother's granddaughter, are members. Other peoples are named only through the metaphors of natural species, places, and houses of the dead.

Spirit-naming of cultivated plant species forms an additional dimension of meaning in *málikai* chants for female initiation. In contrast to the spirits of edible animal species (*umáwari, éenunai,* and *képinai*), the spirits of domesticated plant species are not harmful beings that must be "killed" or "cooked" but benevolent spirits that assist the chant-owner in his search for the initiate's soul. The name of Káali, the mythic originator of manioc and all other cultivated plant species, is used as a categorical term for manioc and other garden products. The varieties of hot pepper are so central to the chants' purpose of purifying the initiate's food that they form a separate category of spirit-names within the general domain of Káali's plant species. Like the naming of different varieties of tobacco in *málikai* chants for the tools and weapons of newborn infants' fathers, the refrain sections of chants for female initiation contain lists of *áati* spirit-names to protect the female initiate.

*Mátsia-karrú mápuru-kanám, rúperru-kanám rúmidza-ká*
So that the sickness does no harm, she licks like this

　*líati-tenám, wárikani-rú iéni-pé.*
　the hot pepper, the new female child.

*Líanawa-dám áati-tenám hlírama-híawa Hér-rí,*
It is called, the reddish hot pepper of Hérri,

　*áati-tenám Hérripina-hiári áa-tí.*
　the cutting, saw-grass hot pepper of Hérri.

*Líanawa-dám líati-tenám hlíaku-ná dzá-wí nápirriku-lí,*
It is called, the name of the hot pepper of the jaguar made from bones,

　*Liápi-dzám hlítada-hwía dzá-wí nápirriku-lí.*
　Then the name of the greenish hot pepper of the jaguar made from bones.

*Liápi-dzám hlíanawa-dám áati-tenám Dzúlipina-hiári áa-tí.*
Then it is called, the cutting, saw-grass hot pepper of Dzúli.

Like tobacco, hot peppers have the power to transform the harmfulness (*línupána*) of edible animal species, and the chant-owner names all reddish and greenish colored varieties of peppers to purify the female initiate's food. However, yellowish varieties of hot pepper are deliberately excluded from these invocations, since the yellowish coloring is said to be harmful to the girl initiate. Spirit-names of two varities of hot pepper are based on the word *pína*, or "saw-grass," a property that makes them useful for metaphorically cutting off the heads of fish and animal spirits.

With one notable exception, spirit-naming of other cultivated plant species is optional, since the spirits of garden produce are not as ritually powerful as those of hot pepper. The chant-owner is obligated to include the spirit-name for manioc bread (*péte*) after naming *Kwaríru-kwá dzákare*, a place on the upper Içana River where manioc cultivation began in mythic times. Manioc bread is the main staple of the indigenous diet, and the breads are eaten together with all other kinds of fruits, vegetables, and meats. When no other foods are available in periods of scarcity, manioc breads keep people alive, and the breads are a ritually safe food for individuals recovering from illness or injury, no matter how severe. The spirit-name of manioc bread, *likáriwa Káali* (the stomach of Káali), expresses its pervasiveness in everyday social life. As the metaphorical stomach of human society, manioc breads are named in female initiation rituals so that the girl eats well and grows rapidly after ending her ritual fast.

Spirit-naming of places and species in *málikai* does not form a closed, mythic order that coldly classifies reality but a dynamic, open-ended musicalization of mythic discourse that explores historically changing realities. Amáru embodies the principle of historical transformation, and indigenous interpretations of history are often grounded in metaphors of female anatomy and physiology. The category of Amáru's hot spirit-names, as we have seen, illustrates how an indigenous metaphor can be creatively extended to provide interpretations of new objects of experience, or steel tools and diseases brought into the Upper Río Negro region by European peoples in the colonial period. In female initiation rituals, performances of *málikai* songs and chants are a type of historical discourse that draws upon the mythic journey of Amáru as a metaphor for exploring the ever-changing patterns of material-political relations among Wakuénai phratries of the Içana-Guainía drainage area. As in *málikai* chants for childbirth rituals, objects that symbolize the beginning of historical relations with European peoples are imbued with great powers and must be named near the beginning of ritual performances. Predictably, however, the chants for female initiation do not focus upon material objects or artifacts but upon animal species and places.

Spirit-names for places inhabited by Europeans are prevalent in chants 3 and 4 during the chant-owner's journey through the second, or downstream, subregion. These spirit-names consist of archaic Portuguese and *lingua geral* names for sites along the Upper Río Negro, such as *Camanão*, Kurukwí, Fortaleza, and San Miguel, followed by the usual ritual suffixes for places (*-kwá dzákare*). Such towns were mission settlements, military outposts, and trading posts near the river port of São Gabriel and they formed the point of entry for European peoples, along with their material culture and diseases, into the Içana-Guainía drainage area during the early years of the eighteenth century (Wright 1981; Hemming 1987). The Europeans also introduced new, domesticated animal species into the Upper Río Negro region, and these species are referred to collectively as *rucámpo ruyéni sAmáru*, or "the pasture-children of Amáru." Under this general heading, two species of livestock receive spirit-names in chants for female initiation. *Hnárekáda éenunai*, or "the whitish forest animal-spirit," designates the pig, and *nátsuwána éenunai* ("the horned forest animal-spirit") is the ritual name for cattle. Aside from their spirit-names in ritual, there are no terms in the everyday dialects of Wáku for these species.[5]

The mythic journeys of Amáru away from Hípana and back to her home at Mútsipáni provide the basic metaphorical frame of reference for the naming of places in female initiation rituals. An initial movement downstream, or away and across the world from the center of mythic space, is completed through a final return to the center. Immediately prior to this return, the chant-owner heaps up the spirit-names of fish and other animal species from the headwaters of the Içana River and brings them to be mixed with animal spirits along the Aiarí River. Through a short series of place-names that excludes the most sacred places along the Aiarí, the chant-owner quickly reaches *Mátsitsi-kwá dzákare*, a place at the headwaters of the Aiarí River where Kuwái created the sweet-smelling *tsipátsi* grass that men wear when they play the sacred flutes and trumpets. Having mixed together the fish spirits from the upper Içana and Aiarí rivers, the two westernmost areas in Wakuénai territory, the chant-owner has finished the naming and mixing together of all the animal spirits in Kuwái's creation. His musical journey through mythic space has followed the sun's path (*Kamúi Yápwaa*, or the Milky Way) from the most easterly, downstream areas along the Río Negro in the chants performed before noon, to the central and northerly territories along the middle Içana and upper Guainía rivers during the early afternoon, and up into the most westerly territories of the upper Içana and Aiarí rivers in the late afternoon.

The sun was low on the horizon as the chant-owner began to name sacred places along the curved stream, called *Dzukwári-kwá dzákare*, that connects the Aiarí River to Mútsipáni, a massive stone hillside where only the most powerful chant-owners and master-shamans may safely travel. As in the opening song-chant, the place-names come one after another in rapid succession without the naming of animal species: *Anáda-kwá dzákare*, a point of land named after the large pestles used to mash sugar cane and other foods; *Máapanai-kwá dzákare*, the place where Kuwái stopped to eat honey; and *Hwáipani-kwá dzákare*, the place where Kuwái made the first *kadápu* whips for initiation rituals. At last, in the final chant of the day, the chant-owner named *Múdipáni-kwá dzákare* (Mútsipáni). *Múdi*, or *mútsi*, is a species of oily white palm-grubs that people harvest after felling palm trees for initiations and other rituals. In myth, *mútsi* grubs were the food that intoxicated Kuwái and led him to reveal his secrets to Kálimátu, a messenger from the world of people below. *Mútsipáni*, or the dance of *mútsi* grubs, is the space-time of Amáru and the women's triumph over Iñápirríkuli in the struggle for control over Kuwái's flutes and trumpets. Like the dark netherworld of spirits of the dead in *íyarudáti*, the place where the sun falls, Mútsipáni is a strangely, almost surrealistically, paradoxical place where the social world is turned upside-down and inside-out. Mútsipáni, in short, is a metaphor for the social contradiction embodied in the female initiate, whose initiation into the cult of Kuwái simultaneously includes her as an adult member of her patrisib and excludes her from it in preparation for the eventual movement to her husband's village.

The final performance of *málikai* for the sacred food of female initiates reverses the initial transformation of sung speech into chanted speech. Using exactly the same set of tones as the opening song-chant, the chant-owner names the places at the center of mythic space to upwardly construct the vertical dimension of mythic space: *Hípana-kwá, hliépule-kwá éenu*, and *líwana-pú éenu*. The *kadápu* whips sound out a prestissimo tempo upon the overturned basket covering the girl's food. The entire village assembled to hear the closing song and witness the final blessing of the food. Stooped over on the ground, the chant-owner prayed that the girl be protected from sickness, and especially the curse of infertility. He paused several times to blow tobacco smoke into the pot of food with the characteristic "Hm-m-m-p-p-f-f" sounds of *ínyapakáati*.

## Musical Dynamics in the Chants for Female Initiation

In opening and closing songs, the chant-owner uses identical tones to construct musically the downward and upward movements of Kuwái. These songs create a stable, tonal center of gravity around which the chant-owner weaves a counterpoint of centripetal and centrifugal movements across the horizontal dimension of mythic space. The semantic processes of moving through places in search of the female initiate's soul and the cumulative growth of animal species through heaping up and mixing together their spirit-names are paralleled by multidimensional processes of musical movement through tones, tempos, volumes, and timbres.

The clearest expressions of musical movement through horizontal space are the use of different starting pitches in different chants and the microtonal rising of pitch within chants. Although the same starting pitch is used at different places in the series of twenty-one chants, no two consecutive performances start on the same pitch. At several points in the series of chants, the starting pitch drops a whole tone interval between consecutive performances. Microtonal rising of pitch within chants augments the movements between different starting pitches. As a general rule, the chants do not rise in pitch by more than a chromatic half-step. Six chants (2, 9, 11, 13, 17, and 19) begin and end on the exact same pitch, while the majority, or twelve, chants (3, 4, 5, 6, 7, 14, 15, 16, 18, 20, and 22) rise a chromatic half-step or less from beginning to end. One chant (21) rises slightly more than a half-step, and two chants (8 and 10) rise more rapidly, ending over three half-steps higher than they began.

The overall pattern of starting pitches and microtonal rising is represented in relation to the stable vertical dimension of sung pitches in opening and closing songs in Figure 5.2. Reading the figure from left to right provides an approximate musical transcription of the chant-owner's day-long series of performances and musical opening up of the horizontal dimension of mythic space. In chant 2, the starting pitch is lower than the principal tones of the opening song-chant, and there is a gradual rising of pitch through the end of chant seven. In chants 8 through 10,

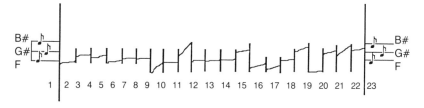

5.2  *Sung pitches of opening and closing songs (1 and 23) and chanted pitches of* málikai *performances for food of female initiates (2 through 22).*

the starting pitches ascend more rapidly through microtonal rising. The pitch continues to fall and gradually rise in a wavelike pattern at fairly regular intervals throughout the remaining chants (11–14, 15–18, 19–22) before returning to the vertical dimension of sung pitches in the closing song. The general pattern of tonal motion in the series of chants roughly parallels the naming of downstream-to-upstream locations in each of the major subregions (see Figure 5.1).

Other dimensions of musical sound support the basic techniques of tonal motion. Gradual acceleration of tempo compresses time and, like the rapid heaping up of names, speeds the performers toward their final destination. The initial tempo of 98 beats per minute is increased to as high as 112 beats per minute. Because of the way *kadápu* whips are used like metronomes to rhythmically pound out the tempo of each chant, even the slightest acceleration is highly noticeable. Like the snowballing, cumulative growth of animal spirit-names, volume increases during each chant, especially in those where tonal rising and tempo change more rapidly.

The most subtle form of musical dynamics in the chants is the alternation between different vocal timbres. A basic contrast is developed between sung speech that is louder, higher in pitch, and more tense and chanted speech that is softer, lower in pitch, and more relaxed. The greater tension of sung speech can be discerned as a more forceful, sudden attacking of notes than in chanted speech, where the attack is smoother. The contrast between sung and chanted timbres is set up during the opening performance through the transformation of higher, sung pitches into lower, chanted pitches. Throughout the set of chants, the same constrast between chanted and sung speech is embodied in two practices. First, the last word of each phrase is sung by the accompanist (or apprentice), whose voice doubles that of the chant-owner. Since the powerful spirit-names of places and categories of natural species (e.g., *dzákare, áati, éenu, éenunai*) are nearly always placed at the end of lines, the effect of the accompanist's singing is to accentuate the rapid movements between places and categories of spirit-names. The other way of employing the sung or chanted speech contrast is only audible in those chants where tonal and rhythmic changes are most pronounced. In these few cases, the two ends of the chanted-to-sung spectrum are effectively bridged by moving gradually from a more relaxed, chanted vocal timbre into a more tense, sung timbre that is on the boundary between chanted and sung speech.

## The Ritual Advice

At the conclusion of the final blessing for the female initiate's food, Hernan removed the overturned manioc basket and slowly stood up with the pot of food in his hands. His brother followed him outside onto the village plaza, carrying the two *kadápu* whips in his right hand. Men, women, and children gathered around the plaza, where the chant-owner set the pot of food down on a small, palm-leaf mat and stood over it with the two *kadápu* whips raised in his right hand. The movement of the sacred food from inside to outside parallels the end of the female initiate's ritual seclusion, and the girl's mother led her outside to the village plaza. The girl's entire body was painted red with *kérawídzu*, and she stood silently next to the food on the palm-leaf mat. As the sun began to set over the forest, the festive atmosphere of laughter and drinking that had prevailed throughout the morning and afternoon gave way to anger and tension. A senior woman set the tone for the initiate's ritual advice by shouting for the chant-owner to start his speech.

The chant-owner commenced his advice slowly and deliberately with a number of comments about the past, before there were white people living nearby. In those days, he explained, before the white men came to interfere with their lives by telling them not to make their children suffer so much, young people fasted for an entire month. In a low, rumbling baritone voice, he exhorted the girl to listen carefully to the advice because these were the same words that his father had given him as a young man and the same ones spoken by the ancient people who lived before the coming of the whites. With rising tension in his voice, Hernan told his granddaughter that she will henceforth act as an adult woman (*ínarru*), not as a child, because she knows the pain of hunger. With his right hand, he angrily gestures toward his granddaughter as he speaks.

*Pihánewátsa kaikána máwitakái!*
You know that it hurts, this hunger!

*Apáda nawíki nahliúkawa panáku, pikápawátsa phiúmi nawíki,*
When other people arrive at your house, you share with all people,

*pikápawátsa phiúmi yárananáitsaka, wanéwe wéyma nápekúriko!*
you share with white people, we live together with all of them!

*Pikápawátsa phiúmi nawíki!*
You share with all people!

*Pakápa páita idzáada, karrútsa panáitukáni!*
When you look upon another's things, do not steal them!

*Pikápa hnúa, pihwérri, karrú hnipáka káidali,*
Look at me, your grandfather, I do not touch poison,

*márikarrúka nuína nunaíki kéwerri!*
I would never kill any person whatsoever!

*Pikápa hnúa, pihwérri, kamátsa nuíñapáka matsiádali,*
Look at me, your grandfather, the only way I blow smoke is good,

*karrú nuínapáka hiwiáti, karrú nuíñuka rumíta nawíki!*
I do not blow smoke to cause harm, I do not kill other people!

*Kwámakátsa pádua ináka phía, karrútsa kérruáka;*
Whenever your mother gives you an order, do not get angry;

*pihepáka pádua, mátsarapitáka ruitáwiyíka phía!*
listen to your mother, for she has worked very hard for you!

*Pikápa hnúa, pihwérri, karrútsa nukúitaka phía;*
Look at me, your grandfather, I am not accusing you;

*máhia pándzarikúita; nukáite pakúitaka phía!*
this is what you think; I advise you, not accuse!

*Pikápa pikhírri, karrútsa kérruáka, kwákadakátsa pípanawátsa,*
Look at your father's brother, do not get angry, whatever he asks of you,

*píshiwáni, áati!*
you plant it, hot pepper!

*Karrú pakáshataka!!*
Do not tell lies!!

*Pikápa hnúa, pihwérri, núnu nuéma ayáha nápekúriko hnatsáka,*
Look at me, your grandfather, I come to live here together with them,

*hnána nawíki, yárananítsaka!*
these people, with white people, too!

*Karrú kwamkwárika dzékatáka máatsia, málinuémaka matsiá!*
Never do I wrong them, so I live well and peacefully!

*Pikápa hnúa, pihwérri, karrútsa kwámkwárika nudáwa,*
Look at me, your grandfather, I never hide things,

*nudáwa nuwíni, nuhniáwada, apáda nawíki pédza nuwíni!*
hide my game meat, my food, from other people!

*Karrútsa pakitsínda kátsapatsáta, phiúmi nawíki!*
It is not just with your family that you share but with all people!

*Pikápa hnúa, pihwérri, yaranáwi hliúkawa nunáku, nualína nuhniáwada!*
Look at me, your grandfather, if a white man arrives at my house, I give him my food!

*Pikápa hnúa pihwérri, hnúa matsiádali, núa pihwérri!*
Look at me, your grandfather, I am good, I, your grandfather!

*Pikapámta mátsiedalíka hnúa, kárrumíta pitáita piépaka nuáku!*
If you saw me as a bad person, you could not receive my word!

*Pikápa hnúa, pihwérri, katsáka kwámkwárika nuínuaka apáda yapídza!*
Look at me, your grandfather, never do I fight with other people!

*Nudiwána kapwámta, katsáka kwámkwárika*
I get drunk, never

*nuinuáka panírri yapídzakámta, nepikhírri yapídzaka!*
do I fight with your father, nor with your father's brother!

By this time, the chant-owner's voice had become extremely agitated, and other elders joined in with additional words of advice. In the twilight, the chant-owner and his granddaughter stood and listened to the elders' advice, their profiles silhouetted against the river's smooth, mirrorlike surface. When the elders had spoken, the chant-owner removed the protective cover of white *yagrumo* leaves from the *káridzámai* and lifted a hot pepper, together with a small morsel of boiled meat, up to the girl's mouth on the ends of the two *kadápu* whips. *"Piéhnewátsa káika máwitakái!"* (You feel the pain of hunger!), interjected one of the girl's grandmothers. With the pain of hunger in her stomach and the burning of hot pepper in her mouth, the female initiate experienced the fiery death and rebirth of Kuwái. Even as two loud cracks of the *kadápu* whip slammed into her back and rang out in the silence of the evening, her face showed no pain.

As a form of verbal art, the ritual advice given to initiates is contextually and stylistically related to performances of *málikai* songs and chants for initiation. The *káridzámai* or sacred food, becomes a substance that binds the chant-owner's musical search for the girl-initiate's soul together with the moral values of a community of people. When the food is taken outside and eventually lifted up to the initiate's mouth in full view of the elders, the dynamic transformation of Kuwái's mythic creation into a plurality of distinct peoples and places is transferred from the realm of poetic, sung, and chanted speech into words and objects that all the adult members of the community can fully understand. The ritual advice for female initiation is not only a statement about the moral values implicit in Kuwái's mythic creation but a performative genre that has musical, poetic qualities. Like the chants for initiation, the ritual advice begins in a relatively low, relaxed vocal timbre that becomes progressively more tense and high-pitched. Both tempo and volume increase steadily during the speech, ranging from relatively soft, slow-paced comments about the historical past at the beginning of the speech to the hyperanimated, forceful commands aimed directly at the female initiate and referring to her senior kin in the final part of the speech.

The ritual advice and whipping of the girl-initiate bring to an end the activities of *wakáiteka iénpiti*, or "we speak to our child." Before she can eat the *káridzámai* to end her ritual fast, the girl must bathe in the river and wash away the red *kérawídzu* paint from her body. Bathing in the river is an act of purification that cools the girl's body after her fiery transformation. In a mythic narrative about the Kuwáiñai, or bee-spirits, bathing in the river at night is the prototypic act of purification and is associated with the making of honey from flowers. In the context of female initiation rituals, the girl's bath marks the achievement of her new status as a young adult, or "newly fasted person" (*wálitáki*), who may safely eat the sacred *káridzámai* food of the ancestor spirits. The girl's mother leads her back home, carrying the sacred food in one arm and the *kadápu* whips in the other. For the initiate, eating the *káridzámai* is not a metaphor for the individual's socialization through internalizing socialized animal nature (as it is for the parents of newborn infants) but a symbolic transformation of the individual's socialization into a collective process of creating and reproducing horizontal relations of exchange among different peoples.

The *káridzámai* is an embodiment of the symbolic overdetermination of exchange relations among Wakuénai phratries, and the ambiguous inclusivity and exclusivity of horizontal exchange relations continues to motivate ritual attention to the newly initiated girl's food for the years between her initiation and marriage. Each new species of food, including wild fruits and garden produce, as well as fish and game meat, is the object of a short *málikai* blessing as it enters the young woman's diet during the months and years after her initiation. Like the shadow-spirits of recently deceased persons in *íyarudáti,* the recently initiated female is no longer just a descendant of the local mythic ancestors but a person whose soul has gone elsewhere and become an Other living among her own kin.

## Málikai *Chants for Male Initiation*

In common with songs and chants for female initiation, those performed in male initiation rituals outline a spatial journey that opens up the horizontal dimension of mythic space between opening and closing songs that construct Kuwái's vertical descent and ascent, respectively. *Málikai* songs and chants for male initiation make use of the same principles of musical movement through tones, timbres, tempos, and volumes. However, the naming of places in male initiation chants reverses and expands the pattern of place-naming in chants for female initiation. In the latter, the series of chants begins at Hípana, the place of mythic emergence, and moves immediately to downstream locations on the Río Negro. Only at the end of the series of chants for female initiation does the chant-owner name places along the curved stream that leads to Amáru's mythic home. In male initiation rituals, the first three performances of *málikai* are devoted to naming places, including Mútsipani, along Dzukwárri stream, and the chant-owner passes directly from the mouth of the Aiarí River up to Hípana in his naming of places during the last three chants. In short, the process of naming places in *málikai* chants for male initiation rituals begins at Mútsipani, the last place named in chants for female initiation rituals.

The opposite directions of place-naming in male and female initiation rituals make sense in terms of Part II of the Kuwái myth cycle. In myth, male initiation was a collective male reversal of Amáru's removal of Kuwái's sacred musical instruments from Hípana to Mútsipáni. Disguised as molítu frogs, Iñápirríkuli and the men traveled to Mútsipani and brought the sacred flutes and trumpets back to Hípana. Thus, male initiation was a further transformation of society and cosmos that took place after Amáru and the women had invented female initiation rituals.

Just as the pattern of spatial movements in *málikai* chants for male initiation reverses the direction of movements in female initiation chants, so also does the timing of male initiation chants reverse that of female initiation chants. *Málikai* chants for female initiation begin in the morning and end just before sunset in the late afternoon. In male initiations, the opening song-chant is performed late in the evening, the time when people usually go to sleep for the night, and the final chant is performed an hour after sunrise the next morning.

The naming of places in *málikai* chants for male initiation also expands the range of geographic space covered in female initiation chants. For male initiation rituals, the chant-owner names places from the headwaters of the Vaupés River all the way down the Río Negro to Manaus and beyond, to Tsówai, the cosmic sea. From there, he returns to the Içana River and in one long, continuous series of place-names, he musically travels from the headwaters of the Içana to the upper Guainía and Cuyarí rivers, down the Guainía to Caño Pimichin, through the Temi and Atacavi rivers, down the Atabapo, Inírida, and Orinoco rivers until finally reaching Tsówai, the cosmic sea (see Figure 5.3).

The expansion of socio-geographic space in *málikai* chants for male initiation is a metaphor for the historical opening up of political relations between Wakuénai phratries of the Içana-Guainía drainage area and other peoples in the Northern Amazon and Orinoco basins. As in *málikai* chants for female initiation, spirit-names for places and natural species provide a discourse for speaking indirectly about the social relations among different peoples. However, the chants for male initiation are concerned with the negation of Otherness among Wakuénai phratries and the unity of adult, initiated males throughout the indigenous territory vis-à-vis neighboring peoples who occupy adjacent territories to the southwest, southeast, northwest, and northeast. By initiating young men from two or more phratries at the same time, male initiation reverses the process of creating Otherness within the language group in female initiation in order to (re)produce political alliances between phratries that can be mobilized against outside ethnolinguistic groups. Indigenous statements

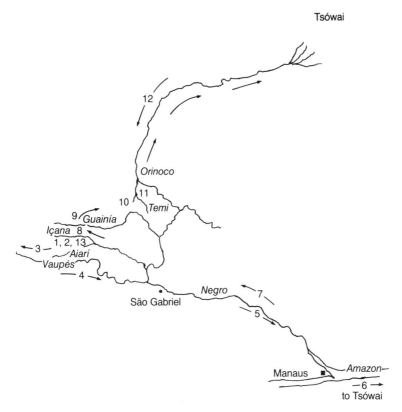

5.3    *Spatial movements in* málikai *chants for food of male initiates*

about warfare and political alliances tend to portray interphratic ties as having had primarily defensive purposes, such as the expulsion of outside intruders. Nevertheless, several narratives point to the ability of the cult of Kuwái and the ancestors to absorb smaller, conquered groups by making them into the lowest-ranked sibs of larger, more powerful and highly ranked sibs. The origins of two "workers," or lowest-ranked sibs, the *Hírridakéna* (Rat's Grandchildren) and the *Makúliéni* (Children of the Makú), are attributed to their defeat in warfare by high-ranking Adzanéni and Waríperídakéna sibs, respectively.

By naming places along the entire length of the Vaupés River in male initiation chants, the chant-owner musically defines a historical frontier area where Northern Arawakan and Eastern Tukanoan peoples have carried out relations of warfare, trade, and intermarriage for many generations. The absorption of two Arawak-speaking phratries as lower-ranked members of the Cubeo social order (Goldman 1963: 26) has effectively created a buffer zone of Eastern Tukanoan speakers who are politically neutral because they are not fully accepted as human beings by either the Eastern Tukanoan phratries of the central Vaupés Basin or the Wakuénai phratries of the Içana-Guainía drainage area. Because the Cubeo do not practice language group exogamy, other Eastern Tukanoan peoples regard them as politically distant Others.[6] The Wakuénai express a similarly neutral, or ambivalent, attitude toward the Cubeo, who are called *Táwináwi* (from *táwi*, a tree species) in *málikai* chants for male initiation. According to myth, Kuwái looked upon the Cubeo people and saw that they did not have power, or danger (*línupána*), so they were able to eat "strong" foods immediately after dancing with sacred flutes and trumpets. Thus, the Cubeo are both included and excluded from Wakuénai political relations, for they were "looked upon" by Kuwái yet did not receive sacred *málikai* songs and chants for harnessing the power of Kuwái.[7] Other Eastern Tukano-speaking groups, such as the Uanano and Desana, who reside along the middle Vaupés also form part of the buffer zone between the Wakuénai and their Eastern Tukanoan neighbors to the southwest.

Irrespective of the defensive or offensive implications of the motif of political-historical expansion embodied in *málikai* chants for male initiation, the cult of Kuwái and the ancestor spirits has continued to serve the Wakuénai as a power resource for negotiating interethnic relations along the lower Guainía River in Venezuela. The inclusion, albeit ambiguous, of Guarequena and Baniwa peoples as subjects of *málikai* chanting and singing was a common practice in 1980–81 and 1984–85. In addition to the Baniwa-Guarequena family who came from Sebucan for a childbirth ritual in 1981, Baniwa, Guarequena, and Yeral-speaking families frequently traveled to Gavilán to be treated with *málikai* counterwitchcraft songs and *málirríkairi* (shamans' songs). The relative ease with which these performances of Kuwái's sacred music allowed the Dzáwinai and Waríperídakéna families of Gavilán to transcend social boundaries between them and other Northern Arawakan language groups in the early 1980s suggests that the cult of Kuwái and the ancestors could have supported the political expansion of Northern Arawakan peoples throughout the Río Negro-middle Orinoco region prior to the arrival of European peoples in the seventeenth and eighteenth centuries.

The arrival of European missionaries, merchants, and slave traders in the Upper Río Negro and Orinoco brought about radical changes in the demography and ethnopolitical relations among colonized indigenous peoples. Like the chants for female initiation, *málikai* chants for male initiation rituals give expression to these colonial transformations through the metaphors of place-naming. In male initiations, the down-stream locations are not limited to the area around São Gabriel but extend the full length of the Río Negro and beyond it to the open sea. *Barcélo-kwá dzákare* or Barcelos, was the name of a major center of Portuguese colonial activity along the lower Río Negro during the 1740s (Hemming 1987:10-11), and *Barrá-kwá dzákare* (Barrá, or Manaus) was the capital through which the colonial government channeled goods and labor from the Upper Amazon, including some 20,000 indigenous slaves taken in the mid-eighteenth century from the Upper Río Negro to plantations in coastal areas. By naming these downstream locations in the chants for male initiation, the chant-owner musically constructs a historical discourse that metaphorically evokes the brutal Portuguese policy of *descimentos* (descents) in the eighteenth century. In addition to the threat of enslavement and forced relocation to downstream sites, the colonial Portuguese and Spanish intensified competition between the Wakuénai phratries and Eastern Tukanoan peoples of the Vaupés by forcing phratries along the Río Negro, lower Guainía, and lower Içana to seek refuge farther upstream in more remote, headwater areas.

## The Musicalization of Mythic Speech as Historical Discourse

In the cycle of narratives about Kuwái and Amáru, the Wakuénai under-stand their history as a dynamic musical transformation of mythic cre-ation. The most powerful, dramatic expression of the mythic creation of history is embodied in long sets of sacred *málikai* songs and chants per-formed during male and female initiation rituals. These performances directly embody mythic movements between the sky-world (*éenu*) and this world (*hekwápiríko*) as well as the movements between various places within this world. Movements between places are accomplished through verbal naming of diverse peoples and places in the special lan-guage of the mythic ancestors as well as through musical processes of movement across tones, tempos, rhythms, and timbres.

Male and female initiation rituals are complex rites of passage in which chant-owners and other senior kin of the initiates symbolically construct Kuwái's second mythic creation of the world. The collective construction of the world as an expansion, or opening up, is applied directly to the transformation of children, who are associated with the mythic primordium and Kuwái's first mythic creation, into fully socialized adults who participate in the social world of exchange relations between kin groups.

The horizontal opening up of the world is also directly embodied in the organization of musical sounds in *málikai* songs and chants. The opening and closing performances are sung rather than chanted or spoken, and by making use of exactly the same pitches, the two songs provide a stable, vertical tonal center around which the more dynamic chants, or "journeys," gravitate. Musical movements between vertically distinct pitches in the opening and closing performances of *málikai* poetically construct the mythic space-time of relations between powerful mythic ancestors in the sky-world and their living human descendants in this world. These vertical musical movements also embody the power to control movements within human society between developmental stages in the life cycle and between older and younger generations.

Between these two songs, the names of all places and animal species are chanted in a long series of performances that lasts for many hours. Horizontal movement, or displacement from the center of the world, is expressed in a variety of musical dimensions. The chants begin on different pitches, and the starting pitch is gradually sharpened through microtonal rising so that the final verses end up on a totally new pitch. The tempo is percussively sounded by striking *kadápu* whips on a basket that covers the initiates' sacred food (*káridzámai*), and the initial tempo is gradually increased during each chant. The chants also exhibit contrasting dynamics between loud and soft sounds, since the principal chanter's voice is doubled at the end of each verse by a second chanter. In male initiation rituals, the chanters' voices are accompanied from time to time by a collage of sounds made on the sacred flutes and trumpets. In short, the musicalization of mythic power uses tonal variation, microtonal rising, acceleration, and instrumental heterophony to directly embody the processes of horizontally journeying to other places, or becoming other peoples, and back. Musicalized mythic power is the poetic construction of a historical space-time through movements away from and back to the center of mythic and tonal space.

The naming of peoples, places, and natural species in *málikai* chants for initiation is a highly dynamic, musical process of "going in search of the names" (*wadzúhiakau nakúna*). Just as Iñápirríkuli had to search through every corner of this world to find Amáru and the sacred flutes, so must the chant-owner explore every nook and cranny of the collective historical experience of his people in searching for the initiate's soul. The more dynamic process of "searching for the names" always operates to-gether with the more stable, classificatory process of "heaping up the names in a single place" (*wakéetaka liakúna papínirítsa*). In the chants for initiation, for example, the chant-owner stops to "heap up the names" of fish, animal, and plant species at a number of key locations during his musical journey in search of the names. The "heap of names" is then brought to another location and "mixed together" with a new set of names, and so on, in a cumulative, accelerating expansion of names and places.

The arrival of European peoples into the Upper Río Negro is not ex-cluded from this musical, historical discourse but given active expression through the naming of places and animal species. Mythic, ancestral names for the places of European colonization are most prevalent in the chants dealing with the Río Negro and other downstream locations to the south and east of Wakuénai lands along the Içana and Guainía rivers at the headwaters of the Río Negro. These towns were mission settle-ments, military outposts, and trading posts near the river port of São Gabriel, and they formed the point of entry for European peoples, along with their material culture and diseases, into the Içana-Guainía drainage area during the early eighteenth century. The musical naming of these places in *málikai* chants for male and female initiation integrates a col-lective understanding of the historical creation of colonial situations of interethnic contact into the mythic creation of human society through the competition between Amáru and the trickster-creator for control over Kuwái's music.

For the Wakuénai, interpreting the history of Western colonial power in the Upper Río Negro region is neither a process of fitting new material into old molds, nor is it the invention of totally new modes of social consciousness. Instead, indigenous historical understanding arises from the transformation of narrative and ritual genres of discourse that explain how evolving, dynamic societies have come to share the same historical space-time. Anthropological discourses that have misrepresented Ama-zonian societies as "cold, mythic societies" (Lévi-Strauss 1966:234) have prevented an understanding of these societies as our historical contem-poraries. The Wakuénai have long since been forced to recognize Western peoples as part of their own history. They have not only preserved the memory of Western colonial power but en-chanted it into the musical reproduction of their social relations and into their narrative representa-tions of the original coming-into-being of human society and history.

In their ritual poetics, the Wakuénai take great care to integrate musical sound as completely as possible with semantic meanings and to en-shrine musical performance at the center of political power relations. His-tory is not just a set of past events recounted in narrative forms but a dynamic process of en-chanting and singing-into-being the imagery of mythic power and transformation. Just as spoken, chanted, and sung speech are deliberately and systematically intermingled to form complex poetic genres of ritual performance, so also is the history of interethnic relations among peoples in the Upper Río Negro region woven together with the mythic primordium and its transformations during the life cycle of the proto-human beings. Musical sounds are not separated from mythic meanings but directly embody the primary sources and relations of power. Vertical movements between distinct tones in sung speech icon-ically embody the movements of individuals between developmental stages in the life cycle, the turning over of generations, and the movement of mythic beings from "up above and outside" to "down on the ground and inside" human social space. Horizontal movements in chanted and sung speech embody the movements "away across" and "back to" the center of social space, movements between different peoples that allow "us" to become "others" and yet return to "ourselves," the Wakuénai, "The People of Our Language."

# 6

# "Going Through the Middle" and "Bringing Back from the Edge"

In childbirth and initiation rituals, spirit-naming and the musicality of spoken, chanted, and sung speech are used to explore the nuances and hierarchical levels of meaning in Kuwái's mythic creations of the world. "Heaping up the names" is coupled to relatively stable, chanted or melodic ways of speaking to socialize the world mythically into a vertical dimension of power between mythic ancestors and human descendants. "Searching for the names" is combined with musically dynamic ways of speaking to transform the vertical dimension of power poetically into an expanding universe of distinct peoples and places. The dynamic, ever-changing character of Kuwái's mythic creation is played against the continuous passing down of ancestral power through an interplay between two poetic processes, the musicalization of mythic speech and mythification of musical sound.

In curing rituals, performances of *málikai* and *málirríkairi*, or shamans' songs, reverse the order of Kuwái's mythic creations. The vertical dimension of power is musically constructed in *málikai* counterwitchcraft songs as a means of transforming the horizontal dimension. In *málirríkairi*, the shamans' musical journeys to the houses of deceased persons in *íyarudáti* do not embody the primordial opening up of the horizontal dimension but the re-opening of cultural separateness between living and dead persons in situations where these two classes of human beings have become "closed" together through illness. In short, curing

| Problem | Treatment | Age and Sex | | Ethnic Group(s) | Results |
|---------|-----------|-------------|---|-----------------|---------|
| Severe diarrhea & weight loss | málikai & málirríkairi | 1 | F | Baniwa-Guarequena | death attributed to evil omens |
| Toothache | málirríkairi | 14 | F | Baniwa-nonindigenous | pains reduced |
| Cough, fever | málirríkairi | 1 | M | Wakuénai (Dzáwinai) | symptoms gone within 3 days |
| Nightmares & tantrums | málikai | 4 | M | Wakuénai (Adzaneni) | child still withdrawn; tantrums alleviated |
| Earache | málikai | 7 | F | Wakuénai (Dzáwinai) | not effective; pain attributed to toothache |
| Stomach pains | málirríkairi | 1 | F | Wakuénai (Dzáwinai) | pains alleviated; no recurrence |
| Menstrual cramps | málikai | 45 | F | Wakuénai (Wariperi.) | pains relieved; resumed normal diet |
| Pains when breathing deeply | málikai & málirríkairi | 18 | F | Wakuénai | pains relieved, fever went down |
| Pains in head & body, fever | málikai & málirríkairi | 57 | F | Wakuénai | pains alleviated but no total cure |
| Stomach pains & fever | málirríkairi | 50 | F | Guarequena | recovered within 2 days |
| Crying | málikai | 1 | M | Guarequena | child had been frightened but recovered well |

6.1    *Curing rituals in Gavilán 1981, 1984*

rituals presuppose the twofold creation of Kuwái's mythic world through the complementary processes of musicalization and mythification in order to restore the cultural differentiation of vertical and horizontal worlds through reversing the order of creation.

Because of the widespread reputation of Hernan and his brother as powerful ritual healers, people came to Gavilán from villages and towns throughout the southwestern region of Venezuela's Amazon territory in 1980–81 and 1984–85. In addition, the two men practiced curing rituals for members of their own community during the measles epidemic of 1980, at the climax of heavy thunderstorms in September 1981, and whenever anyone in the village became seriously ill. Thus, in contrast to childbirth and initiation rituals that were held only on the special occasions of major life cycle transitions, curing rituals were performed at relatively frequent intervals in the early 1980s (see Figure 6.1). For the most part, these rituals consisted of brief performances of *málikai* or *málirrí-kairi* that did not require either specialist to refrain from everyday social interaction and subsistence activities. On two occasions, however, both specialists became fully occupied with ritual curing activities for several consecutive days and nights. The measles epidemic of early 1980 triggered a prolonged curing ritual in which Hernan and his brother worked together with a medical doctor from Maroa to bring their people through a collective crisis. The epidemic was still a frequent topic of conversation when I arrived in Gavilán in 1981, since it had resulted in the death of one adult male (an in-law visiting from the Içana River) and had temporarily crippled the entire village population. A second prolonged curing ritual developed in August 1981, when both Hernan and his brother worked for several consecutive days in an unsuccessful attempt to avert the death of an infant girl, whose parents had brought her from their village along the upper Orinoco River.

In addition to the many subgenres of *málikai* and *málirríkairi* performances, curing rituals bring into play a complex and richly varied range of dream symbolism, mythic narratives, ritual substances, and situational factors. Since a complete analysis of all these ethnographic materials would require monographic treatment, the following discussion of curing rituals is not intended as an exhaustive summary but only a highly selective analysis of shamanistic performances. In essence, curing rituals outline a process of "turning around" (*ikápukúita*) the causes of illness, misfortune, and death by reversing the order of Kuwái's mythic creation of vertical and horizontal worlds. The two principal ways of reversing the mythic creations are "going through the middle of the world" by reconstructing a vertical relationship with the Kuwáiñai ("Kuwái-people," or bee-spirits) and "bringing back from the edge of the world" by reopening the overly close relations between the living and the dead. Although each of the two processes of reversal draws implicitly upon imagery of creation in the cycle of narratives about Kuwái, their mythic prototypes are explicitly described in a set of narratives about curing substances, death, and evil omens. These narratives construct a third, more recent mythic space-time that is closer to the world of living people than the distant past of Iñápirríkuli at Hípana and the transformational space-time of Kuwái and Amáru. Through exploring the relations between living humans, the Kuwáiñai, and spirits of the dead, indigenous storytellers create a reversible, shamanistic space-time that forms the immediate context within which ritual curing practices unfold. Accordingly, the following analysis focuses on the ritual processes of "going through

| Ritual name of species | Secular name of species | Distinctive Traits | Uses |
|---|---|---|---|
| Kuwáiñai mádahĕwrri lidánam | kámaradápani | long proboscis | very sweet, red honey; larva eaten |
| Kuwáiñai kánerráma-dawánai | kwemápani | very long proboscis | useful wax; resin cooke[d] for medicine |
| Kuwáiñai kúmarúli | éenui | large, black body; hive attached to outside of tree, high above ground | bitter, red honey used only for curing; resin burned during epidemic |
| Kuwáiñai néperámadána | kerrádi | yellow color of queen; live inside of trees | very sweet, clear honey useful wax |
| Kuwáiñai píapiányai | manápi | hive inside trees | honey only in dry seaso[n] useful wax and eggs |
| Kuwáiñai dzáwi-dakéna | dzáwihiwída | hive is black and attached to branches | sweet honey |
| Kuwáiñai pétulédani | kétuli | bite itches like mosquito | useful wax |
| Kuwáiñai dzámadáperri | mapíwa | very small, yellowish body | very sweet honey usefu[l] for curing |

6.2   Sacred bee species and their uses

the middle of the world" and "bringing back from the edge" in tandem with the narrative construction of a reversible, shamanistic space-time.

## "Going Through the Middle of the World"
### Who are the Kuwáiñai?

In the most literal sense, the Kuwáiñai consist of eight species of bees that produce honey used for curing witchcraft victims. Two of these species also make resins that are cooked or burned in curing rituals, and the waxes made by several of the species are used in making ceremonial musical instruments, caulking leaky canoes, and in other practical activities. In a more metaphorical sense, the term Kuwáiñai is a generic category of spirit-names that is invoked in *málikai* counterwitchcraft songs and that includes all eight bee species (see Figure 6.2). In a still broader sense, the Kuwáiñai are spiritual beings that embody a retrospective, or reversed, perspective of the mythic opening up of the world in the transformational space-time of Kuwái and Amáru. A general association between Kuwáiñai spirits and Kuwái was established in Part I of the Kuwái myth cycle, where the buzzing, humming sound of bees was compared with the humming sound of Kuwái's voice. This comparison receives further elaboration in a narrative about a man whose greed for large quantities of honey brought him into contact with the Kuwáiñai. Like Part I of the Kuwái myth cycle, this narrative about the Kuwáiñai begins with an initial removal of the individual to a place that is outside of and above human society and works through a series of downward and upward movements until the individual has been brought down to the ground and inside human society.

There were people who went chopping down the trees wherever they found bees' nests. Several times they went and chopped down the hives, getting a little honey each time. Then one day, one of the men took a large clay pot and went to look for another hive. He heard talking in the forest and saw a group of little old men who were only as tall as young adolescent boys at the age of initiation. The old men were picking flowers from tall *yebaro* trees. When they saw the man, they asked him what he was looking for. "The home of the bees," he replied. So the old men decided to take him to their home after they had finished gathering enough of the *yebaro* flowers by dropping them down to the ground for their wives to collect.

The old men took the man to their home and told him that they were bees who picked flowers to make honey with the nectar. Their home, *Máapakwá Makákui* (Large Honey-Place), was an enormous village at the headwaters of the Guainía River, filled with all kinds of flowers and honey for curing sick people. The headman of the bee-people, Kuwáiñai *dzámadáperri* ("Two-brothers"), spoke for his people: "We are the bee-people, the Kuwáiñai." Their visitor grew frightened upon learning that his hosts were not people, but the headman calmed him by offering to fill his pot with honey. The Kuwáiñai stuffed the man's pot full of *yebaro* flowers and told him never to tell his family or friends that he had seen the Kuwáiñai and their village. "When you want some honey, come see us again. But don't tell anyone else about us, for to do so would be extremely dangerous."

The man returned to his village and hid the pot of flowers inside his house. After bathing in the river in the middle of the night as the Kuwáiñai had instructed him to do, the man opened the pot and found that the flowers had turned into the purest honey. He ate honey all day long but without letting any of his family or neighbors share it.

They could not figure out how he had brought so much honey back from the forest, since they were never able to collect more than a tiny bit of the precious honey.

The man went again to the home of the Kuwáiñai and asked for more honey, and the Kuwáiñai filled his pot with flowers of all the different trees in the forest. Again it turned into honey after the man bathed in the river at night. The other people of his village became very curious to know how the man was getting so much honey when all they could find was a tiny amount. So they made a strong, fermented drink and got the man very drunk, hoping that he would tell them his secret. After he had gotten very drunk, his brothers asked him, "How do you always get so much honey?" "I don't know, I guess I'm just lucky and chop down the largest hives," he answered. The others knew he was lying and persisted in their questioning. Finally, the man could not stand their pestering any longer, so he told them about his meeting with the Kuwáiñai and other details about the making of honey from flowers. He even told them about the bee-peoples' warning never to tell anyone about these things. The group went back to drinking until the man went outside to urinate. There he was bitten by a poisonous snake and died instantly.

Ever since then, people have only encountered a tiny bit of honey in beehives. On the rare occasions when a man cuts down a tree and finds a large quantity of honey inside the hive, it is considered to be an evil omen (*hínimái*), and the man who cut down the tree will inevitably become sick and die within a short time.

The overall sequence of spatial movements in this narrative is identical to the pattern of movements in Part I of the Kuwái myth cycle. The movement from inside to outside of social space is established in the initial setting, where a group of men go out into the forest to collect honey. An individual man, hoping to find larger quantities of honey, splits off from his kin group, thereby completing the inside-to-outside movement. The solitary man has unwittingly crossed a vertical, mythic boundary and comes into contact with the Kuwáiñai, who are described as old men whose bodies are no taller than those of young male initiates. This description of the Kuwáiñai is a further reference to Part I of the Kuwái myth cycle, where Kuwái was portrayed as appearing to be very old even though he was still very young. However, in the Kuwáiñai narrative, this portrayal is reversed: the Kuwáiñai appear to be young men even though they are very old. In a sense, the Kuwáiñai embody the reversal of growth, aging, and socialization processes that were created as natural, irreversible forces in the primordial human life cycle of Kuwái.

After the initial removal of the individual from inside to outside of human society, the Kuwáiñai take him up to their village, called *Máapakwá Makákui,* or "Large Honey-Place." In the remainder of the Kuwáiñai narrative the man's spatial movements continue to parallel those in Part I of the Kuwái myth cycle. On his first return to the village below, the man remains outside social space through his refusal to share his abundant supply of honey with any of his kin. Like Kuwái, the man then goes back up to the sky before finally returning to his death down on the ground and inside human society.

At the same time as the Kuwáiñai myth replicates the basic pattern of spatial movements in Part I of the Kuwái myth cycle, the narrative also reverses many of the specific causal and temporal relations in the Kuwái myth cycle. In the latter, a group of men (Iñápirríkuli and his brothers) removed the individual child (Kuwái) from human society, whereas in the Kuwáiñai narrative an individual man removes himself from human society by departing from a group of men. In the Kuwáiñai narrative, the man's act of eating large amounts of honey does not have the same fatal result as the three boys' act of eating *guaco* fruits dropped into their initiation hut by Kuwái. Instead, it is the man's refusal to share honey that alienates him from his kin group and ultimately proves lethal. As the ritual advice given to initiates makes frighteningly clear, adult sociality presupposes the activity of sharing food with one's own kin and other people (*Pikápawátsa phiúmi nawíki!*). In narrative, the individual's refusal to share honey reverses the expected pattern of adult behavior and leads to the eventual sharing of forbidden knowledge about the Kuwáiñai. Finally, the man's second return to the ground from Máapakwá Makákui contains many of the same elements as Kuwái's second return from the sky but in reverse order. Kuwái communicated his secret powers to men before they got him drunk and killed him, whereas the man's kin group got him drunk so that they could pressure him into speaking about the Kuwáiñai, which in turn led to the man's death by poisonous snakebite. Agentivity, intentionality, causality, and temporality are all reversed. Kuwái willingly gave *málikai* songs and chants to Dzúil and in full knowledge that Iñápirríkuli would subsequently kill him. The protagonist of the Kuwáiñai narrative, on the other hand, has to be forced to share his knowledge about the Kuwáiñai, and even as he does so he remains ignorant of the consequences of his action.

The reversal of causal relations is also evident on a more general level of the Kuwáiñai narrative. Unlike Part I of the Kuwái myth cycle, the individual's movements up to the sky and down to the ground do not create, or open up, a vertically differentiated cosmos but are merely travels up and down between a preexisting order of places. Moreover, the Kuwáiñai narrative provides no model of mediation between these worlds, since the power of the Kuwáiñai to make honey from flowers is never truly given to people on the ground but remains up in the sky at Máapakwá Makákui. The narrative is about the failure of the individual to mediate successfully between these two worlds, the progressive alienation and death of an individual who has unwittingly crossed the boundaries of mythic space-time and, through speaking about his secret experiences in the world above, disrupted the proper relations between ancestors and human descendants. The protagonist is a sort of antihero whose greed for honey, the food of the ancestor spirits in paradise, embodies an excessive individualism and desire for immortality that are punished by supernatural death.

On an implicit level, the Kuwáiñai narrative suggests that flowers and honey are substances that are capable of mediating between the two worlds. Even though the protagonist fails in the end of the narrative, he did succeed in bringing flowers and honey down into his village and in eating honey without causing harm to himself or others during his first return from Máapakwá Makákui. It was not honey per se but the man's greed and stinginess that led to his alienation and death. Finding large quantities of honey is an action that symbolizes both the man's excessive individualism and his failure to obey the injunction against speaking about the Kuwáiñai to people in his village. As an unsolicited intrusion of ancestral power into the world of living people, finding of honey in large amounts becomes the prototypic evil omen, a disruption of the vertical dimension of power relations between mythic ancestors and human descendants.

The Kuwáiñai narrative also indirectly implies the need for some form of communication other than everyday speech that enables people to make use of the bee-peoples' curing powers. Unlike everyday speech, which results in a blurring of spatio-temporal boundaries in the vertical dimension of generations and developmental stages, this alternative form of communicating the curing powers of bee-spirits must embody within itself the principle of movement between a pre-existing order of vertically distinct places. *Málikai* counterwitchcraft songs provide just such an alternative, since they consist of a singing-into-being of mythic journeys between the vertically separate worlds of living people and the "Kuwái-people." Like the opening and closing performances of *málikai* for initiation, the *málikai* counterwitchcraft song is a breakthrough into sung speech and uses the musical technique of movements between distinct tones to embody the parallel movement between vertically distinct places in the cosmos, generations in the social order, and developmental stages in the individual human life cycle. However, the musical embodiment of vertical journeys in *málikai* counterwitchcraft songs reverses the order of creation in Part II of the Kuwái myth cycle. The vertical dimension of body, society, and cosmos now becomes a transformational source of power that radically alters the horizontal dimension.

### Singing the Myth of Kuwaikánirri

The *málikai* song for treating victims of witchcraft consists of a single, wavelike arc of descending melodic intervals that continues until the chant-owner has named all classes of bee-spirits, honey, and flowers. As in other contexts, exhalations of tobacco smoke and the aspirated, voiced sounds of *ínyapakáati* are the means of transferring musical naming power in *málikai* to ritual subjects and their foods. The process of naming various classes of bees, flower, and honey resembles the "heaping up" of spirit-names for edible animal species in childbirth and initiation rituals. However, in curing rituals, Kuwái's musical naming power works in the reverse order. Instead of protecting ritual subjects from the potentially harmful effects of hot, sharp, loud, and other powerful kinds of spirit-names, the goal of naming bees, honey, and flowers is to protect ritual subjects by bringing them into contact with the cooling, sweetening, and purifying effects of these curing substances.

| Néniwátsa-a | núhwa nuputídza | límidzáka | ikálenáwa |
| There | I sat, I sweetened | for him | his heart, |

etc. *a fine*

| likálewáutsenhe | Kuwaikánirrí. |
| his body-spirit, | Kuwaikánirri. |

*Awátsa liédakuétewátsa wakúlukuiká hnétewátsa núma*
There they embarked, at Kurukwí, I wanted

 *nuputídza límidzáka ikálenáwa.*
 to sweeten    for him    his heart.

*Kádzu kárumi námaka límidzáka ikálewa hliéhe Kuwáikanirrí.*
Thus it was that they searched for his heart, that Kuwaikánirri.

*Néni námaka likálewa liédakuéte wakúlukuiká.*
There they searched for his heart, starting in Kurukwí (São Gabriel).

*Néniwátsa núaka núma límidzáka lidákináwa hlíawatséhne
Kuwáikanirrí.*
There I went and searched for his body, the body of this
Kuwaikánirri.

*Néniwátsa núaka nuputídza límidzáka ikálenáwa líywátsa cóco
idónia.*
There I went and made his heart sweet, like this coco nectar.

*Líyuwátsa núhwa nuputídza límidzáka likálena yúdza,*
Like this I sat and made his stomach sweet,

 *nalátsa idónia íyuwátsa.*
 like this orange nectar.

*Núhwa nuputídza límidzáka likálena.*
I sat, I sweetened his heart.

*Awátsahna liédakuéte wakúrukwi-ká,*
There they embarked, in Kurukwi,

 *"an" mánga idónia íyuwátsa núaka nuputídza límidzáka likálena,*
 "an" mango nectar, like this I went and sweetened his stomach,

 *"an" táparéwa idónia íyuwátsa núaka nuputídza límidzáka
 likálena,*
 "an" jobo-fruit nectar, like this I went and sweetened his stomach,

 *"an" kakáwa idónia íyuwátsa núaka nuputídza límidzáka likálena,*
 "an" cacao nectar, like this I went and sweetened his stomach,

 *"an" idzépu idónia íyuwátsa núaka nuputídza límidzáka likálena,*
 "an" wild cocoa nectar, like this I went and sweetened his stomach,

"an" *kahméru idónia íyuwátsa núaka nuputídza límidzáka*
  *likálena.*
"an" garden cocoa nectar, like this I went and sweetened his
  stomach.

*Awátsa liédakuéta wakúrukwi-ká.*
There they embarked, at Kurukwí.

*Kádzu kárumi námaka límidzáka ikálewa Kuwáikanirrí.*
Thus they searched for the body-spirit of Kuwaikánirri.

*Néniwátsa núhwa nuputídza límidzáka ikálewa.*
There I sat, I sweetened his stomach for him.

*Wadéemta hliákani liwanáita éenu,*
So that the splinter-sickness did not come,

  *wadéemta hliákani likáiteri lítsidapúkuka éenu,*
  so that the anaconda-hair poison did not come,

  *wadéemta hliáka kahyúkana yúmahniúka límidzáka ikálena,*
  so that the rawness-sickness did not enter his stomach,

  *hliáwa núhwa nuputídza liúdza, núhwa nuputídza liakúna.*
  I went, sitting and sweetening for him, sitting and sweetening the
    spirit-name.

*Néniwátsa núhwa núma límidzáka ikálenáwa,*
There I sat, searching for his spirit,

  *makáli hírakatsáutsa, makáli ítudakáitatsáutsa,*
  so he did not fall unconscious, so he was not touched by sickness,

  *núhwaka nútuhluéta liúdzani.*
  I sat, I cast it out of him.

*Awátsa liédakuétawátsa wakúrukwi-ká.*
There they embarked, at Kurukwí.

*Hnétewátsa núdzenéeta límidzáka ikálena*
Afterwards, I brought for his stomach

  *awátsa natídzahwíalikwátsa hnáa Kuwáiñai.*
  the canoe made from honey and wax of the Kuwáiñai.

*Matsiá kárua núkadáka límidzáka likálewa*
It was good that I carried for his spirit

*awátsa nátupiálerikwátsa hnáa Kuwáiñai.*
the bed made of honey and wax of the Kuwáiñai.

*Kádzu karúnpida nádzuhwíaka náma likálewa Kuwáikanirrí,*
Thus it was that they curved about in search of the spirit of
    Kuwaikánirri,

*"an" lídzarúnawátsa limutúka-kwá wacáyalíka.*
"an" the flower-medicine at the mouth of the Vaupés River.

The story of Kuwaikánirri, the first victim of witchcraft, begins at Ku-rukwí (São Gabriel) on the Upper Río Negro and moves gradually up-stream to the mouth of the Vaupés River and eventually to the Içana River and the central regions of Wakuénai territory. Iñápirríkuli gathers flower nectar from various species of fruit trees at Kurukwí to sweeten his younger brother's heart, or body-spirit, and brings a canoe and bed made of the bee-spirits' wax and honey for him to lie upon. The sweet-ening, cooling effects of flowers, wax, and honey calm the witchcraft victim's fear of death and cool the body's fever. Iñápirríkuli continues to paddle the beeswax canoe up the Río Negro and stops to gather flower-nectar belonging to different species of bee-spirits. Although the two brothers' mythic journey is frequently described as a search for the lost spirit of Kuwaikánirri, the process of searching, or naming places in the world, is clearly overshadowed by the more empowering processes of sweetening and cooling Kuwaikánirri's body-spirit.

Throughout the first part of the mythic journey, Iñápirríkuli's activity of sweetening his younger brother's body-spirit is closely connected to the activity of sitting. Sitting down is the initial posture for curing victims of witchcraft and undergoes important changes in later stages of the mythic journey. Upon arriving at *litípikwa*, a mythic home of the bee-spirits along the lower Içana River, Iñápirríkuli gives his brother a canoe paddle made from the bee-spirits' wax.

*Néniwátsa núdzenéeta liakúna likáiteri litípikwá,*
There I brought him to the place named litípikwa,

*námidzákakwápida nátidzakwápida hnáa Kuwáiñainai.*
the village of the canoe paddle of the Kuwái-people.

*Ikénawátsa hliáka watídzakwa-ká wetípikwa-ká,*
Then we arrived there in the paddle-place, wetipikwa,

*kénpida yáku hía Kuwáiñainai.*
as the Kuwái-people call it.

*Néniwátsa núhwa hniréeta hotsón límidzáka ikálena, límidzáka*
*ídakína.*
There I sat, I rose upright for his stomach, for his body.

*Núkapawáutsa kádzukáruni hlirétaka lidákiwa nahliú Kuwáiñainai.*
I sat up, thus it was, and he raised his body with the Kuwái-people.

*Néniwátsa núkaka hniréeta núkapáwa límidzáka idákináwa,*
There I sat up, I saw his body,

   *líwatséhne mídzawánirri.*
   the sick person.

*Nénikáruwátsa núma núkapáwa lirríu wátsa nátidzáitawátsa*
There I searched, I saw him grasp the paddle of wax

   *náhna Kuwáiñainai; nakáiteri ñápekáiteka.*
   of the Kuwái-people; they called it coldness.

*Núma núkapáwa lirríuwátsa núhwakéna hniréeta límidzáka*
*likálewa.*
I searched, I saw him grasp it, I stood upright for his body-spirit.

*Himénawátsa núkakéna hniréeta límidzáka likálewa.*
He heard me stand upright for his body-spirit.

*Hotsó liakúna límidzáka nudzéemanáwa dzéema.*
To make the name stand up for him, I blew tobacco smoke.


Grasping the paddle of wax in his hands cools down the sick body of Kuwaikánirri, and he sits up to join his older brother in paddling the canoe up the Içana toward its mythic destination. At *litípikwa*, Iñápirrí-kuli gathers many different kinds of flower-nectars to sweeten his brother's stomach. The brothers' first contact with the bee-spirits at *litípikwa* has resulted in a visible improvement of Kuwaikánirri's health but has not effected any comparably profound changes in the external world of places.

At a place called *dzáwakápikwa* on the upper Içana River, the two brothers' mythic journey is suddenly transformed from a continuous, upstream movement into an abrupt, vertically displaced leap through horizontal space. They go through the middle of the world and arrive at *Máa-*

*pakwá Makákwi* (Large Honey-Place), a place where the most powerful bee-spirits reside.

> *Néniwátsa núdzenéeta límidzáka ikálena lídzarúnawátsa*
> There I brought for his stomach the medicine

>> *lipámudzuakákwa éenu, likáiteri dzáwakápikwáka;*
>> from the middle of the sky-world, the place called *dzáwakápikwa;*

>> *kátsapída likáiteri lipámudzuakákwa.*
>> thus it is called, the middle-place.

> *Néniwátsa núaka nuputídza núkapawátsani nádzawakéwiale*
> There I went and sweetened, I arrived with the dzáwakána flowers,

>> *íyuwátsa hnáa Kuwáiñaináika dzáwakéwirrinái.*
>> like these Kuwái-people of the dzawakana flowers.

> *"An" lídzarúnawátsa Máapakwa Makákui,*
> "An" the medicine from the Great Honey-Place,

>> *awátsa hlíwidálewátsa Wápadzáwidzáka.*
>> there at the headwaters of the Guainía River.

> *Nénipída nénika nátidzákwa makákui.*
> There they came to a great village.

> *Nénipída wátidzákwa makákui, kénpida yáku hía Kuwáiñainai.*
> There was "our great village," as the Kuwái-people called it.

> *Hnésrewátsa núka núma límidzáka ikálena núkapawáutsa.*
> There I went and searched for his spirit as I arrived.

> *Néniwátsa núka núma mátalápikún liakúna.*
> There I went and searched to get rid of the name.

> *Néniwátsa núma tapíriri búwa líakawa.*
> There I wanted the witchcraft-sickness to fall off.

> *Néniwátsa núka núma liakúnawátsa Máapakwa Makákui.*
> There I went and searched in the name of the Great Honey-Place.

>> *"An" awátsa ítidzákwa kátsapída ímidzákakwáka hía Kuwáiñainai,*
>> "An" there in the great village, the home of the Kuwái-people,

>>> *katsáwa núkakéna nuputídza liakúna.*
>>> thus I arrived and sweetened the name.

*"An" núakawa nudzúhwia nukúpia límidzáka ikálenawátsa,*
"An" I sat and walked in circles looking for his spirit,

*línakuwátsa itíyawátsa hía Kuwáiñainai.*
like the honey of the Kuwái-people.

The two brothers have gone through "the middle of the sky-world" and arrived at the Great Honey-Place, the center of the bee-spirits' power. The vertical movement up to the bee-spirits' realm is paralleled by a vertical change in body posture, since Iñápirríkuli now stands up and walks around in Máapakwa Makákui. This shift from riverine to terrestrial locomotion is accompanied by a profound transformation in the horizontal dimension of mythic space, which becomes a series of geographically separate places in remote headwater areas rather than a continuous set of places located along major rivers. Going through the middle of the world has brought the two brothers up to a new plane of horizontal space that scarcely resembles the world they have left behind. In this vertically removed horizontal space, Iñápirríkuli names the witchcraft sickness, the source of Kuwaikánirri's illness, and expels it from his brother's sick body-spirit. The cure is almost complete.

The witchcraft victim remains in a situation of life-threatening danger even though the source of illness, or bewitchment, has been identified and expelled from the body. Witches are master-shamans (*dzáwináitairi*) who belong to enemy groups, and they come back to destroy their victims' body-spirits after their first attempts have been counteracted through the sweetening, cooling process of *málikai*. Accordingly, the mythic journey of Iñápirríkuli and Kuwaikánirri does not end at Máapakwá Makákui but continues through a second leap across horizontal space to the headwaters of the Vaupés River, a place where the victim's body-spirit is hidden beneath manioc leaves and left under the protection of a surrogate mother.

*Netédaliwátsa núdzenéeta límidzáka ikálewa híwidálewátsa*
*Wakáyalika.*
Afterwards, I brought his body-spirit to the headwaters of the
Vaupés.

*Néniriwátsa núkakéna nudáwa límidzáka ídakína.*
There I arrived and hid his body for him.

*Néniwátsa núkakéna núma límidzáka haduánawa,*
There I arrived and searched for their mother,

*sruawátsa srú númiyalerú.*
an old woman named *númiyalerú.*

*Matsiákaruátsa rudáwaka límidzáka ídakína awátsa*
It was good that she hid his body there

*srípuledáli yápitewátsa srú númiyalerú.*
underneath the manioc leaves of *númiyalerú.*

*Kádzukárunpída rudáwaka límidzáka ídakína, hlie Kuwáikanirrí.*
Thus it was that she hid his body, that Kuwaikánirri.

*Rudáwakapidáni nádzani, hnáa dzáwináitairi.*
She hid him from them, those master-shamans.

*Apidáta srípuledáli yápite "an" núdawáutsa límidzáka ídakína*
There underneath the manioc leaves "an" I hid his body

*awátsa nádzuliápoleríko hnáa pátunúmanai*
there in the pathway of the leaf-cutter ants

*"an" hnáa ínipodzuákanai.*
"an" the army ants.

*Kátsapída hía mákapákanálitsa íkapáka ímidzáka ídakináwa.*
Thus he could not be seen as he walked, his body-spirit.

*Núdawáutsa límidzáka ídakína tánhawátsa rútupéaliti.*
I hid his body with her palm leaf mat.

*Idánamiwátsa hnáwatsa nádanámawátsa hnáa kéepinai.*
His shadow-spirit became the small *gallineta* bird.

*Néniwátsa núdawa límidzáka ídakína nádzawátsa hnáa dzáwináitairi."*
There I hid his body from those master-shamans.

The singing of the myth of Kuwaikánirri ends at the headwaters of the Vaupés River, where Iñápirríkuli leaves his younger brother to recover in the safety of an old woman's manioc garden. Kuwaikánirri can walk from one place to another, but only by staying under a covering of leaves carried by ants can he remain safely invisible to the jaguarlike master-shamans, or witches. Nevertheless, this restricted, or diminished, form of terrestrial locomotion signals the restoration of Kuwaikánirri's body-spirit to its proper place and the completion of his three-stage transformation from an invalid lying down in bed to a recuperating patient able to sit up and grasp a paddle, to an autonomous person who is able to stand up and walk.

The myth of Kuwaikánirri describes the gradual reempowerment of an individual who has come dangerously close to death by witchcraft. Through the special naming processes and musicality of *málikai,* the potentially lethal effects of uncontrolled contact between people and the bee-spirits are turned around in order to avert supernatural death. The reconstruction of vertical relations of power unfolds simultaneously in the individual's body, the social order, and the cosmos. The change in body postures from lying down to standing upright is a renewal of life, an echo of the child's self-empowerment through natural processes of growth and development in the first years of life. At the same time, a generation of time depth is added to the initial, single-generational relationship between older and younger brother when Iñápirríkuli transfers his protective function to an old woman, or mother. Instead of expressing the severance of social relations between parent and child as in Part I of the Kuwái myth cycle, the myth of Kuwaikánirri asserts the need to reestablish, at least temporarily, the witchcraft victim's childlike relationship of dependency on a protective, nurturing maternal figure. The vertical dimension thus serves as a metaphor for generational time, but the meaning of the vertical dimension in the myth of Kuwaikánirri is the reverse of its meaning in Part I of the Kuwái myth cycle.

Singing the myth of Kuwaikánirri also reempowers the cosmos by restoring properly mediated relations between upper and lower worlds and their respective inhabitants, the bee-spirits and human beings. The mythic journey through the middle of the world is a vertical movement that powerfully transforms the horizontal dimension of cosmic space from a continuous, riverine movement through downstream regions into a discontinuous, terrestrial movement between remote headwater areas. This spatial transformation has numerous resonances with other patterns of spatial movement in *málikai* songs and chants. Most directly, the myth of Kuwaikánirri reverses the pattern of horizontal and vertical movements that are sung and chanted into being during male and female initiation rituals. In the latter performances, a pair of downward and upward vertical movements envelops a long series of horizontal movements away from and back to the center, or "navel," of mythic space. In the myth of Kuwaikánirri, a pair of horizontal movements back to and away from the middle of mythic space envelops a single vertical movement up to the realm of bee-spirits at Máapakwá Makákui. By reconnecting the vertical dimension of cosmic space, the myth of Kuwaikánirri reverses the process of horizontally opening up the social world of the child into that of an adult to create a protective sanctuary for the sick person's return to full health.

At a more implicit level, the myth of Kuwaikánirri establishes a general contrast between downstream, easterly areas, where life-threatening diseases afflict the body, and remote, westerly headwater areas where these diseases are expelled and kept away from the body. Given the intimate connections between place-naming and historical consciousness in *máliakai* songs and chants, the mythic journey from downstream to upstream locations makes sense as a metaphor for the historical reempowerment of indigenous peoples through turning around, or escaping, the disasterous effects of epidemics of disease that first entered the Içana-Guainía region from downstream areas along the Río Negro during the colonial period. Kurukwí, or São Gabriel, was the major point of interethnic contact between European and indigenous populations in the early to mideighteenth century. At the Jesuit mission in São Gabriel, the Wakuénai and other indigenous groups of the Upper Río Negro region were taught to speak *Neengatú,* or *lingua geral,* a trade language based on Latin syntax and Tupinamba vocabulary that Jesuit priests had concocted in their earlier missions in coastal and downstream areas of Brazil. The historical origins of *lingua geral* are metaphorically expressed in Part II of the Kuwái myth cycle as a mythic dialogue between Amáru and Iñápirríkuli that took place near São Gabriel. And in *málikai* songs and chants for initiation, the arrival of Europeans in early colonial times forms part of the opening up of historical relations of exchange between peoples through the naming of domesticated animal species and places along the Río Negro.

Although there are no comparable metaphors of historical change in *málikai* counterwitchcraft songs, the naming and metaphorical cutting in half of the Europeans' diseases, *rupápera srú Amáru,* provides additional support to the interpretation of Kuwaikánirri's mythic journey as a historical metaphor for the collective migrations of downstream peoples to places of relative safety in remote, headwater areas. Upon finishing the myth of Kuwaikánirri, the chant-owner utters a brief prayer in which he "cuts in half" (*n'tedáhe liakúna*) the spirit-name of Amáru's paper. Written historical documents from the eighteenth century describe a series of pandemics in which measles, influenza, smallpox, and other diseases introduced by the Europeans devastated indigenous peoples of the Upper Río Negro region (Sweet 1974; Wright 1981). During the pandemics that erupted in the 1780s, the main channels of the Vaupés, Negro, and Içana rivers were abandoned as survivors fled to safety in more remote areas.

The calming, cooling effects of bee-spirits, honey, beeswax, and flowers are directly embodied in the musicality of sung mythic speech through the continuous repetition of a single, four-tone melodic phrase. The descending melodic phrase is repeated more than a hundred times without any variation in loudness, pitch, rhythm, or tempo. Like the canoe paddle made of wax that Kuwaikánirri grasps in his hands, the singing of mythic speech is an embodiment of coldness, or a frozen space-time in which the same, simple movement unceasingly repeats itself, like a heartbeat or a breath of air.

The four-note melody of *málikai* counterwitchcraft songs remains unchanged throughout the duration of each curing ritual and also stays the same from one ritual to the next. A determination of pitches used in *málikai* curing songs performed in two curing rituals that took place in August and October of 1981 revealed that the chant-owner employed exactly the same four pitches on both occasions. After recording the same song in August 1984, a determination of pitches showed that Hernan was still using exactly the same four pitches as in the 1981 performances. By implication, stability of pitch over time acts as a musical center of gravity, or "middle of the world," through which a myriad of specific contexts are integrated. In short, the chant-owner is the keeper not only of sacred names and naming processes but also of the sacred musical tones.

The chant-owner's bodily movements add to the musical effects of "coldness" through minimal changes of pitch, rhythm, tempo, and volume. The chant-owner sits in a hammock while performing *málikai* curing songs and does not stand up until the end of the prayer with which he concludes his performance. During the singing of the myth, the chant-owner sits rigidly still except for the unconscious, somatic movements of respiration and occasional eye-blinking. In the brief interlude between the end of the song and the beginning of the prayer, the chant-owner restricts his movements to the minimal hand and body motions necessary for bending over to pick up a pot of manioc drink (*pačáka*), raise the lid, and set it back on the floor. Furthermore, the chant-owner always sings the myth of Kuwaikánirri inside a house. In short, his performances are a process of restricting all conscious body movements to a minimum and of temporarily shutting out all sense perceptions except for the sound of *málikai* and the smell of tobacco smoke.

Singing the myth of Kuwaikánirri reverses the order of Kuwái's mythic creations of the world by "going through the middle of the world." Like the related process of "heaping up the names in a single place," "going through the middle of the world" is a relatively stable, hypotrophic performative process in which the classificatory, vertical dimension of mythic speech acts upon the musicality of language, resulting in a minimum of dynamic musical change. "Going through the middle of the world" turns around the bodily, emotional destruction of individual witchcraft victims by transforming mythic images of fear, physical weakness, and death into verbal and acoustic instantiations of empathy, reempowerment, and life. Before going on to discuss the complementary, musically dynamic process of "bringing back from the edge of the world," a brief account of the connections between lightning, witchcraft, and epidemics will demonstrate how *málikai* is used in turning around collective witchcraft that threatens the existence of the entire community.

## Lightning, Epidemics, and Collective Witchcraft

The individual victim of witchcraft is a person who suffers physical, emotional collapse as a result of an enemy master-shaman who has deliberately attacked the person's dream-soul (*líwarúna* or *rúarúna*). A witch attacks at night while the victim is asleep and dreaming. The dream-soul is metaphorically described as a tiny, infantile fish, bird, or animal of the same species as a person's patrilineal sib name (*nanáikika*). A witch, or enemy master-shaman, travels in his dreams at night to the hammock of the intended victim, where he cuts in half the animal-shaped body of the victim's dream-soul. Dream interpretation was an important, daily activity in Gavilán, and Hernan elicited and interpreted the dreams of witchcraft victims before singing the myth of Kuwaikánirri, collecting honey, or other therapeutic activities. Nightmares and other powerful dreams were always attributed to witchcraft, and when Hernan experienced bad dreams, the entire village interpreted them as a sign of collective witchcraft.[1]

In contrast to individual witchcraft, collective witchcraft is the result of a total breaking down of the mediated, vertical relations of power between the sky-world of mythic ancestors and the social world of human descendants on the ground. Collective witchcraft operates aleatorically by attacking peoples' dream-souls during the night and causing serious illnesses and deaths to many people. When people are dreaming at night, their dream-souls wander about and interact with other dream-souls in the village. Collective witchcraft is a randomly destructive force that cuts in half wandering dream-souls and destroys the collective emotional spirit of the entire community. Like lightning, which can instantly kill a whole family of people in their sleep, collective witchcraft is an extremely powerful blast of life-taking energy from the sky-world of mythic ancestors. And like epidemics of measles, influenza, and other contagious diseases, collective witchcraft can spread with incomprehensible speed through a village, leaving a trail of sickness and death in its wake.

The chant-owner cannot protect people from collective witchcraft by singing the myth of Kuwaikánirri, a performance that can only turn around the effects of deliberate, individual witchcraft. Instead, he must put into practice the most powerful, direct means of turning around the life-taking, destructive energy of mythic ancestors by enlisting the protective powers of the most powerful species of bee-spirits, called *éenui*, or *dzáwi kumáruli Kuwáiñainai*. When an epidemic of contagious disease threatens the village, the chant-owner leads a group of adult men into the forest at night to cut down a tree where the *éenui* have built a hive. Before he can strike his axe against the tree, he blows tobacco smoke and utters a special *málikai* prayer at the *éenui* so that they do not become angry and attack the group of men. When the tree falls, a small fire of sticks and leaves is used to remove the *éenui* bees from the hive, but the insects are extremely persistent and some follow the men all the way back to the village. The hive is broken open to extract tiny amounts of bitter, red honey, the only form of medicine that is effective against collective witchcraft. The men also extract large chunks of brown, aromatic resin from the hive. After everyone in the village has eaten some of the bitter honey, the chant-owner leads a group of men from house to house, burning some of the resin inside each dwelling to make a protective barrier of smoke under the thatched roofs. Inside his own house, he performs a special *málikai* prayer to turn around the lightning-epidemic, or collective witchcraft.

*Núma númanani piakúna, pía limawénukápi mawénuli.*
I want to silence your name, you, the owner of thunder.

*Néniwátsa núka hnitíkani pidánawátsa liwáwa inyákim dzáwi*
　　*kumáruli,*
There I sat and burned, you hid us inside the belly of the *éenui* bees,

　*hnitíkani pidánawátsa lítsurúiriko éenu.*
　burning, you hid us beneath the roof of the sky.

*Néniwátsa núhwa hnitíkani wadánawátsani.*
There I sit and burn so that we are hidden.

*Néniwátsa núma menúnan liakúnawátsa.*
There I want the silencing name.

*Néniwátsa núma mákalirúnan liakúna.*
There I want the wind-stopping name.

*Néniwátsa núhwa núkapukuíta nudzáwa límidzáka ínumánaa*
There I sit, I turn away from me like this the mouth,

  *áwatsáatan litáhinsrewátsa Hérri.*
  towards the eastern horizon of the sky.

*Nérrewátsa núkapukuíta wámidzáka, wádakína liúdzawátsa.*
There I turn it away from us, from our body-spirit.

*Néniwátsa núma mápalenán piakúna, néni númešínka piakúna.*
There I want your name to be without gunpowder, without munition.

This *málikai* prayer continues the themes of hiding and making people invisible to protect them from witchcraft, the final situation of the first witchcraft victim in the myth of Kuwaikánirri. However, the activity of hiding has become generalized from the individual's body to a collectivity of bodies (*wádakína*, "our body"), and the turning around of witchcraft is much more directly and urgently expressed (*núkapukúita*, "I turn around"). In turning around the collective witchcraft, the chant-owner metaphorically compares the source of thunder and lightning to an enormous shotgun coming from the eastern horizon, the direction from which most thunderstorms and other weather fronts enter the Upper Río Negro region. The goal of the prayer is thus to deflect thunder and lightning back to its source by turning the mouth of the shotgun back toward the east. Other names seek to deprive the metaphorical lightning-shotgun of its power by negating its supply of munition and powder.

Lightning comes in a variety of colors and visual shapes, so the chant-owner names each different kind of lightning and cuts its spirit-name in half.

*Néniwátsa núhwa núkapukuíta piakúna.*
There I sit and turn around your name.

*Néniwátsa núma hníta dákadáka piakúna pímaliyápuli,*
There I want to cut in half your name, lightning,

*hníta dákadáka pímoniápuwátsa,*
then to cut in half the quickly flashing lightning,

*hníta dákadáka píperukápuwátsa,*
then to cut in half the shimmering lightning,

*hníta dákadáka pirráikápuwátsa,*
then to cut in half the reddish lightning,

*hníta dákadáka pílekápuwátsa,*
then to cut in half the whitish lightning,

*hníta dákadáka piéewakápuwátsa."*
then to cut in half the yellowish lightning.[2]

Having named the kinds of lightning and cut them in half, the chant-owner approaches the point of directly identifying and negating the mythic sources of collective witchcraft. The metaphorical lightning-shotgun coming from the eastern horizon evokes Amáru. However, before naming the shotgun and other hot things belonging to Amáru, the chant-owner identifies another, equally dangerous mythic source of thunder and lightning: the place where Kuwái was burned.

*Wadéemta pipwámaka wámidzáka ídakínanáku,*
So that you do not come to harm our body,

*wadéemta línakúka likáiteri lipukwámta máhnekánari yénipe,*
so that he does not come here, the one called the place where Kuwái was burned,

*wadéemta línakúka pipwám wámidzáka ídakínanáku,*
so that he does not come to harm our body,

*liáwa núma númanáni liakúna.*
I want to silence the name.

By naming the place where Kuwái was burned, the chant-owner evokes the most powerful moment of mythic creation, when the world was turned inside-out and upside-down. This transformation forms the highest level of meaning in the Kuwái myth cycle, since it is the passageway leading from vertical to horizontal dimensions of mythic creation. The burning of Kuwái resulted in a total synthesis of life-giving and life-taking powers of the jaguar-ancestors, and Kuwái's fiery death led to the emergence of humanly controlled, objectified instruments of ancestral power. However, the creative, life-renewing powers of the sacred flutes and trumpets were not the only product of Kuwái's fiery death, since his body also released poison (*mahnéti*), disease (*wáramápwa*), and other dangerous substances. As his body burned, Kuwái created a powerful thunderstorm and urinated on the fire. Wind and rain nearly put the fire out, and thunder and lightning would have killed Iñápirríkuli and the others at Hípana were it not that Dzúli had already learned the art of *ínyapakáati dzéema* and could protect everyone from Kuwái's wrath by performing *málikai* prayers. The chant-owner's naming of the place where Kuwái was burned is thus an urgent attempt to confront the mythic source of collective witchcraft by negating Kuwái's negation of the turning inside-out and upside-down of the cosmos.

The other mythic source of collective witchcraft is Amáru, the mythic owner of shotguns and other hot things. The chant-owner negates this mythic danger and turns it around, away from the people of his village.

*Wadéemta piákani pía rúmawénukápi srú Amáru,*
So that you do not come here, you the thunder-rifle of Amáru,

> *padánta piáka pía límawénukápi,*
> so that you do not come, the owner of thunder,

> *padánta piáka pía srímukápi srú Amáru,*
> so that you do not come, the hot shotgun of Amáru,

> *piáwa núhwa núkapukuíta ínumána núdzawátsa.*
> I sit and turn your mouth away from me.

After cutting in half the spirit-names of various classes of lightning for the second time, the chant-owner concludes his prayer with the usual "H-h-m-m-p-f-f" sounds of *ínyapakáati dzéema,* only this time he blows smoke over a piece of resin from the *éenui* beehive.

Hernan led the people of Gavilán in the ritual negation of collective witchcraft on two occasions during 1980–81. The measles epidemic of early 1980 struck during a fishing and hunting expedition along Caño San Miguel. Several men, women, and children returned to Gavilán with high fevers, and Hernan's older brother contracted the sickness through his shamanistic curing practices. Hernan led the remaining men into the forest where they chopped down an *éenui* hive and brought it back to the village. Soon afterwards, Hernan and the remaining healthy adults became ill, and for several days the entire village sweated out high fevers in their hammocks. Fortunately, a young medical doctor from Maroa brought food, drink, and aspirin to Gavilán so that all but one person survived the epidemic. Hernan and other members of the village spoke with great respect for the young doctor, but they also felt that the *éenui* bee-spirits and *málikai* were the real basis of their survival and recovery.[3] The man who had died, they reasoned, was a victim of his own ignorance, for he had gone to bathe in the river before the fever had completely subsided.[4]

The harvest of *éenui* honey in early 1980 had also produced an abundant supply of the powerful, sweet-smelling resin, and Hernan had kept some of this material in his house for protection against future outbreaks of collective witchcraft. In September 1981, a nasty thunderstorm moved through the Upper Río Negro region, bringing high winds and continuous peals of thunder for three consecutive nights. Loud claps of thunder were followed by several minutes of uninterrupted low rumbles that slowly built up to steady roars of sound until another loud clap started the cycle over again. For hours at a time, lightning flickered on and off as it danced between clouds or struck trees in nearby forests. No one, not Hernan, not I, nor anyone else, got much sleep, and several people, including Hernan, began to speak of bad dreams during the night. On the fourth night, Hernan stayed up to burn some *éenui* resin and perform the *málikai* prayer against collective witchcraft. The storm finally moved on to the northwest sometime after midnight, and skies were crystal clear at dawn. A Catholic missionary on her way from San Carlos de Río Negro to Maroa stopped by Gavilán later in the morning with the news that a family of eight people had been killed, along with dogs, pigs, chickens, rats, and all other living creatures, in a downstream village that had been struck by lightning the night before.

## *"Bringing Back From the Edge of the World"*
### The Mythic Basis of Chthonian Power

*Málirríkairi,* or shamans' songs, form a distinct genre of sung speech that complements *málikai* songs and prayers for turning around witchcraft. Shamans (*malírri*) are ritual curers whose main activity is that of "bringing back" the body-spirits of sick persons from the houses of the dead in *íyarudáti*. Coughs, toothaches, gastro-intestinal problems, and a number of other ailments are attributed to the antisocial behavior of poison-owners (*máhnetímnali*) who have introduced a foreign, disease-causing agent into the foods or bodies of their victims. Unlike witches who work through dreams, poison-owners act materially and consciously against other people by shooting them with invisible splinters, urinating in places where they walk, or tossing poisonous hairs into their food. Shamans seek to reverse the damage of poisoning through direct, physical removal of splinters, hairs, and other poisonous substances from peoples' bodies. Shamans' songs are performances that link the removal of physical substances in the microcosmic space of peoples' bodies together with the retrieval of body-spirits in the macrocosmic space of *íyarudáti*.

In Gavilán, shamanistic curing rituals were always performed in the open spaces behind households lining the eastern shore of the island-village. Invariably, the shaman faced the eastern horizon when singing *málirríkairi*. The morning hours were sometimes used for taking hallucinogenic snuff, smoking tobacco, and singing into being various classes of spirits in the east, but patients and their families were only treated after noon, when the shadow-spirit (*lidánam*) becomes increasingly visible due to the decline of the sun in the western sky. Shamanistic curing rituals lacked much of the aura of secrecy that surrounded *málikai* singing, chanting, and praying. People in Gavilán and other nearby villages tended to regard the shaman, Hernan's older brother, in very practical terms, similar to the way contemporary Americans consider physicians. Once the shaman had entered into his special, altered state of consciousness and completed work on a patient, other people would come for cures, just as people go to medical doctors during office hours. Like medical doctors, shamans received a material gift, or payment (*dawáinaku*), in return for their curing services. However, the Wakuénai and neighboring Arawakan peoples of the Guainía River are far more egalitarian in their financial dealings than Western capitalists, and they only allowed the shaman to keep a payment if the cure was successful.[5] Payments also formed one of the magical forces of attraction through which the shaman sought to bring back his patients' body-souls from *íyarudáti*. Moreover, the shaman helped to promote himself as a healer whose supernatural powers were subordinate to practical concerns by referring patients to medical doctors in Maroa when he did not believe his own curing powers sufficient to improve peoples' physical health.

The more pragmatic character of shamanistic healing is reflected in both the genre of shamanistic singing (*málirríkairi*) and the narratives that describe the mythic origins of shamanism. Unlike the densely metaphorical language of spirit-naming in *málikai* songs, chants, and prayers, the language used in shaman's songs is readily intelligible to any competent speaker of Wáku. The genre of *málirríkairi* is limited to sung speech with percussive instrumental accompaniment rather than the sprawling array of sung, chanted, and spoken speech that makes up the complex genre of *málikai*.

Corresponding to these contrasts in performance and style is an equally profound difference in the mythic origins of *málirríkairi* and *málikai*. The origin of *málikai* clearly and unambiguously took place during the first initiation ritual when Kuwái came down to the ground at Hípana and taught Dzúli the sacred songs and chants for initiating children into adulthood. *Málirríkairi*, on the other hand, did not explicitly originate during the transformational space-times of Kuwái and Amáru but was only implicitly created as a by-product of Amáru's prototypic female initiation ritual. Unlike the mythic origin of *málikai*, a supersocialized act of instilling the life-giving and life-taking powers of ancestor spirits into human social consciousness, the mythic origin of *málirríkairi* was a mere nuance, a wrinkle of meaning, insinuated into the void created by Amáru's powerful movements down-under-across the world, the opening up of a chthonian underwold. Amáru created *íyarudáti*, an underground world inhabited by spirits of the dead, female initiates, forest animal-spirits, and bird-spirits, all spatially separated from the aquatic, chthonian place where mythic ancestors had emerged at the center of the world in the distant mythic past of Iñápirríkuli. The shaman merely travels to and from the netherwold of *íyarudáti*, re-opening the houses of the dead so that animals and birds can return to the forests and people can return to their villages.

Shamanistic journeys to retrieve body-spirits from *íyarudáti* are hallucinogenic, musical transformations of relations between the world of living people and the underworld of recently deceased persons. Shamanistic musicalization of the shadow-spirits is a process of using the horizontal dimension of cosmic space to reverse the vertical dimension. The shaman's musical journeys down-under-across the world, from here to there and back, transform the vertical descent of human body-spirits down to the underworld into the opposite movement, or a return from down-under to up on the surface. Although there are no narratives in which the process of shamanistic reversal is directly explored, a narrative about the origin of *bocachico* trumpet-dances of *pudáli* ceremonies explains the fate of an individual whose body-spirit has descended into the underworld without the mediating powers of shamanistic musicalization.

In the late dry season, when the *bachaco* ants had wings and were flying, three *bocachico* fish went to invite a woman to dance at their *pudáli* festival, saying that they were short one dancer. The woman refused to go with them, so the three fish left to find the woman's husband and some other people who were away catching *bachaco* ants to use as fish bait. The woman's husband agreed to attend the fishes' dance. His companions stayed behind and put up a *cacuri* fish trap in the spot where the fish were holding their dance.

Under the river, the fish threw feathers of the white heron and other birds into the fish trap, and the feathers turned into fish. The Headman of the village, a *guabina* fish-person, invited the man and the three *bocachico* fish inside his house because the people on the surface of the river were killing the fish-people in the village below. When they entered the host's house, they went deeper into the river. The host's headman was angry that people had killed and eaten so many of his sons, and he vowed to seek revenge by killing and eating the man who had come down from the surface. The man heard these angry words and coughed on some water that had entered his *máwi* flute as he was dancing.[6]

His three *bocachico* friends told him to continue playing so that the *guabina* headman would not be able to identify him. After the dance was over, the *bocachico* fish calmed the *guabina* headman's anger by persuading him that there were only fish, not humans, among the visitors at the ceremony. In the late afternoon, the ceremony came to an end, and the *guabina* headman invited his guests to attend another ceremony in his village next year. The man went back up to the surface and returned to his house. His wife had been looking for him all day but could not find him anywhere. He told her that he had been fishing all day but hadn't caught anything. The three *bocachico* fish had strictly forbidden him to tell anyone where he had been and what he had seen in the fish-people's village under the river. Finally, the man's wife gave him some food to eat, and the man vomited. His wife could smell liquor when he vomited, and she knew now that he was lying to her. She asked him where he had been drinking during the day. The man could not hide the truth from his wife and told her that he could no longer live with her because he had broken his promise to the *bocachico* fish. He left the house and was bitten by a poisonous snake. He turned into a *bocachico* fish and went to live in the river with other fishes.

Like the Kuwáiñai narrative, this story about the origin of *bocachico* trumpet-dances is concerned with the alienation and death of an individual who fails to mediate relations between the world of living people and a mythic realm inhabited by semi-human, semi-animal beings. However, the myth of the origin of *bocachico* dances reverses the social, bodily, and spatio-temporal processes outlined in the Kuwáiñai narrative. Instead of the individual person becoming frightened upon learning that he is in contact with mythic beings (the bee-spirits), one of the fish-people becomes angry upon sensing that there is a human being present at the ceremony. And instead of a man's kin group getting him drunk and pestering him into revealing his secret knowledge of the bee-spirits, a man's wife discovers that he was drinking at a ceremony when he vomits some food she has given him. In both narratives, the individual goes outside and is bitten by a poisonous snake, but with opposite consequences. The antihero of the Kuwáiñai narrative dies instantly, whereas the man who danced with the fish-people turns into a *bocachico* fish-person and goes to live under the river.

The parallels and contrasts between these two narratives could be elaborated upon still further, but the most important point for understanding shamanistic curing is how the narratives demonstrate that victims of poisoning embody a process of alienation that is the reverse of witchcraft victims' deaths. Witchcraft, or unmediated contacts between people on the ground and mythic beings in the sky-world overhead, is essentially a disruption of the vertical dimension of power relations between mythic ancestors and human descendants. Poisoning, on the other hand, is a disturbance of the horizontal dimension of exchange relations between groups of people that results from a failure to mediate between "we people here" and "those other (i.e., fish) people there."

The pattern of movements in the narrative about *bocachico* dances shows that poisoning transforms a person into a mythic Other, or fish-person, through horizontal movements away and across the world to the Others' village and back across the world to the initial point of departure. This pair of outward and inward horizontal movements envelops a downward vertical movement as the person enters the Others' house, allegedly for protection against people on the river's surface who are killing the fish-people. Once he has gone inside the Others' house, the person has become one of the fish-people, and his return to the surface world is a movement *deep* down-under-across that is removed to a deeper vertical plane of horizontal space (see Figure 6.3). The man's return across hori-

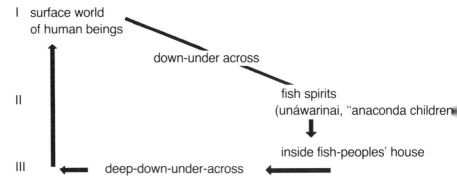

6.3    *Spatial movements in the myth of* bocachico *dances*

zontal space abruptly reverses the two-fold vertical movement down into
the depths of the other world, but his ascension to the surface world of
people results in a reiteration of the transformation of human being into
fish-person rather than a restoration of the man's humanness. When he
eats the human food (i.e., fish) prepared by his wife, he has become a
cannibal, a fish-person who kills and eats fish, a rottenness that makes
him vomit up the fish-people's liquor and divulge his secret knowledge.
Unlike the victim of witchcraft, the victim of poisoning displays a full
awareness that he can no longer remain in the world of living people, and
he knowingly goes outside to his "death," or transformation into a fish.

This narrative resonates with the symbolic overdetermination of fish as
the mediating substance par excellence of horizontal relations of exchange between different kin groups. The spawning runs of *bocachico*
fish species at the beginning of long wet seasons are a release mechanism
that triggers the bringing, heaping up, and redistribution of surplus fish
and other foods in *pudáli* exchange ceremonies. Like the movements of
fish from downstream to upstream areas, ceremonies bring and mix together peoples from different territories. However, like the bee-spirits'
honey, fish is a mediating substance that can kill as well as nourish. What
is conspicuously absent from the narrative of the fish-people is a means
of communicating about the other world that allows the returning fish-
person to recover his fully human identity. Speaking about the fish-people
in the language of everyday speech destroys the individual person and
permanently alienates him from the world of living people. By implication, the individual requires a form of verbal communication that embodies within itself the horizontal transformation, or reversal, of vertical

movements down to the depths of a chthonian underworld into opposite movements up to the human social world.

## *Shamans' Songs* (Málirríkairi)

Shamans' songs are musicalizations of the mythic journey between *íyarudáti* and *hekwápríko*, the world of living people. As in *málikai* songs, the vertical dimension of mythic space is constructed through musical movements between vertically distinct tones in *málirríkairi*. Unlike *málikai* songs, however, in which the vertical dimension of tonal movement is rigidly stable, vertical tonal movements in shamans' songs are constantly moving across the horizontal dimension of mythic space through microtonal rising, use of different starting pitches, and other musically dynamic processes. The majority of shamans' songs belong to a subgenre called *íyarudáti* and are based on simple tonal structures, each consisting of three distinct tones (see Figure 6.4).

The most frequently used tonal structure, or Variant A, is made up of three tones that divide the interval of a fourth into two, unequal smaller intervals (a whole step and a minor third). Variant A is reproduced on four different levels of pitch that are a chromatic half-step apart. A second tonal structure, or Variant B, consists of three tones in which a minor third is divided into two whole-tone intervals of equal size. Variant B is reproduced at five different levels of pitch separated by a chromatic half step. As a general rule, lower starting pitches (e.g., A1, A2, B1, B2) are used in the early stages of shamanistic curing when the shaman is entering an altered state of consciousness and beginning to perceive and manipulate spirit-beings in the eastern sky. Higher starting pitches (e.g., A4, B4, B5) are used in later stages of curing rituals, after noon and the arrival of patients. Within each song, the pitch rises gradually through microtonal intervals so that the tonal structure has been sharpened by a chromatic half-step by the song's end. Thus, the progression from lower to higher starting pitches in the course of curing rituals is not a stepwise, upward motion but a continuous process of displacing the vertical tonal structures by microtonal intervals. In short, the horizontal journey through microtonal intervals and different starting pitches transforms the vertical structures of tonal movement from a frozen upward and downward pattern into a musically dynamic movement of melodic patterns.

In addition, shamans' songs exploit a number of other elements of musical sound to embody the process of constant horizontal displacement.

Shamans make use of dynamic contrasts between loud and soft voices to express their musical journeys to *íyarudáti*. After singing each phrase aloud, the shaman, like a ventriloquist, sings a faint echo of the phrase so that his song appears to be coming back to him from far off in the distance. Shamans also use sacred rattles to produce a variety of percussive, rhythmic accompaniments to their songs. These sounds have the effect of speeding up or slowing down the tempo at different moments of the curing ritual.

The lyrics of shamans' songs are less ritually powerful than the dynamic musical processes outlined above. Unlike the secret, powerful, and richly poetic processes of spirit-naming in *málikai,* the language of *málirríkairi* songs consists of mere verbal representations of the shaman's curing activities. In opening stages of curing rituals, the songs speak of looking at the sky, smoking tobacco, and retrieving the lost body-spirit. Later, when the shaman is actually curing patients through sucking physical objects from their bodies and vomiting them into his hands, the songs describe these activities. Throughout curing rituals, the dominant theme of musical lyrics is that of bringing back (*-idiétakáwa*) from *íyarudáti,* as in "I bring back from tapir-house" (*nudiétakáwa liúdza héemapánadali káuli*) and "we bring back from the place where the sun falls" (*wadiétakáwa liúdza hlíakawa hérri*). In short, the power of shamans' songs is based on the horizontal displacement of vertical, sung speech rather than poetic processes of spirit-naming that are embedded in language itself.

## Combined Curing Rituals

In the great majority of cases, only one or the other of the two genres of curing music is performed for a patient, depending upon what are the symptoms. *Málikai,* or singing the myth of Kuwaikánirri, is the prescribed treatment for diseases of the genital organs, neurological disorders, nightmares, and children's behavioral problems (e.g., temper tantrums or frequent crying). In addition, there are several shorter *málikai* chants for treating specific diseases, such as severe headaches and skin rashes. *Málirríkairi* songs belonging to the subgenre called *íyarudáti* are performed for persons who suffer from toothaches, stomach pains, intestinal disorders, and coughs. For the most part, curing rituals are brief events in which either *málikai* or *málirríkairi* songs are performed for only a few minutes. However, when a person suffers from severe, life-threatening illness, curing rituals become prolonged events in which both ritual curers, the chant-owner and the shaman, combine their powers in an effort to avert death.

A prolonged ritual of this type developed in August 1981, when a Baniwa man and his Guarequena wife brought their infant daughter to Gavilán from their home at Quitare, a village on the upper Orinoco River. Everyone knew from the start that the child was too sick to live much longer, but the parents offered a highly valued payment to Hernan and his brother. Other ritual healers and doctors had treated the severe diarrhea that was killing the one-year-old girl, but all their efforts had failed. The girl's family turned to Hernan and his brother in desperation, and the two men responded with an all-out effort to save the dying child.

Soon after their arrival in the village, Hernan led the girl's family to the vacant guesthouse where they could hang up hammocks and rest before the commencement of ritual curing activities. Hernan instructed all five visitors (the parents, a grandmother, a brother, and the sick girl) to refrain from eating any foods until he had sung *málikai* and blown tobacco smoke over a mixture of manioc flour and water for them to drink. A few minutes later, the shaman brought out his bag of curing implements, set up two small benches behind the visitors' house, and lit a smoldering fire off to one side of the little clearing. He lit a strong, filterless cigarette on an ember and stood up to stare at the clear, mid-afternoon sky. Then he sat down on a low bench and blew smoke over each ritual object as he removed it from his bag. He poured *dzáato* snuff (*Virola callophylla*) into the palm of his left hand, scooped it into a V-shaped bone tube, and self-snorted several blasts of the purplish powder into each nostril. With the sacred rattle in his right hand, he picked up a smooth red stone, called *éenu íshu* ("sky-hook," or lightning), in his left palm and clasped a long tube of paper between his fingers. He began to shake the rattle in large, slow circles and to sing a low, gently descending melody, his eyes constantly scanning the eastern horizon. At the end of his song, he pushed out into the air with both arms and exhaled loud breaths as though clearing away invisible layers of fog that hindered his view of the sky. Standing up, he held his rattle high up over his head and peered at the sky through its colorful toucan feathers.

The shaman worked alone in the clearing behind the guesthouse before bringing out the payment, in this case a hand-powered sewing machine in almost new condition. He called for the visitors to come outside with the sick child, and they sat down on the bench beside the sewing machine. The shaman lit a cigarette, waved it in circles overhead, inhaled a puff of smoke, and held in his breath while walking over to blow smoke on the heads of the patient and her family. He waved his rattle over the girl's body, using the feathers like a fan to cool down her fever. After several more rounds of smoking, snorting snuff, and singing, he began to suck on the patient's stomach. Sucking the patient's body was followed by standing up to peer at the sky through the feathers of the sacred rattle and scooping up invisible disease-spirits with the hands. Then he walked to the bushes at the edge of the clearing, bent over, and forcefully vomited into his hands. Several repeated attempts to suck out and vomit up the object causing the girl's sickness failed to produce anything solid.

The shaman turned his full attention back to the sky, where a dark thundercloud had come into view on the eastern horizon. A strong wind began to cool down the blazing heat of afternoon sun. The shaman worked to capture the cooling winds with his cigarettes, stones, and rattle. When the wind stopped, the air became sultry and still, and he sang at the sky. The storm cloud blocked out all sunlight and dropped heavy rains over the gardens only two hundred meters away across the river channel. The shaman finished his song and rose to talk to the storm cloud, mumbling questions through the feathers of his rattle until a loud crash of thunder obliterated the sound of his voice. For several minutes, he spoke to the storm cloud that hung over the manioc gardens. The child screamed and cried, and her family and a growing number of local people gathered to observe the shaman's magical conversation with thunder and lightning.

When at last the heavy rains swept across the channel and into the village, everyone except the shaman moved into the wall-less, covered cooking area behind the visitors' house. The shaman's singing was joined by a crackling roar of rain striking the crisp, sun-dried palm thatch overhead. The patient's family went back outside to resume their previous positions as soon as the cloudburst had ended.

Meanwhile, Hernan was starting on a long series of *málikai* songs in a front room of the visitors' house. He sat in the patient's hammock and placed a small pot of manioc beverage at his feet. With a cigarette burning in his uplifted hands, he fixed his eyes on a blank wall across the room and sang the mythic journey of Kuwaikánirri through the middle of the world and up to Máapakwá Makákui, the great honey-place of the bee-spirits. At the end of each part of the musical journey, he lit another cigarette and promptly raised the pot of manioc beverage to his mouth. Accompanied by high-pitched, descending "h-h-m-m-p-f-f-" sounds of *ínyapakáati dzéema*, he released thick veils of tobacco smoke into the pot and resumed his song. The sounds of the shaman's rattling, singing, and vomiting faintly penetrated the front room. Finally, the shaman finished his day's work, and the patient and her family came into the room where Hernan was singing *málikai*. After completing the mythic journey of Kuwaikánirri, the chant-owner prayed directly into the pot of manioc beverage, cutting in half the paper of Amáru, the source of other peoples' diseases. Then he lit another cigarette and blew tobacco smoke over the heads of the patient and all members of her family before instructing them to drink the pot of manioc beverage.

Both specialists continued to work, sometimes together and other times alone, for two more days. The shaman began his work in the mid-morning of the second day and spent more than two hours taking *dzáato* snuff, smoking, singing, and pushing shadow-spirits in the eastern sky. Shortly before noon, he went inside to fetch the sewing machine and sang once more before staring up at the bright sun through the feathers of his maraca. When he brought out the mother and her sick child, the time was exactly noon. After an hour of *íyarudáti* songs, snuffing, and blowing smoke, he embarked on a prolonged session of sucking and vomiting, but still he could not manage to come up with any solid object. By now he had snuffed *dzáato* well over twenty times in each nostril and had entered the deep-down-across world of the dead, an altered state of consciousness in which his voice no longer seemed to come from his body but instead from somewhere else. Behind us, the descending melody of Kuwaikánirri's mythic journey became faintly audible from inside the visitors' house.

The shaman glared angrily at the dying girl's body and abruptly interrupted his singing with a series of questions directed at her frail, tiny body. "Who or what has made this evil omen?" (*Kwákada wátsa hínimánali?*). The mother, who was holding the sick girl on her lap, did not understand the shaman's aggressive interrogations, and she became visibly upset as the questioning continued. Hernan emerged from the visitors' house and sat down beside the frightened woman to explain that Dzulíhwerri, the mythic owner of *dzáato* snuff, was speaking through his brother and demanding that she reveal any unusual events or dreams that she or her family had experienced in recent weeks. The mother resisted at first but then recalled how she and her husband had heard a rooster "sing" in exactly the same voice as the crying of their daughter during the first week of her illness. The father had immediately killed the rooster, since they were frightened by the strange resemblance of its voice to their daughter's crying.

The mother's revelation did not make a strong impression on the shaman, who had started a third kind of *málirríkairi* song, called *hínimái*. Dzulíhwerri was angry that he had not been told the truth, and he demanded a raise in payment as a show of greater cooperation by the family of the sick child. The mother pulled out two twenty-*bolívar* notes and handed them to the shaman, who placed them on top of the sewing machine. The singing and interrogation intensified until at last both parents revealed a far more serious event. The father admitted that he had wished his daughter's death out loud in a quarrel with his wife. The child's constant crying had annoyed him day and night until he had angrily told his wife that he would rather see his daughter die than continue to hear her crying.

The revelation of this pair of evil omens had a profound effect on the shaman, who would not have continued his efforts to save the dying child without the parent's confession. After another round of sucking the girl's body and vomiting into his hands, the shaman found a hairlike piece of stomach-sickness (*iwálikunám*) that was interpreted as either a sorcerer's poison (*mahnéti*) or the rawness of a fish-spirit (*umáwari*). The shaman appeared to suffer great pains when this hairlike object came out of his mouth, and he cleaned it and examined it for a minute before showing it to the patient's family. He sang several closing songs after everyone else had left and blew tobacco smoke over each of his sacred objects before putting them away.

In the evenings and early morning hours, Hernan sang *málikai* and blew tobacco smoke over manioc beverages for the visitors. The third day was very rainy, and the two curers worked at different times to revive the dying child. Her condition had not changed either for better or worse since the start of the curing ritual three days earlier. At the end of the day, Hernan announced that he and his brother had done everything in their powers to cure the infant girl and that they would not work any more until they could see some change in her condition. He predicted that an improvement in her condition on the fourth day would mean that she would eventually recover but that a new onset of diarrhea and fever would mean certain and speedy death. Throughout the night and following morning, the child's health remained steady. Shortly after noon, in the hottest hours of the day, her condition suddenly took a turn for the worse, and she very nearly died. Hernan stood by his prediction of the previous day and sadly gave up hope of saving the child's life. He sent her father upstream to Sebucan to summon the mother's Guarequena kin to Gavilán to mourn the child's death.

Hernan's brother, however, surprised everyone by holding an emergency curing session in the clearing behind the visitors' house. The child lay in her mother's arms, her cries reduced to the pathetically weak voice of an infant who was closer to death than life. Everyone brought out their most valuable possessions and heaped them into a pile on top of the sewing machine. Shotguns, clothes, money, and other modern articles of value (including the anthropologist's typewriter) were piled up to please Dzulíhwerri and help the shaman bring back the girl's body-spirit from the netherworld. Oddly enough, the infant girl began to show some improvement after the unplanned curing ritual and, for the time being, people were happy that Hernan's gloomy prediction had not come to pass.

The girl's father returned with a number of Guarequena men and women just before dawn. They had all been far up Caño San Miguel at their single-family gardening and fishing sites. Although they were relieved to find the girl still alive, they also seemed resigned to accept that she could not survive another recurrence of the fever.[7] They began to formulate an alternate explanation for the child's illness and the inability of Hernan and his brother to do more than postpone her death by a few days. The failure, they reasoned, clearly meant that the sorcerer had been a nonindigenous person, a *velero* (candle-manipulator) who had conspired to kill the child out of hatred toward the parents. That night, they lit five candles, one for each of the five visitors from Quitare, and set coins about two inches away from each candle. They left the five candles burning all night. One man dreamed that he saw the child's mother surrounded by burning candles inside a church, and his dream reinforced a reading of the candlewax in which it was claimed that the candle representing the sick child had left a fairly round pattern, a sign of the inevitability of her death. The candles representing the other four family members had all left patterns that showed little arms of wax extending toward the nearby coins. In the morning, the Guarequena from Sebucan agreed that a *velero* had cast an evil spell upon the infant girl and that there was no longer any hope of saving her life. They took her to Sebucan, and she died there early the next morning, nearly a week after the curing ritual had begun in Gavilán.

## The Social Construction of Death

The prolonged curing ritual of August 1981 demonstrated that the two genres of musical curing, as well as the corresponding processes of alienation through witchcraft and poisoning, are complementary ways of understanding the reversal of Kuwái's mythic creations. Taken separately, *málikai* counterwitchcraft songs and *málirríkairi* songs are musical embodiments of a turning around of the patterning of vertical and horizontal dimensions of power, arrangements that have become disrupted through unmediated contacts between different levels and places in the cosmos. At a higher level of meaning, the two genres of ritual curing music can be juxtaposed within a single context to confront death and to construct a nexus of meanings that shows how the death of an individual's body is part of a wider situation of social and cosmic contamination. Evil omens and the juxtaposition of *málikai* and *málirríkairi* songs are a ritual process of constructing the space-time of death, a higher level of meaning at which contrasts between different curing processes are synthesized into complex images of the total reversibility of the cosmos.

The most powerful and direct embodiment of the space-time of death is the simultaneous performance of *málikai* and *málirríkairi* songs. Sitting in the cooking area behind the guests' house was a study in the juxtaposition of contrasts: on the one hand, the chant-owner sat inside the house and sang the frozen musical tones of Kuwaikánirri's mythic journey through the middle of the world; on the other hand, the shaman sang outside at the eastern sky to bring back the child's body-spirit, his voice meandering across a decentered journey of microtonal intervals and softly echoing back from the underworld. The chant-owner sat rigidly still and stared straight ahead, while the shaman paced around the little clearing and searched every corner of the sky. On first hearing, the juxtaposition of *málikai* and *málirríkairi* songs felt like a chaotic clashing of voices, each moving through different space-times and in different directions. As the ritual curing process unfolded, this initial impression gradually transformed into a feeling that the two voices had become fused into a single, coordinated musical journey through the space-time of death.

The first indication of an emerging synthesis was the shaman's magical conversation with thunder and lightning. Shamans do not normally deal with these forces, since they are primarily in the domain of vertical relations of power, witchcraft, and the chant-owner's musical uses of bees and honey. Yet there was the shaman, master of underworld spirits and horizontal down-under-across journeys, directly addressing the thunder and lightning witch that had come to finish off a dying child.

6.4    *Tonal variants of shamans' songs* (málirríkairi) *and* málikai *song for counteracting witchcraft*

The emerging revelation of evil omens on the second day of the curing ritual was a process of socially constructing the space-time of death, or the total reversibility of bodily, social, and cosmic processes of creation. When confronted with an evil omen, the shaman sang a special subgenre of *málirríkairi*, called *hínimái*. Unlike the other shamans' songs, or *íya-rudáti*, the evil omen song consisted of four tones that divide the interval of a fourth into three smaller intervals (whole step, whole step, and half step). The shaman performed this song three times during the second day, and each time he used exactly the same pitches. Nor were there any horizontal movements through microtonal intervals in the three performances of the *hínimái* song. Like the chant-owner's singing of the myth of Kuwaikánirri, the shaman's evil omen song was composed of repeated movements between unchanging, vertically distinct tones. Indeed, the vertical tonal structure of the shaman's evil omen song was identical to that of the chant-owner's counterwitchcraft song, only transposed a major third higher (see Figure 6.4). In the evil omen song, the shaman reversed the reversal of poisoning, a contamination across the horizontal dimension of space, into a vertical musical journey. The shaman had musically broken through to the vertical dimension of power relations between mythic ancestors and human descendants. Together, the shaman and the chant-owner had constructed the space-time of death, a musically defined place that lies hidden inside the black box of bodily, social, and cosmic transformation, the primordial murk where "going though the middle" and "bringing back from the edge" of the world become fused into the utter transformability and reversibility of the entire universe.

# 7

## The Poetics of Ritual Power

Ritual power in Wakuénai society is a poetic process of using the musicality of spoken, chanted, and sung speech to explore the nuances and hierarchical levels of mythic meaning. The "felt consubstantiality" (Friedrich 1986:39) between language music and mythic meaning emerges through the interplaying of more-to-less powerful ways of speaking: from "going in search of the names" to "heaping up the names in a single place"; from "going through the middle of the world" to "bringing back from the edge." It is important to understand the interrelations between these different ways of speaking as a relative hierarchy of more-to-less powerful ways of poeticizing bodily, social, and cosmic processes rather than an absolute, binary opposition between powerful and powerless modes of poetic speech. In Wakuénai ethnopoetics, there is no categorical distinction between "mythic meaning" and "language music," since both more and less powerful modes of poetic speaking are sensuous, performative processes in which musical sounds and mythic meaning act upon and transform into one another. The poetic nexus of language music and mythic meaning, or of music within and about myth and myth about and within music, is anchored in the primordial "h-m-m-p-f-f" sounds of *ínyapakáati dzéema*, a releasing of breath and chanted tones from inside the body into the external world of objects, foods, and persons.

The relativity of ritual power is evident at a number of different levels. Within each performance, more powerful, dynamic ways of speaking are always interacting with less powerful ways of speaking. In the same manner, the relative contrast between more-to-less powerful ways of speaking operates at the level of sets of performances within a single ritual context, at the level of subgenres between different ritual contexts (e.g., *málikai* chants performed in childbirth and initiation rituals), and at the level of comparison across genres and contexts.

Although it is impossible to draw a clear distinction between mythic meaning and language music at the level of empirical phenomena, an analytical contrast between more and less powerful ways of speaking can be made according to the relative weightings of musicality and mythic meaning. In less powerful ways of speaking such as "heaping up the names," taxonomies of mythic being are dominant over the musicality of speech, resulting in a minimum (but not an absence) of musical dynamics. In more powerful ways of speaking such as "going in search of the names," musical movements through microtones, tempos, rhythms, timbres, and volumes of speaking transform taxonomies of mythic being into an expanding montage of powerful names. For want of better terms, I have called these two contrasting processes "mythification" and "musicalization," respectively. "Mythification" is a transformation of the categories of mythic speech into relatively stable lines of chanted and sung speech. "Musicalization" is the complementary process of transposing mythic speech into relatively dynamic lines of spoken, chanted, and sung speech.

Mythification, or transforming the powerful sounds of language music into mythic speech, is a miniaturizing process, an inscription of the macrocosmic creation of natural species into the microcosm of individual human bodies. The socialization of individuals is a process of converting raw, animal-like, incestuous sexual relations into a fully human, vertical dimension of power relations between mythic ancestors and human descendants. Fasting, "heaping up the names," and eating the sacred food (*káridzámai*) are activities that define the humanness of individuals and link them into the ritual hierarchy of ancestors, specialists, elders, children, and grandchildren. Giving birth, fasting, and eating are the processual matter through which the macrocosmic opening up of a vertical structure of worlds, generations, and human developmental stages is engraved into the geography of microcosmic, bodily space. What sets the macrocosmic creation in motion is the raw, unsocialized, musical naming power of Kuwái, or the "powerful sound that opened up the world" (*kémakáni hliméetaka hekwápi*). Individual humanness and vertical power relations in human society are emergent properties of the transformation of powerful musical sounds into socialized genres of mythic speech, such as dialogue and the internalization of sacred names into social consciousness. Mythification is thus the creation of a distinctly human social world through the transformation of language music into a mythic, classificatory order of relatively steady, chanted and sung speech. To control mythification is to be a keeper of the formative principles that generate and mediate between vertically differentiated "worlds," or generations and developmental stages.

Childbirth rituals provide the clearest illustration of how mythification works. In the first set of chants, the chant-owner's search for a newborn infant's ancestral tobacco spirits sets in motion a dynamic, expansive process of linking the body's soft flesh to the hard bones at the base of the spine through metaphorically constructing an external world of hot, powerful-sounding, sharp, and otherwise dangerous mythic beings. In the second set of *málikai* chants, the dynamic musicalization of a newborn infant's overly close ties to the parents is transformed into a more static process of mythification, or the miniaturization of the powerful sounding macrocosmos into a pot of hot peppered, boiled meat (*káridzámai*). The vertical "heaping up" of spirit-names into the pot of food mediates the relations between animal nature and individual humanness by integrating the newborn infant and its parents into the vertical dimension of power relations between mythic ancestors and human descendants. The newborn infant (*kérramu*) is an ambiguously dangerous and endangered being because it has only recently come outside the maternal womb. "Heaping up the names" transforms the biologically and socially ambiguous process of birth, or externalization, into an opposite process of internalizing socialized animal nature.

Musicalization, or transforming the taxonomies of mythic speech into dynamic language music, is a turning inside-out and upside-down of mythification. Musicalization is a process of expanding, opening, and augmenting the miniaturized vertical creation into a horizontal dimension of exchange relations among a plurality of peoples from different places. Through musicalization, the female initiate's loss of blood, the male initiate's fulfillment of bride service to his future affines, and the ceremonial bringing and mixing together of foods and peoples create a cultural landscape of rivers, peoples, and places, including the chthonian underworld of spirits of the dead. Social movements of goods, services, and persons across the collective boundary between one's own kin group (*nukítsiñápe* or *nukitsínda*) and "other people" (*apána náiki*) are embodied in the musical movements of chanted and sung speech through a variety of "places," or microtones, starting pitches, tempos, rhythms, and timbres. Musicalization produces and mediates between collective, social categories of Others through placing both "us" and "them" into the framework of naturalized, or animalized, social being. To control musicalization is to be a custodian of Amáru's chthonian powers to open up a horizontal world of distinct peoples, to travel from here to there and back again, to become Other to one's own people and yet return to one's own social being.

Male and female initiation rituals are contexts in which musicalization is brought to bear upon young adults who are leaving the relatively stable, "mythified" world of childhood and entering the more dynamic world of exchange relations among distinct peoples. The sacred food is no longer an embodiment of socialized animal nature but of naturalized social being, or Otherness, and the social principle of exchange with Others. "It is not just with your own kin that you must share but with all people!" (*Karrútsa pakitsínda kátsapatsáta, phiúmi nawíki!*). The long series of *málikai* chants for initiates' food creates an expanding montage of powerful spirit-names, a "bringing together" and "mixing" of natural species and places, all in a perpetual state of musical motion.

Added to the musicalization of mythic speech is an external, instrumental layer of musical sound, the sharp percussive tappings of *kadápu* whips on the overturned manioc basket that covers the initiates' sacred food. Like the self-empowerment of children who must endure the pain of fasting in order to break through the vertical threshhold between developmental stages, the percussive sounds of the *kadápu* whips break through the cosmic space separating mythic ancestors in the sky from their human descendants on the ground at Hípana, the "navel" of the world. Once this vertical transformation is completed, the *kadápu* whips are used to delineate the temporal dimension of accelerating movements away-across and back-down-under the expanding world of species and places. After giving the ritual advice to initiates, the chant-owner uses the *kadápu* whips to lift morsels of sacred food up to the initiates' mouths. The whips are thus an embodiment of the horizontal space that has been opened up between the giver and receiver of food substances, a social lifeline of food sharing that complements the vertical umbilical cord through which ancestral power nourishes humanity. Finally, the *kadápu* whips sound out two fortissimo "thwacks" across the initiates' backs, transforming their bodies into percussive musical instruments that contain within themselves the horizontal distance between "us" and "them," giver and receiver, gain and loss. In essence, musicalizing the Other is a way of opening up the microcosm of individuals' bodies into a macrocosmic, musical expansion of natural species and places.[1]

The analytical contrast between mythification and musicalization is equally important for understanding the various reversals of creation performed in curing rituals. However, in curing rituals, both processes are embodied in genres of sung speech, whereas *málikai* performances in childbirth and initiation rituals bring into play a greater diversity of spoken, chanted, and sung speech. Furthermore, the relative hierarchy of musicalization to mythification, or more-to-less powerful ways of speaking is reversed, or "turned around," in the two genres of curing songs. The *málikai* counterwitchcraft song is a transposition of mythic speech into a frozen pattern of melodic tones, a mythification of musical sound in which the mythic journey through the middle of macrocosmic space is miniaturized into the reempowered body of Kuwaikánerri, the primordial victim of witchcraft. Taken together with the *málikai* prayer for "turning around" collective witchcraft, or lightning, the subgenre of *málikai* performed in curing rituals is more powerful than the shaman's musicalization of relations between living and dead persons. Curing rituals are contexts in which the vertical and horizontal creations are turned around through reversing the relative hierarchy of more-to-less powerful ways of speaking. The more musically dynamic processes of shamanistic journeys through the chthonian underworld are less powerful than the musically stable, densely poetic ways of turning around witchcraft in *málikai* songs and prayers.

The parallel yet reversed usage of mythification and musicalization in curing rituals is illustrated in Figure 7.1 and includes a broad range of stylistic and contextual elements. In general, the left-hand side of Figure 7.1 displays more musically stable ways of speaking that are primarily concerned with the vertical dimension of power relations between mythic ancestors and human descendants. The right-hand side of the figure lists more musically dynamic ways of speaking in which horizontal displacements of chanted and sung speech embody the opening up of an ever-changing, growing social world of exchange relations among distinct peoples. In childbirth and initiation rituals (the top half of Figure 7.1), *málikai* encompasses the entire spectrum of spoken, chanted, and sung speech as well as the subtle shadings of spoken chanting and chanted singing. The more powerful processes of musicalization and "going in search of the names" consist of complex, dynamic interweavings of spoken-and-chanted or chanted-and-sung speech. The less powerful processes of mythification and "heaping up the names" are less ambiguously

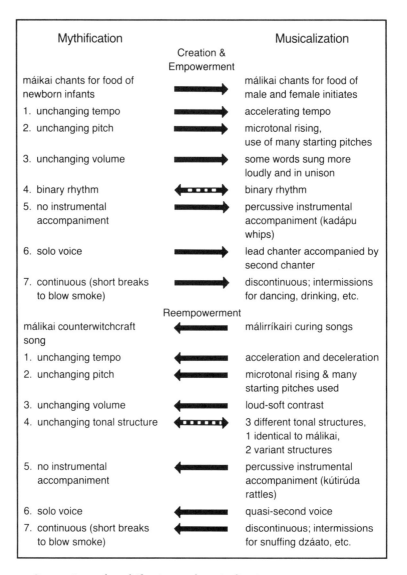

| Mythification | | Musicalization |
|---|---|---|
| | Creation & Empowerment | |
| máikai chants for food of newborn infants | → | málikai chants for food of male and female initiates |
| 1. unchanging tempo | → | accelerating tempo |
| 2. unchanging pitch | → | microtonal rising, use of many starting pitches |
| 3. unchanging volume | → | some words sung more loudly and in unison |
| 4. binary rhythm | ←····→ | binary rhythm |
| 5. no instrumental accompaniment | → | percussive instrumental accompaniment (kadápu whips) |
| 6. solo voice | → | lead chanter accompanied by second chanter |
| 7. continuous (short breaks to blow smoke) | → | discontinuous; intermissions for dancing, drinking, etc. |
| | Reempowerment | |
| málikai counterwitchcraft song | ← | málirríkairi curing songs |
| 1. unchanging tempo | ← | acceleration and deceleration |
| 2. unchanging pitch | ← | microtonal rising & many starting pitches used |
| 3. unchanging volume | ← | loud-soft contrast |
| 4. unchanging tonal structure | ←····→ | 3 different tonal structures, 1 identical to málikai, 2 variant structures |
| 5. no instrumental accompaniment | ← | percussive instrumental accompaniment (kútirúda rattles) |
| 6. solo voice | ← | quasi-second voice |
| 7. continuous (short breaks to blow smoke) | ← | discontinuous; intermissions for snuffing dzáato, etc. |

7.1   *Comparison of mythification and musicalization*

composed of smooth, flat lines of chanted speech, the mid-point in the spoken-to-sung spectrum. The various subgenres of *málikai* performed in childbirth and initiation rituals are musically integrated by the technique of splitting, or cutting in half, each word of chanted speech in the performances for sacred food (*káridzámai*). Even without the slightest knowledge about the spirit-names and naming processes used in *málikai*, it is immediately obvious to any listener that the long series of chants for initiates' food is a transformation of the chants for the food of newborn infants and their parents.

The musical integration of *málikai* and *málirríkairi* songs performed in curing rituals is a much subtler process of juxtaposition and the use of a common melodic structure in the subgenre of *málirríkairi* called *hínimái*. The more powerful process of "going through the middle of the world," or singing the myth of Kuwaikánirri in a frozen melodic pattern, is juxtaposed with the less powerful, more musically dynamic process of "bringing back" from the chthonian underworld. Nevertheless, in the special circumstances of an evil omen, shamans can break through to the more powerful, vertical dimension of bodily reempowerment by singing the evil omen song. The most powerful way of speaking in curing rituals is the musically flat mythification of thunder and lightning in *málikai* prayers to turn around collective witchcraft, a supreme example of transforming powerful sounds into mythic speech.

In sum, performances of *málikai* in childbirth and initiation rituals explore the full spectrum of spoken, chanted, and sung speech. More powerful ways of speaking move away from the central position of flatly chanted speech into ambiguous, musically dynamic modes of spoken-chant and chanted-song. The power of creation is the power to move up the scale of language music from mythification to musicalization. In curing rituals, the more powerful way of reempowering the body is to move down the scale of language music and into the realm of densely poetic, mythic speech. The most powerful means of reempowering body, society, and cosmos is spoken speech, or prayer, invoking the protection of *éenui* bee-spirits in the struggle against lightning, epidemics, and collective witchcraft. Reempowerment, in other words, is a movement from musicalization to mythification.

## The Doubly Reversed Transformation

By turning around the processes of creation in curing rituals, the chant-owner and shaman use the musicality of language to explore the highest level of meaning in the Kuwái myth cycle. At the outer limit, the Kuwái myth cycle embodies a double-edged prism of miniaturizing and expanding worlds. Although at one level these two processes of creation are separated by the implosion of the first creation after Kuwái's fiery "death," the two creations form part of a single, compound process of cosmogenesis at the highest level of meaning. In the Kuwái myth cycle, this highest level of meaning is packed into the tri-fold imagery of Dzúli's "supersocialized" act of memorizing Kuwái's sacred ways of speaking (*málikai*), the "oversocialization" of Kuwái through fiery transformation, and Hérri's eating of the "supernaturalized" food (*káridzámai*), or the newly imploded world of Kuwái's first creation. At this level, the relationship between vertical and horizontal dimensions of Kuwái's musico-mythic creation is no longer only a unidirectional transformation, or turning upside-down and inside-out of the world, but becomes a doubly reversible transformation that is capable of producing the opposite result: the turning outside-in and rightside-up of bodily, social, and cosmic processes.

This doubly reversed transformation is the space-time of death, the darker side of Kuwái's mythic creation, the space-time of the thunder and lightning with which Kuwái tried to kill the people at Hípana and the rainstorm of urine with which Kuwái tried to extinguish the fire of life. In the space-time of death, individual humanness is desocialized beyond the raw, unsocialized sexuality of incest into a rottenness of seduction, betrayal, and witchcraft-poisoning. Instead of supersocialized, musicalized speech (*málikai*), or the powerful sound that created life, speech becomes desocialized, or naturalized, into the sounds of death. The space-time of death is like a "black box" that contains the principle of total reversibility. In a narrative about the origin of evil omens, the Wakuénai explore the contents of this black box.

Iñápirríkuli was in love with the daughter of Kunáhwerrim and went to visit the woman in her father's village. The woman's two brothers told her to seduce Iñápirríkuli in the forest at night so that they could come to kill him in his sleep. Iñápirríkuli and the woman left Kunáhwerri's village together. When they had gone half-way to Iñápirríkuli's village, the woman said, "It's getting very late. Let's sleep here tonight and arrive early in the morning." She had brought along only one hammock. Iñápirríkuli had brought along his blowgun and a cartridge completely full of poison-tipped darts. He knew that the woman's two brothers would come to kill him in the night, so he took two of the darts and hid them inside his blowgun. The woman asked to see Iñápirríkuli's cartridge of poisoned darts so that she could count them and put cotton "heads" on each one.

While the woman was finishing this task, Iñápirríkuli went and cut a large *platanilla* leaf and some firewood. He built a fire and lay down on his *platanilla* leaf across from the woman's hammock. She

invited him to sleep with her in the hammock, but Iñápirríkuli refused. She spread her legs and invited Iñápirríkuli to make love to
her, but he knew that she wanted to make him fall asleep so that her
brothers could easily kill him. He pretended to fall asleep by closing
his eyes and snoring, and the woman fell asleep. While she was sleeping, Iñápirríkuli got up and blew tobacco smoke over the woman to
make her sleep very heavily.

Iñápirríkuli heard the brothers coming in the treetops. Their dream-
souls had assumed the form of nocturnal monkeys (*kúto*). The monkeys saw Iñápirríkuli's campfire and made a sound like "kwi-kwi."
Iñápirríkuli loaded his blowgun and saw one of the two monkey-
brothers. They took out their poison and threw it down over Iñápirríkuli, but he jumped out of the way. He shot the two monkeys with his
blowgun, and they ran away into the forest. Then Iñápirríkuli blew
tobacco smoke over the woman to wake her up and returned to his
*platanilla* leaf to pretend that he was sleeping. The woman woke up
and saw Iñápirríkuli sleeping. Just as she got out of her hammock,
she heard two loud "thump" sounds as the two monkey brothers fell
to their death on the forest floor. She tried desperately to awaken Iñápirríkuli and finally succeeded after kicking him as hard as she could.
Iñápirríkuli pretended to be waking up from a deep sleep, rubbing
his eyes and exclaiming, "I was sleeping like a dead man." The
woman pointed to where the two sounds had come from and asked
Iñápirríkuli, "This couldn't be my brothers that you have killed?"
"No, they're far away from here. How could I do that to them?" Iñápirríkuli replied. The woman asked for his cartridge of darts to count
them and see if any had been used while she slept. She counted and
found that none of the darts was missing, and Iñápirríkuli convinced
her that she had only heard some dead branches falling in the forest.
The woman went back to sleep, and Iñápirríkuli blew tobacco smoke
over her again to make her sleep like a drunkard.

Iñápirríkuli took a burning log to go search in the forest for the
two dead monkey brothers. He found the first monkey, cut off the
head, and stomped on the severed head until it was all the way underground. He left the body to rot on the ground. Then he found the
other monkey and did the same thing. The heads of the two monkey
brothers turned into enormous fruit trees called *dzápura*. Iñápirríkuli
went back to his camp and slept.

When Iñápirríkuli woke up in the morning, he told the woman that
he had dreamed that a very bad thing had happened to her family. "I

think they fell ill," he said to her. "Let's go back and see how they are," said the woman. So they turned back on the trail leading to Kunáhwerri's village. The woman walked in front of Iñápirríkuli, who took a little stick and picked his teeth with it. He threw the stick ahead of the woman on the trail, and she smelled a foul odor. "This is an evil omen for you meaning that someone in your family is sick," explained Iñápirríkuli. The woman began to run ahead of Iñápirríkuli, and he secretly placed his blowgun across the trail in front of her. She tripped over the blowgun and fell to the ground. "This is another evil omen for you, and I think it means that someone in your family has died," said Iñápirríkuli. From that time on, there would always be evil omens in the world.

The woman was running faster than ever toward her father's village. She was far ahead of Iñápirríkuli, who took some knots off a *guambé* vine and threw them across the trail in front of the woman. The knots turned into little white-throated birds (*házde*). "This is another evil omen for you, a very bad one this time. Your entire family is in great danger, so let's hurry up," Iñápirríkuli told the woman.

The woman was running ahead of Iñápirríkuli as they drew near to Kunáhwerrim's village. Iñápirríkuli did not want to arrive there with her, so he told the woman that his leg hurt and that he had to walk slowly behind her. He came to a log across the path that was covered with worm shit. He grabbed a couple of handfuls and formed it into a ball. He pushed it under his loincloth against his hip and called the woman to come over to where he was sitting. "Look at how swollen I am. I can't walk anymore." Iñápirríkuli shouted in mock pain and told the woman to go ahead to Kunáhwerrim's village without him. As soon as she was out of sight, Iñápirríkuli threw away the ball of worm shit and departed as quickly as possible for his village on the other side of the forest. The woman ran by herself into her father's village. There her father, Kunáhwerrim, told her that her two brothers had died suddenly in their sleep during the night. They had had sharp pains in their stomachs as though shot by arrows.

The narrative about evil omens demonstrates how an initial situation of totally desocialized human relations is gradually turned around into a process of discovering death through sound, dream, smell, touch, vision, and speech.[2] An initial movement out into the forest at night, or from inside to outside social space, depicts a process of desocialization that works directly against the process of creating socialized human individuals. Rather than transforming incestuous, animal-like sexuality into the imagery of food, fasting, and eating within the center of social space, the narrative about evil omens shows the perversely antisocial transformation of incestuous sexuality into a deadly scheme of seduction, betrayal, and murder in the extrasocial space-time of the forest at night. As in other narratives, the trickster-creator is a master of deceit, and he fools the would-be seductress by hiding two darts inside his blowgun and allowing the woman to count the darts in his cartridge before and after he slays the two monkey brothers.[3]

When the two monkey brothers arrive late at night to kill Iñápirríkuli in his sleep, the incest-tinged plan to use their sister's sexuality as a trap backfires. Using tobacco like a switch that turns on and off individual consciousness, Iñápirríkuli puts the woman into a deep sleep and jumps out of the path of poison thrown down at him by the two monkey brothers. Like witches, the two brothers come to kill the animal-shaped dream-soul at night, yet they also use poison to destroy their victim's body-spirit. The image of poison thrown down to the ground in the nocturnal forest is a protrait of totally desocialized humanness, a rottenness in which vertical and horizontal processes of alienation, or witchcraft and poisoning, become fused into an ambiguous whole. The downward motion of the two monkey brothers' poison foreshadows their own deaths and the falling of their bodies down to the ground.

The initial movement from inside to outside social space is thus doubled by the two brothers' nocturnal journey into the forest as poison-wielding witches. The double movement out into the forest, or double alienation, is then followed by a pair of downward movements from up in the forest's canopy to down on the ground. The pivotal episode of the narrative comes at the moment when Iñápirríkuli wakes up the dead brothers' sister so that she can hear the loud thumping sounds of their bodies striking the forest floor. Hearing the brothers' deaths is the first step in a two-fold process of reversing the double alienation of witchcraft-and-poisoning, a turning outside-in and rightside-up of body, society, and cosmos. Although the woman suspects the true meaning of the two "thump" sounds, she is persuaded that Iñápirríkuli has not killed her brothers by counting his blowgun darts and finding that none are missing.

Before he can turn around the horizontal dimension of space by making the woman return to her village, Iñápirríkuli must complete the reversal of vertical space by returning to cut off the heads of the two witches. Paradoxically, the way to reverse the downward falling of poison and dead bodies is through a further downward movement from the surface of the ground down into the chthonian underworld of the dead. The severed heads spring up into giant trees, an image of new life returning from the space-time of doubly alienated death. With this first return to life, Iñápirríkuli has turned around the vertical descent of death. Although the cosmos is still inside-out, it is now rightside-up.

The turning around of horizontal space begins when Iñápirríkuli relates his bad dream to the woman, frightening her into turning back toward her father's village. As we have seen in the previous chapter, telling and interpreting dreams in the morning are important activities that connect the invisible, nocturnal world of dream-soul interactions to the everyday social world. Bad dreams are evidence of witchcraft and require individuals to temporarily withdraw from social and economic activities into the protective sanctuary of bee-spirits, honey, flowers, and a surrogate mother. In the narrative about evil omens, Iñápirríkuli's activity of relating a bad dream is the connection between the vertical, nocturnal reversal of witchcraft-poisoning and the horizontal, diurnal reversal of seduction-betrayal. Recounting the dream sets in motion a process of returning back-across horizontal space in which the woman becomes progressively more aware of, and frightened by, the knowledge that her two brothers have died during the night. Whereas she went out into the forest on the first day with the anticipation of Iñápirríkuli's death, she returns from the forest on the second day with the suspicion of her brothers' deaths.

The woman's return to her father's village is analogous to a process of self-empowerment or reempowerment, since she ends up running by herself into the village. She has become "self-propelled," but the motor that pushes her backward across the world is an increasing level of fear, a reverse mirror image of the calming, cooling, and sweetening through which Iñápirríkuli reempowered his mortally wounded younger brother, Kuwaikánirri. The woman's return is a process of re-humanization, a return to the mesocosm of human life through reactivating the senses of smell, touch, and vision. Iñápirríkuli knows how to transform the woman's guilt into fear and, in doing so, to convert the would-be seductress into the star witness for her own prosecution.[4] The pathway of rehumanization is strewn with life's unpleasant obstacles: foul smells, banged-up shins, disturbing visions, and cunning deceptions. At the end of the stinking, bumpy journey lies an equally unpleasant verdict, the learning and knowing of death.

In spite of the overwhelmingly negative flavor of this narrative, a comforting message of rehumanization emerges from the inky shadows of witchcraft-poisoning, seduction-betrayal, and doubly alienated death. The cosmos is rehumanized by turning around the doubly alienating movements out into the forest at night into an opposite movement back to the village in the day, or turning the world outside-in and downside-up. Even the foulest, most antisocial and dehumanizing behaviors can be turned around to rehumanize individual, society, and cosmos.

As a performance, the narrative about evil omens was literally a return to laughter for the people of Gavilán. Hernan narrated the story to a gathering of men, women, and children on the evening after the week of the prolonged curing ritual in August 1981, a context in which an infant girl's death had been attributed to evil omens experienced by her parents. Like the narrative process of rehumanization, the ritual process of confessing evil omens to the shaman began as a revelation of sounds heard at night, or the strange resemblance between a rooster's crowing and the sick child's crying. And like Iñápirríkuli's recounting of bad dreams in the narrative, the crucial act of ritual confession was the parents' recounting of a bad argument in which the father had openly wished for his daughter's death. The failure of Hernan and his brother to prevent the little girl's death had created an ambience of grief in Gavilán and neighboring villages. When the evil omens were diagnosed and confessed on the second day of the curing ritual, children and young people had stopped playing their usual noisy games. Several days later, in his performance of the narrative about evil omens, Hernan led his children and grandchildren back from the sickening, double alienation of witchcraft-poisoning to the everyday world of human social life. His skillful verbal and bodily renderings of the trickster-creator's mythic act of picking his teeth evoked a few mirthful chuckles. The most comic moment of the performance came when Hernan imitated Iñápirríkuli's use of worm shit to trick the woman into running by herself back to her father's village. With a look of mock pain on his face and a feigned weakness in his voice, Hernan rolled an old rag into a ball and stuck it under his pants against his hip. The old chant-owner, master poet and musician among his people, could also play the role of stand-up comedian, and howls of laughter filled the big front room of his house.

In addition to its situational meaning as a collective return to laughter, the narrative about evil omens contains a profound insight into the ethnopoetics of ritual power. Rehumanization is itself a poetic process of transforming evil thoughts and bad dreams into a sensuous world of socialized natural species and objects. The alienated, invisible sounds of death are gradually transformed into socialized, verbal ways of learning and knowing through the intermediate stages of recounting dreams, smelling, touching, seeing, and deceiving. The narrative is a process of constructing a poetics of poetic speech, or a hierarchy of more-to-less powerful ways of experiencing and conceiving natural and social phenomena that cuts across all the various subgenres and genres of more-to-less powerful ways of speaking. This metatrope of ritual power shows how the most powerful modes of knowing, or hearing and dreaming, are connected to the least powerful mode of knowing, or interpreting speech, through a mesocosm of smelling, touching, and seeing.

Hearing and dreaming are the most powerful ways of knowing because they alone can transform the double contaminations of witchcraft-poisoning and seduction-betrayal into a doubly reversed, rehumanized world. Smelling, touching, and seeing are intermediate ways of knowing the mesocosm, or human life world. Through speech acts that link each of these three sense modes to the human social world, the external world of objects and species is rehumanized into a tapestry of meaningful signs. Speech acts and their interpretation are the least powerful ways of knowing, since the spoken word is equally useful for hiding knowledge through irony and deceit as it is for imparting accurate knowledge.

## Keepers of the Sacred Chants

Mythification and musicalization are ways of creating and exploring the micro- and macrocosmic space-times that infuse and surround the human mesocosm of smells, tastes, textures, and visions. The simultaneously expanding and contracting world of Kuwái and the jaguar-ancestors is not a mystifying, bewildering pantheon of spirits that are abstractly imposed upon the human mesocosm but a process of humanizing, empowering, and reempowering the mesocosm through poeticizing the same basic objects, species, and life experiences that constitute it. In sociological terms, the human mesocosm is the qualitative, cultural space-time into which the individual is socialized and re-socialized throughout the human life cycle and through which the dispersion of an egocentrically conceived kin group is made into the pattern of institutions for collectively reproducing the social order (Turner 1985).

Performances of *málikai* transform everyday speech into Kuwái's powerful ways of speaking through spirit-naming, or esoteric taxonomies of mythic beings, and musicalization, or highly formalized techniques of transposing mythic speech into the tones, timbres, volumes, and rhythms of language music. However, the processes of transforming everyday speech into supersocialized, musicalized ways of speaking do not create a separate reality of mythic beings but integrate the world as experienced into a hyperanimate world of empowerment. The musical journeys out of the human mesocosm into the outer limits of micro- and macro-cosmic space are always turning—around, inside-out, upside-down, down-under, away-across, back-across, and so on. Musical travel out of the mesocosm is at the same time a journey into the inner workings of socialization and social reproduction. Sounds, beginning with the inchoate human vocalization of *ínyapakáati dzéema* ("H-m-m-p-f-f") and spreading out to embrace the entire natural and social soundscape, are the pathways into and out of the microcosm of dream-souls and the macrocosm of shadow-spirits from the mesocosm of human beings. Ultimately, to control sounds, dreams, and the musicality of speech is to hold the power of transformability: every formative or transformative process is reversible through the transposition of musical sounds into mythically empowered speech or the complementary transposition of mythic speech into musically empowering sound patterns. Mythification and musicalization are poetic genres of discourse that enable individuals and groups to sensuously experience the ongoing creation and reempowerment of a fully human world of bodily, social, and cosmic processes.

Clearly, chant-owners and shamans have greater participatory powers than other individuals who experience these comings-into-being and renewals of life as ritual subjects rather than specialists. However, the specialist-to-subject relationship, like the interrelations between more and less powerful ways of speaking, is relativized in a number of ways. The exercising of ritual power is not only a one-way, monological activity but also includes the subjects' communications of dreams, unusual events, physical symptoms, and other information to the specialists. These specific, contextual details are not external to ritual power but are actively sought out and integrated into the twin processes of mythification and musicalization. Chant-owners and shamans are masters of participatory discrepancies (Keil 1987), those small but highly significant alterations that make each performance unique and situationally adjusted to specific circumstances and individual differences.

In addition to the open-ended, dialogical negotiation of meaning in highly sacred ritual contexts, the relationship between specialists and nonspecialists is relativized through the direct, sensuous participation in mythification and musicalization in a number of less high-powered contexts. By making and playing musical instruments, adult men take part

in mythification and musicalization on a collective scale in initiation rituals, *kwépani* ("Kuwái-dance"), and *pudáli* exchange ceremonies. In the
musical dialogues between *molítu* flute players and women, for example,
the single musical tone of *molítu* flutes is transformed into a genre of
quasi-speech, or stress patterns, that carry semantic messages from men
to women. Semantic meaning and musical sound are intentionally and
totally merged into musicalized communication. Dancing and singing *kápetiápani* ("whip-dance") is a collective performance of musicalization,
or the transformation of Kuwái into external objects (e.g., whips) and the
expansion of the social world through the movement of male and female
dancers from inside to outside the ceremonial house. In *pákamarántakan*
song duels, adult women musicalize their marginal situation in the female
initiation ritual by singing animal names (e.g., currassow and tapir) to
produce a discourse on Otherness, or naturalized social being. In short,
collective singing and dancing in ceremonial and ritual contexts are ways
of generalizing the poetic processes of mythification and musicalization
to entire communities of nonspecialists (see Hill 1993a).

Even the language of everyday speech embodies poetic relations of
ritual power and mythic meaning. The verbal activity of counting, or
enumerating, is governed by formal principles of nominal classification
in all five dialects of Wáku.[5] The juxtaposition of nouns within numeral
classifier sets is based upon the esoteric meanings attributed to species
and objects in sacred narratives and ritually powerful ways of speaking.
Tobacco, for example, is classified together with arrows, darts, hooks,
nails, and other sharp objects. This allocation of nouns makes little or
no sense in terms of the actual, physical properties of tobacco but becomes perfectly intelligible in light of the ritual uses of tobacco and tobacco spirits to "cut off the heads" of animal spirit-names and to "cut
in half" lightning, the "paper of Amáru," and other disease-causing spirits. Through numeral classifiers, children are socialized into a world of
subject-object relations that implicitly specifies micro- and macro-cosmic
processes of empowerment within and about the human mesocosm.

The chant-owner's exceptional skills as a master of musical, poetic
ways of speaking do not alienate him from the social world of nonspecialists, who are only partially aware of the names and sounds of empowerment. The chant-owner cannot act alone in empowering and humanizing the world but only as *primus inter pares*. He is a master of poetic
ways of speaking in a social world of men, women, and children who all
participate in Kuwái's powerful ways of speaking. They are Wakuénai,
the People of Our Language, keepers of the sacred chants.

# Notes

## 1. An Introduction to Wakuénai Ritual Poetics

1. The project was called "Man and the Biosphere Pilot Project Number 1 on Tropical Rain Forests," or MAB-UNESCO, and consisted of approximately ten years of scientific studies on soils, nutrient cycling, natural plant communities, regeneration of disturbed forests, energetics of swidden horticulture, and a variety of secondary topics. In addition to support from UNESCO, the project received funding from the National Science Foundation through the Institute of Ecology, University of Georgia, and was logistically based at the Venezuelan Scientific Research Institute (IVIC).

2. A major controversy over the activities of the New Tribes Mission had erupted in the national press shortly before my first visit to Venezuela in 1980. I am very grateful to Dra. Nelly Arvelo-Jimenez at the Department of Anthropology, IVIC, for inviting me to join her ongoing research into processes of missionization among indigenous peoples of Venezuela. I remain in awe of Dra. Arvelo-Jimenez's courageous and lucid criticisms of the national government's support for the New Tribes Mission, and I am thankful for the opportunity she gave me to understand the national context within which my fieldwork with the Wakuénai and other Arawakan peoples of the Upper Río Negro region was to take place.

3. Throughout this study, proper names of indigenous villages and individuals have been changed to comply with the Protection of Human Subjects Act.

4. See Hill and Moran 1983 for a detailed analysis of social and economic relations in Punta Bella.

5. See Hill and Moran 1983 for a comparison of social and economic relations in Gavilán and Punta Bella.

6. Listening copies of my original field recordings can be ordered for research purposes at the Archives of Traditional Music, Morrison Hall, Indiana University, Bloomington, Indiana 47405. The accession number for recordings made during doctoral research in 1980–81 is 82-418-F, cassettes number 1817–1833. The later set of recordings made by Siderio are listed under accession number 85-526-F, cassettes number 1–12. In addition, copies of the 1980–81 recordings were made in 1981 on open reels (VEN 866-874 M) at the Instituto Interamericano de Etnomusicologia y Folklore, which has since become part of the National Folklore Institute of Venezuela.

## 2. *The Regional and Historical Contexts of Wakuénai Ritual Poetics*

1. The litany of sib names can be understood as a way of bridging the gap between powerful, poetic ways of speaking in *malikái* and conversational speech. As Friedrich noted, "In conversation, lists are common, whereas a taxonomy, while rare in conversation, is often built into primitive poetry and may serve as a mnemonic device" (1986:32). The litany of sib names is a metapoetic performance, or a way of speaking about poetic ways of speaking through using the relative hierarchy of "going in search" and "heaping up the names" to arrange lists of sib names.

2. I also elicited a version of this narrative in Spanish from the Camico family of Maroa and Puerto Ayacucho. The narrator was a great-grandson of Venancio Camico. Along with my coauthor, Robin Wright, I have previously published two interpretations of this narrative (Wright and Hill 1986, Hill and Wright 1988). Terence Turner, Norman Whitten, and the contributors to Rethinking History and Myth have all helped me to deepen and refine my understanding of the narrative.

## 3. *The Genesis of Ritual Power*

1. The indigenous word for shotgun, *múkawa*, is derived from the word for "hot" (*hámukáni*) and is an interesting case of the creation of a novel lexical item through the process of generic classification, or spirit-naming, in performances of *málikai* (see Chapter 4). Also, the Wakuénai attribute collective witchcraft, or lightning, to Amáru's mythic shotgun, an interpretation that has interesting resonances with the associations between lightning-ancestors and firearms in the Central Andes (see Silverblatt 1988).

2. These songs are what later came to be reproduced on the two pairs of ancestor trumpets of Kuwái. These instruments make a deep, hissing sound that is associated with huge jaguars (*dzáwi*) and are named after these animals (*dzáwiñápa*, "jaguar-bone," and *dzáwiñápa íhwerrúti*, "gigantic jaguar-bone"). These jaguar sounds embody the completion of Kuwái's creation of the world, the jaguar

being seen as the last animal species that Kuwái created prior to his "death," or fiery transformation.

3. My understanding of the Kuwái myth cycle has been greatly improved through studying recent works on narrative structure by Terence Turner (1985, 1988). In particular, I have benefited most directly from Turner's treatment of narrative structure as a process of self-embedded, internalized transformations that encode processes of socialization and social reproduction. Also, Turner's sensitive analysis (1985) of spatial movements and dimensions as metaphors for developmental and institutional processes in Northern Kayapó social organization has proven immensely useful in my interpretation of the Kuwái myth cycle.

4. This is very similar to the situation of the hero of Kayapó myth as analyzed by Turner (1985). In the Northerth Kayapó myth, the hero's acts of slaying his jaguar-mother and receiving cultural artifacts of adult masculinity (e.g., bow and arrows, cotton, and cooking fire) are analogous to the refusals to receive food and shelter by the Wakuénai first initiate.

5. Alternatively, this can be read as a metaphor for the individual's learning to control his sexuality. See Rubel and Rosman 1978 for an exploration of the uses of food as a substance for defining the incest taboo and relations of exchange in various New Guinea societies.

6. *Déetu* is also the namesake of a type of flute played during the late-night, transitional period of *pudáli* ceremonies. In this context, the imitiation of the *déetu* weevils' natural feeding behavior is both an implicit evocation of shamanistic curing practices on a collective scale and a symbolic process of collapsing images of eating and reproducing into an ambiguous, metonymic whole (see Hill 1987a, 1987b, 1993a).

7. In the version of the Kuwái myth cycle narrated by Hohódeni elders to Robin Wright, Kuwái is described as "very old" in this narrative.

8. Also, it is interesting that the image of "three outer fingers" returns here from the space-time of mythic beginnings, when Iñápirríkuli and his brothers were created from the bones of their slain father's outer three fingers. The five fingers embody the wholeness of the father and son after their initial separation at the beginning of the Kuwái myth cycle. The number five is also the ideal number of patrisibs making up each phratry.

9. Matos Arvelo (1912:180) described the behavior of women secluded inside a house during *kwépani* ceremonies but without specific reference to *molítu* flutes. According to him, pregnant women acted out the process of childbirth even if the time of parturition was still weeks away, believing that their rehearsal would act in combination with the music of sacred flutes to make their labor pains as slight as possible and to prevent other complications. Other women grated manioc tubers inside their house in the belief that their work would be easier in the future.

10. The Wakuénai use of *molítu* frogs' singing as a timing device for horticultural activities is strikingly similar to the use of toads' singing as a means for

deciding when to begin the main planting in the Central Andean community of Misminay (Urton 1981).

11. The strong relation between young men's success as gardeners during bride service and their ability to become fully adult, married men was tersely and eloquently summarized by Matos Arvelo. "La mujer se adquiere por la fuerza del conuco" ["A woman is acquired through the 'strength' of the manioc garden"] (1912:44, my translation).

12. *Lingua geral*, or *Neengatú*, was a trade language created by Jesuit missionaries among indigenous groups of coastal Brazil and later introduced by them in the Upper Río Negro region during the eighteenth century.

13. According to Matos Arvelo 1912, the soul always re-unites with the sacred animal soul of its ancestors, but a violent death preceded by large losses of blood is considered to prolong the period of painful separation from the ancestor soul. Matos Arvelo attributed the low rates of violence and murder among the Wakuénai and other Arawakan groups near Maroa to these beliefs. Only three murders took place in his fifteen years as Prefect of Maroa (1912:97).

14. The manioc garden is the usual place where husbands and wives meet to have sexual intercourse. Since husbands and wives work together in all burning, planting, and weeding phases of gardening, they have a lot of free time on their own in the gardens. The garden is thus the place of adult heterosexual intercourse, the place of conceiving children, and the place of cooperative male-female productive labor.

15. In ceremonial songs and speeches, houses are referred to as "bodies" and doors as "house-mouths." This metaphorization of houses is based upon the style of single longhouse settlements that were common to both Arawakan and Tukanoan groups of the Northwest Amazon region until Catholic missionaries forced indigenous peoples to replace them with criollo-style, mud-walled houses for each nuclear family.

## 4. Birth and the Art of Microtonal Rising

1. Passive voice is used in translating verbs in cases where the third-person, singular, masculine subject (*li-*, *hli-*) does not appear to denote any specific being. Active voice is used with the third-person female pronoun (*ru-*, *sru-*) because it obviously denotes Amáru.

2. Stripping bark off trees is also related to the making of large, jaguar-bone (*dzáwinápa*) ancestor trumpets for male initiation rituals. The bark of *yebaro* trees is lashed around a framework of poles to create large cavities, or resonators, that amplify the trumpets' sound.

3. *Máhnekánari*, or "Nobody knows," is a circumlocution that refers to the fact that no one knew the identity of Kuwái's father when he was born.

4. These sticky fibers also make excellent bandages for flesh wounds. Due to

the extremely high humidity and acidity of the Upper Río Negro, it takes much longer for such wounds to heal than in drier regions. The danger of infection is therefore much higher.

5. In *The Raw and the Cooked*, Lévi-Strauss suggested a tentative definition of the social meaning of culinary symbolism in sacred rituals. "The individuals who are 'cooked' are those deeply involved in a physiological process: the new-born child, the woman who has just given birth, or the pubescent girl" (1969:336). This definition, along with the examples of "cooking the pains" in curing rituals of the Yurok and "roasting" mothers of newborn infants in Southeast Asia, provide interesting analogues to the use of cooking metaphors in Wakuénai rites of passage.

6. The spawning of *Leporinus* species is a basic metaphor in ceremonial dances of *pudáli* (Hill 1987a, 1987b). Large ceremonial trumpets named after *kulírri* (a species of large catfish) are played by groups of men as they arrive in a hosts' village with an offering of smoked fish and game meat. The low, rumbling sound of the trumpets imitates the sound of a stream filled to the brim with spawning, migrating *Leporinus* fish.

7. Hunger, scarcity, and heaping up the names are also tightly connected in the myth of Uliámali, an anaconda child who caused a cosmic flood. More generally, the importance of ritual fasting in all sacred ritual contexts is related to the frequency with which the Wakuénai experience scarcity of fish and game meat during long wet seasons. By making the ability to demonstrate control over hunger into a sacred axiom for defining humanness, sacred rituals and ceremonies provide an alternative, more hierarchical mode of social organization based on differential control over nonmaterial power resources (e.g., *málikai*) (see Hill 1984b).

8. The connection between Amáru, the anaconda, and salt is another clue indicating that the Wakuénai might have had relations of trade or other contacts with Quichua-speaking peoples of the Northern or Central Andes prior to the arrival of European peoples in South America. The word *amáro* denotes "anaconda" or "serpent" in Quichua, and the Wakuénai myth of the origin of salt metaphorically juxtaposes the terms Amáru and anaconda (*umáwari*). In precontact times, Northern Andean peoples mined salt and exchanged it with Central Andean peoples and neighboring lowlands groups.

9. Friedrich has noted the tendency of literary critics "to ignore the music of the poems they are reviewing and even the issue of whether and how a poem or poet is musical. . . . Most poets—as is often transparent from interviews on their craft—are reticent, inarticulate, cryptic, or astutely devious when it comes to this subject" (1986:36–37). The latter observation is entirely accurate for Hernan and other poets among the Wakuénai, even though their verbal art is part of a nonliterate, sacred tradition rather than the written, secularized literature produced by poets in the industrialized societies of the West.

## 5. *Initiation into the Cult of Kuwái and the Musicalization of Mythic Speech*

1. In male initiation rituals, each of these calls is answered by a blast of flute and trumpet sound, the collective voice of Kuwái. On the fourth call (Dzo-re), the instruments begin to play melodies.

2. This narrative can be interpreted as an inversion of the Kuwái myth cycle (Hill 1983).

3. Chernela (1985) has reported a strong correlation between the social ranking of patrilineal sibs and access to downstream areas that are far richer in fishing resources among the Uanano. This hierarchical zoning of sibs was not in evidence among the Wakuénai of Venezuela in the 1980s nor among the Hohódeni (a Wakuénai phratry of the Aiarí River in Brazil) in the 1970s (Wright 1981).

4. See Hill 1987, 1993a, for detailed interpretations of the emergence of shamanistic power in *pudáli*.

5. The fact that pigs and cattle are classified as *éenunai* but not chickens hints at an alternative translation of *umáwari, éenunai*, and *képinai* as a form of locomotive taxonomy instead of habitat taxonomy. *Eenunai* are creatures that move about by walking on four legs, *képinai* are those that fly with wings, and *umáwari* are those that swim with fins or other body parts.

6. This indigenous sentiment of political distance between the Cubeo and other Eastern Tukanoan groups corresponds to the measurable linguistic drift of Cubeo language away from other Eastern Tukanoan languages (Jackson 1983: 172–73; Sorensen 1967).

7. This ethnoanthropological observation is entirely consistent with Goldman's descriptions (1963) of Cubeo narratives about Kuwái. For the Cubeo, Kuwái is merely a culture hero, or one mythic being among many others, rather than the source of life-giving ancestral powers.

## 6. *"Going Through the Middle" and "Bringing Back from the Edge"*

1. The Wakuénai have a number of standardized formulae for interpreting common dream imagery, and these establish many of the same metaphorical comparisons that are constructed in the various forms of spirit-naming in *málikai*.

2. These spirit-names for lightning resemble Central Andean beliefs in *Illápa*, the lightning ancestor-fathers, or powerful spirits formally associated with the great emperor of Cuzco. In particular, the concern for different shades, or colors, of lightning in *málikai* is similar to the legendary hero Tumayricapa: "When Tumayricapa saw the herders approach, he snorted white hail (one of Illápa's meteorological specialties) from one nostril and pinkish hail from the other" (Silverblatt 1988:181).

3. Whole families died in villages along the Río Negro, the Casiquiare, and the

Guainía rivers in early 1980. Perhaps 20 percent of the young children in the region died during the epidemic. The number of deaths went much higher in San Carlos de Río Negro and surrounding villages, in part because the local doctor refused to give adequate medical treatment to the "Indios" and failed to understand the seriousness of the epidemic's effects on a subsistence-oriented economy where little or no food is stored.

4. Notice the similarity of this explanation to the Kuwáiñai narrative. In both, bathing in the river alone amounts to an unmediated contact with the Kuwáiñai that leads to supernatual death. Also, several people mentioned that the man had died because the doctor in Maroa had told everyone not to bathe in the river until their fevers had totally subsided. Thus, the man who died of measles in Gavilán in 1980 was doubly fitted into the interpretive framework of the Kuwáiñai narrative.

5. Clothes were by far the most common form of gift that patients and their families offered to Hernan and his brother in return for curing rituals in 1981 and 1984. When the unusual case of a shotgun valued at 1,500 *bolivars* is excluded from the sample, the analysis of these transactions (n = 38) is as follows: clothing (67% of value), food items (17%), miscellaneous articles (5%), cash (3%), matches (3%), fishhooks (2%), soap (2%), and cigarettes (1%).

6. Coughing or gagging is the sign of persons who swallow poison in their food. Pieces of hair or splinters of wood are said to get stuck in the victims' throats, causing them to choke.

7. The nearest medical doctor would ordinarily have been in Maroa. However, the young doctor who had saved many lives during the measles epidemic of 1980 had finished his rural medical service by mid-1981, and his replacement had not yet arrived in Maroa.

## 7. The Poetics of Ritual Power

1. A similar process of poetically comparing the human body to a musical instrument was explored in the following poem by Basavanna, a political activist who lived in the tenth century in India: "Make of my body the beam of a lute of my head the sounding gourd of my nerves the strings of my fingers the plucking rods. Clutch me close and play your thirty-two songs O lord of the meeting rivers!" (Ramanujan 1973:83).

2. The progression of sense modes in this narrative is strikingly similar to an indigenous North American myth called "The Wife Who Goes Out Like a Man" (Hymes 1981).

3. Counting in Wáku is a highly significant activity in which nominal classification is used to categorize different classes of things. These nominal classifiers embody relations of ritual power and mythic meaning.

4. Lévi-Strauss discussed a similar story about the confessions of a Zuñi boy accused of witchcraft. "First of all, we see that the boy tried for witchraft, for

which he risks the death penalty, wins his acquittal not by denying but by admitting his alleged crime. . . . By his confession, the defendant is transformed into a witness for the prosecution, with the participation (and even the complicity) of his judges" (1963 : 173–74).

5. Counting is closely related to hearing and dreaming, the two most powerful ways of knowing, in the narrative about evil omens.

# References

Arhem, Kaj. 1981. *Makuna Social Organization.* Uppsala Studies in Cultural Anthropology, 4. Stockholm, Sweden: LiberTryck.

Basso, Ellen. 1985. *A Musical View of the Universe: Kalapalo Narratives and Ritual Performance.* Philadelphia: University of Pennsylvania Press.

Brown, Michael. 1985. *Tsewa's Gift: Magic and Meaning in an Amazonian Society.* Washington, D.C.: Smithsonian Institution Press.

Chernela, Janet. 1983. "Hierarchy and Economy of the Uanano (Kotiria) Speaking Peoples of the Middle Uaupés Basin." Ph.D. dissertation, Department of Anthropology, Columbia University.

———. 1985. "Indigenous Fishing in the Neotropics: The Tukanoan Uanano of the Blackwater Uaupés River Basin in Brazil and Colombia." *Interciencia* 10(2): 78–86.

Clark, Kathleen, and Uhl, Chris. 1988. "Farming, Fishing, and Fire in the History of the Upper Río Negro Region of Venezuela." *Human Ecology* 15(1): 1–26.

Dixon, Robert. 1983. *Where Have All the Adjectives Gone?* Amsterdam: Publishers Mouton.

Drummond, Lee. 1981. "The Serpent's Children: Semiotics of Cultural Genesis in Arawak and Trobriand Myth." *American Ethnologist* 8(3): 633–60.

Eco, Umberto. 1990. *The Limits of Interpretation.* Bloomington: Indiana University Press.

Federmann, Nicolas. 1945 [1530]. *Narración del Primer Viaje de Federmann a Venezuela.* Caracas: Lit. y Tip. del Comercio.

Friedrich, Paul. 1986. *The Language Parallax: Linguistic Relativism and Poetic Indeterminacy.* Austin: University of Texas Press.

Galvão, Eduardo. 1959. "Aculturação Indígena no Río Negro. Boletim do Museu Paraense Emilio Goeldi, N.S.," *Antropologia* 7:1–60.

———. 1964. "Encontro de Sociedades Tribal e Nacional no Río Negro, Amazonas," in *XXXV Congreso Internacional de Americanistas, Actas y Memorias,* 329–39. Mexico City: International Congress of Americanists.

Gebhart-Sayer, Angelika. 1986. "Inca Tales of the Shipibo-Conibo." Ms. Voelkerkundliches Institut. Tuebingen: Univ. of Tuebingen.

Goldman, Irving. 1963. *The Cubeo: Indians of the Northwest Amazon.* Urbana: University of Illinois Press.

Graham, Laura. 1986. "Three Modes of Shavante Vocal Expression: Wailing, Collective Singing, and Political Oratory," in *Native South American Discourse,* Joel Sherzer and Greg Urban, eds., pp. 83–118. Amsterdam: Mouton de Gruyter.

Hemming, John. 1987. *Amazon Frontier.* Cambridge, MA: Harvard University Press.

Herrera, Rafael, Carl Jordan, Ernesto Medina, and Hans Klinge. 1978. "Amazonian Ecosystems: Their Structure and Functioning with Particular Emphasis on Nutrients." *Interciencia* 3:223–31.

Hill, Jonathan. 1983. "Wakuénai Society: A Processual-Structural Analysis of Indigenous Cultural Life in the Upper Río Negro Region of Venezuela." Ph. D. dissertation, Department of Anthropology, Indiana University.

———. 1984a. "Los Misioneros y las Fronteras." *America Indigena* 44(1): 183–90.

———. 1984b. "Social Equality and Ritual Hierarchy: the Arawakan Wakuénai of Venezuela." *American Ethnologist* 11:528–44.

———. 1985a. "Myth, Spirit-Naming, and the Art of Microtonal Rising: Childbirth Rituals of the Arawakan Wakuénai." *Latin Music Review* 6(1): 1–30.

———. 1985b. "Agnatic Sibling Relations and Rank in Northern Arawakan Myth and Social Life," in *Working Papers on South American Indians,* Judith Shapiro, ed., pp. 25–33. Bennington: Bennington College.

———. 1987a. "Representaciones Musicales Como Estructuras Adaptativas. Traducida por A. Pollak-Eltz y Yolanda Lecuna." *Montalban* 17:67–101.

———. 1987b. "Wakuénai Ceremonial Exchange in the Northwest Amazon." *Journal of Latin American Lore* 13(2): 183–224.

———. 1989. "Ritual Production of Environmental History among the Arawakan Wakuénai of Venezuela." *Human Ecology* 17(1): 1–25.

———. 1990. "Myth, Music, and History: Poetic Transformations of Narrative Discourse." *Journal of Folklore Research* 27 (1–2): 115–32.

————. 1993a. "Metamorphosis: Mythic and Musical Modes of Exchange in the Northwest Amazon." In *A Universe of Music: A World History*, Malena Kuss, editor. Washington: Smithsonian Institution Press.

————. 1993b. "Cosmology and Situation of Contact." In *Cosmology, Value, and Inter-Ethnic Contact in South America*, Terence Turner, editor. South American Indian Studies, No. 9, pp. 46–55. Bennington: Bennington College.

Hill, Jonathan, editor. 1988. *Rethinking History and Myth: Indigenous South American Perspectives on the Past*. Urbana: University of Illinois Press.

Hill, Jonathan, and Moran, Emilio. 1983. "Adaptive Strategies of Wakuénai Peoples to the Oligotrophic Rain Forest of the Río Negro Basin," in *Adaptive Responses of Native Amazonians*, William Vickers and Raymond Hames, eds., pp. 113–35. New York: Academic Press.

Hill, Jonathan, and Wright, Robin. 1988. "Time, Narrative, and Ritual: Historical Interpretations from an Amazonian Society," in *Rethinking History and Myth: Indigenous South American Perspectives on the Past*, Jonathan Hill, ed., pp. 78–105. Urbana: University of Illinois Press.

Hugh-Jones, Christine. 1979. *From the Milk River*. New York: Cambridge University Press.

Hugh-Jones, Stephen. 1979. *The Palm and the Pleiades*. New York: Cambridge University Press.

————. 1988. "The Gun and the Bow: Myths of White Men and Indians." *L'Homme* 106–7:138–158.

Humboldt, Alexander von. 1852. *Personal Narrative of Travels to Equinoctial Regions of America, during the years 1799–1804*. Translated by Thomasina Ross. London: Henry G. Bohn.

Hymes, Dell. 1981. *"In vain I tried to tell you": essays in Native American ethnopoetics*. Philadelphia: University of Pennsylvania Press.

Jackson, Jean. 1983. *The Fish People: Linguistic Exogamy and Tukanoan Identity in Northwest Amazonia*. New York: Cambridge University Press.

Jordan, Carl. 1979. *Nutrient Dynamics of a Tropical Rain Forest Ecosystem*. Annual Report to NSF: Institute of Ecology, University of Georgia.

Jordan, Carl, and Chris Uhl. 1978. "Biomass of a 'Tierra Firma' Forest of the Amazon Basin." *Oecologia Plantarum* 13(4): 387–400.

Journet, Nicolas. 1981. *Los Curripaco del Río Isana: Economía y Sociedad*. *Revista Colombiana de Antropología* 23:125–81.

————. 1988. "Les Jardins de Paix." Unpublished Ph.D. dissertation, Universite de Paris.

Keil, Charles. 1987. "Participatory Discrepancies and the Power of Music." *Cultural Anthropology* 2(3): 275–83.

Key, M. R. 1979. *The Grouping of South American Indian Languages*. Tubingen: Gunter Narr Verlag.

Koch-Gruenberg, Theodore. 1909. *Zwei Jahre unter den Indianern.* Stuttgart: Strecker and Schroder.

Landaburu, Jon, and Pineda, Roberto Camacho. 1984. *Tradiciones de la Gente del Hacha: Mitología de los Indios Andoques del Amazonas.* Yerbabuena, Colombia: Instituto Caro y Cuervo/UNESCO.

Laughlin, Charles. 1974. "Deprivation and Reciprocity." *Man* 9:380–96.

Laughlin, Charles, and Ivan Brady. 1978. "Introduction: Diaphasis and Change in Human Populations." In *Extinction and Survival in Human Populations,* Charles Laughlin and Ivan Brady, eds., pp. 1–48. New York: Columbia University Press.

Lévi-Strauss, Claude. 1963. "The Sorcerer and His Magic," in *Structural Anthropology,* vol. 1, pp. 167–85. New York: Basic Books.

———. 1966. *The Savage Mind.* Chicago: University of Chicago Press.

———. 1969. *The Raw and the Cooked.* Trans. John and Doreen Weightman. "Introduction to a Science of Mythology," 1. New York: Harper & Row.

Matos Arvelo, Martin. 1912. *Vida Indiana.* Barcelona: Casa Editorial Mauci.

Mauss, Marcel. 1968. "Essai sur les Variations Saisonnaires de Sociétés Eskimos. Etude de Morphologie Sociale." In *Sociologie et Anthropologie,* pp. 389–478. Paris: Presses Universitaires.

Munn, Nancy. 1969. "The Effectiveness of Symbols in Murngin Rite and Myth," in *Forms of Symbolic Action,* R. F. Spencer., ed., pp. 178–206. Seattle: University of Washington Press.

Murphy, Yolanda, and Robert F. Murphy. 1974. *Women of the Forest.* New York: Columbia University Press.

Nimuendajú, Kurt. 1950. "Reconhecimento dos Ríos Içana, Ayarí, e Uaupés. Relatorio Apresentado ao Serviço de Proteção aos Indios do Amazonas e Acre, 1927." *Journal de la Société des Americanistes,* N.S. 39:128–70.

Oliveira, Adelia. 1975. "A Terminologia de Parentesco Baniwa—1971. Boletim do Museu Paraense Emilio Goeldi, N.S.," *Antropologia* 56:1–36.

Oliveira, Adelia, and Galvão, Eduardo. 1973. "A Situação Atual dos Baniwa (Alto Río Negro)—1971." *O Museu Goeldi no Ano do Sesquicentario* 20: 27–40.

Piñeda Camacho, Roberto. 1985. *Historia Oral y Proceso Esclavista en el Caqueta.* Bogotá: Banco de la Republica.

Ramanujan, A K. 1973. *Speaking of Siva.* Baltimore: Penguin Books Inc.

Reeve, Mary-Elizabeth. 1988. "Cauchu Uras: Lowland Quichua Histories of the Amazon Rubber Boom," in *Rethinking History and Myth: Indigenous South American Perspectives on the Past,* Jonathan Hill, ed., pp. 19–34. Urbana: University of Illinois Press.

Reichel-Dolmatoff, Gerardo. 1971. *Amazonian Cosmos.* Chicago: University of Chicago Press.

———. 1975. *The Shaman and the Jaguar.* Philadelphia: Temple University Press.

———. 1985. "Tapir Avoidance in the Northwest Amazon," in *Animal Myths and Metaphors in South America*, Gary Urton, ed., pp. 107–44. Salt Lake City: University of Utah Press.

———. 1987. "The Great Mother and the Kogi Universe: a Concise View." *Journal of Latin American Lore* 13(1): 73–113.

Roe, Peter. 1988. "The Josho Nahuanbo Are All Wet and Undercooked: Shipibo views of the Whiteman and the Incas in Myth, Legend, and History," in *Rethinking History and Myth: Indigenous South American Perspectives on the Past*, Jonathan Hill, ed., pp. 106–35. Urbana: University of Illinois Press.

Rubel, Paula, and Rosman, Abraham. 1978. *Your Own Pigs You May Not Eat.* Chicago: University of Chicago Press.

Saake, Wilhelm. 1968. "Mitos Sobre Inapirikuli, el Heroe Cultural de los Baniwa." *Zeitschrift fur Ethnologie* 93: Heft 1–2.

Saldarriaga, Juan, and D. C. West. 1987. "Holocene Fires in the Northern Amazon Basin." *Quaternary Research* 26: 358–66.

Sanford, Robert, Juan Saldarriaga, Kathleen Clark, Christopher Uhl, and Rafael Herrera. 1985. "Amazonian Rain-Forest Fires." *Science* 227: 53–55.

Seeger, Anthony. 1986. "Oratory Is Spoken, Myth Is Told, and Song Is Sung, But They Are All Music to My Ears," in *Native South American Discourse*, Joel Sherzer and Greg Urban, eds., pp. 59–82. Amsterdam: Mouton de Gruyter.

Sherzer, Joel. 1983. *Kuna Ways of Speaking: an Ethnographic Perspective.* Austin: University of Texas Press.

Sherzer, Joel, and Greg Urban, eds. 1986. *Native South American Discourse.* Amsterdam: Mouton de Gruyter.

Sider, Gerald. 1987. "When Parrots Learn to Talk, and Why They Can't: Domination, Deception, and Self-Deception in Indian-White Relations." *Comparative Studies in Society and History* 29: 3–23.

Silverblatt, Irene. 1988. "Political Memories and Colonizing Symbols: Santiago and the Mountain Gods of Colonial Peru," in *Rethinking History and Myth: Indigenous South American Perspectives on the Past*, Jonathan Hill, ed., pp. 174–94. Urbana: University of Illinois Press.

Smith, Richard. 1977. "Deliverance from Chaos for a Song: A Social and Religious Interpretation of the Ritual Performance of Amuesha Music." Ph.D. dissertation, Cornell University, Department of Anthropology.

———. 1984. "The Language of Power: Music, Order, and Redemption." *Latin American Music Review* 5(2): 129–60.

Sorensen, Arthur P., Jr. 1967. "Multilingualism in the Northwest Amazon." *American Anthropologist* 69:670–84.

Spruce, Richard. 1970. *Notes of a Botanist on the Amazon and Andes*. New York: Johnson Reprint Corporation.

Sullivan, Lawrence. 1988. *Icanchu's Drum: An Orientation to Meaning in South American Religions*. New York: Macmillan.

Sweet, David. 1974. "A Rich Realm of Nature Destroyed: The Middle Amazon Valley 1640–1750." Ph. D. dissertation, University of Wisconsin.

Taussig, Michael. 1984. "Culture of Terror, Space of Death: Roger Casement's Putumayo Report and the Explanation of Torture." *Comparative Studies in Society and History* 26(3): 467–97.

————. 1987. *Shamanism, Colonialism, and the Wild Man*. Chicago: University of Chicago Press.

Tavera Acosta, B. 1927. *Río Negro: Resena Etnográfica, Historica, y Geographica*. Maracay, Venezuela: Imprenta del Estado.

Turner, Terence. 1985. "Animal Symbolism, Totemism, and the Structure of Myth," in *Animal Myths and Metaphors in South America*, Gary Urton, ed., pp. 49–106. Salt Lake City: University of Utah Press.

————. 1988. "Commentary: Ethno-Ethnohistory: Myth and History in Native South American Representations of Contact with Western Society," in *Rethinking History and Myth: Indigenous South American Perspectives on the Past*, Jonathan Hill, ed., pp. 235–81. Urbana: University of Illinois Press.

Urban, Greg. 1986. "Ceremonial Dialogues in South America." *American Anthropologist* 88(2): 371–86.

————. 1991. *A Discourse-Centered Approach to Culture*. Austin: University of Texas Press.

Urton, Gary. 1981. *At the Crossroads of the Earth and the Sky: an Andean Cosmology*. Austin: University of Texas Press.

Vidal, Silvia M. 1987. "El Modelo del Proceso Migratorio Prehispanico de los Piapoco: Hipotesis y Evidencias." Unpublished Master's Thesis, Depto. de Antropología, Instituto Venezolano de Investigaciones Científicas.

Villas Boas, Orlando, and Claudio Villas Boas. 1973. *Xingu: the Indians and Their Myths*. New York: Farrar, Straus, and Giroux.

Whitten, Norman E., Jr. 1978. "Ecological Imagery and Cultural Adaptability: the Canelos Quichua of Eastern Ecuador." *American Anthropologist* 80: 836–59.

————. 1985. *Sicuanga Runa: the Other Side of Development in Amazonian Ecuador*. Urbana: University of Illinois Press.

Wilbert, Johannes. 1966. *Indios de la Region Orinoco-Ventuari*. Instituto Caribe de Sociología y Antropología, Caracas: Fundación La Salle.

Wolf, Eric. 1982. *Europe and the Peoples Without History*. Berkeley: University of California Press.

Wright, Robin. 1981. "History and Religion of the Baniwa Peoples of the Upper Río Negro Valley." 2 Volumes. Ph. D. dissertation, Department of Anthropology, Stanford University.

Wright, Robin, and Hill, Jonathan. 1986. "History, Ritual, and Myth: Nineteenth Century Millenarian Movements in the Northwest Amazon." *Ethnohistory* 33:31−54.

# Index

12, 142; ethnographic studies on, 26–27; pandemics on, 178–79; in ritual place naming, 44, 138, 139, 157, 172

New Tribes Mission, 26, 32, 88, 217 n. 2

Nightmares, 180

Office of Indigenous Affairs (DAI), 28

Omens: evil, 118–19, 168, 195, 196, 199, 207, 208–13

Origins, 33–34. *See also* Emergence

Orinoco River, 44, 50, 154

Otherness: negation of, 154–55, 204–5

Otiarírria, 37

Paca, 84

*Pákamarántakan,* 216

Palms: in initiation ritual, 135, 138; *macanilla,* 68, 121; *moriche,* 109–10; role of, 113–14; *seje,* 121, 137; symbolism of, 78, 106–7, 132

Panama, 14

Pandemics, 178–79

Panoan groups, 60

Papers, 6, 38, 195

Paradise: celestial, 72, 94, 115

Parents: in childbirth ritual, 97, 99–100, 113, 115, 121

Patients: in curing ritual, 193–97

Patrisibs, 9, 47, 155, 219 n. 8, 222 n. 3

Payments, 186

Peccaries, 107, 120

Peppers, hot, 68, 81, 140; in childbirth ritual, 101, 115–18; in initiation rituals, 135, 137, 143, 144

Performance, 14–15, 16, 18, 25–26

Peru, 59, 60

Petroglyphs, 77

Phratries, 46, 47, 157; Arawak-speak-ing, 155–56; hierarchically ranked, 9–10; and male initiation rites, 154–55; survival of, 42, 45. *See also by name*

Piapoco, 38

*Píci,* 101

*Pína,* 144

Place naming: and historical context, 44–45, 178; in initiation rituals, 132, 137, 138–39, 146, 152–53, 153–54, 156–57; in ritual jour-neys, 43–44

Places, 105, 145, 149, 168

*Plantanilla,* 110

Plantations, 46

Plants, 58, 108, 140; flute and trum-pet, 68–69, 72; in initiation rites, 135, 138–39, 144; Kuwái as, 83, 131; as metaphors, 109–10. *See also by type*

Pleiades'-Grandchildren. *See* Waríperídakéna

Poetry, 17, 20, 221 n. 9

Poison, poisoning, 196, 198, 213, 223 n. 6; in mythic narratives, 188, 189, 190, 211; origins of, 184, 185–86

Poison-owners, 185–86

Politics, 156; and socio-geographic space, 154–55; Venezuelan, 40–41; of whites, 38–39

Portuguese, 44–45

Pottery, 63

Pottery making, 61

Power, 51, 215, 221 n. 7; and human society, 202–3; indigenous, 52–53; kinship and, 127–29; Kuwái's, 78–79, 81–82; musical, 60, 126, 207; mythic, 16–17, 21–22, 46–47, 136, 158; ritual, 6–7, 130, 201–2; of sound, 63–64, 126; of whites, 35–36, 46–47. *See also* Musical naming power

# About the Author

JONATHAN D. HILL has been an associate professor in anthropology at Southern Illinois University since 1990. In addition to his interest in Amazonian ethnomusicology, he has published articles on indigenous social organization and history in journals such as *American Ethnologist, Human Ecology,* and *Ethnohistory.* He has a Ph.D. in anthropology and ethnomusicology from Indiana University.

He is a contributing editor for the Ethnology of Lowland South America, *Handbook of Latin American Studies,* U.S. Library of Congress, and a member of the Editorial Council of *American Anthropologist.*